Bringing Eurasia Back In?

Mireno Berrettini, Davide Borsani (eds.)

Bringing Eurasia Back In?

The Resilience of the Western-Centric Alliance System Between History and Politics

PETER LANG

Lausanne · Berlin · Bruxelles · Chennai · New York · Oxford

Library of Congress Cataloging-in-Publication Data
A CIP catalog record for this book has been applied for at the
Library of Congress.

**Bibliographic Information published by the
Deutsche Nationalbibliothek**
The Deutsche Nationalbibliothek lists this publication in the
Deutsche Nationalbibliografie; detailed bibliographic data is
available online at http://dnb.d-nb.de.

ISBN 978-3-0343-4525-5
ePDF 978-3-0343-4734-1
ePub 978-3-0343-4735-8
DOI 10.3726/b20888

© 2023 Peter Lang Group AG, Lausanne
Published by: Peter Lang Editions Scientifiques Internationales
- P.I.E., Brüssel, Belgien

info@peterlang.com - www.peterlang.com

Index

Mireno Berrettini – Davide Borsani
Introduction

The Introduction explains the scope and content of the volume, giving a short description of each chapter. It also describes the elements of continuity and transformation in the history of the Western-centric alliance system in light of an international Eurasian scenario that actually differs from that of the Cold War and is still in evolution.

Since the end of the Second World War, the role of the United States on the international scene, including in Eurasia, has appeared to be closely linked to the stability and sustainability of the system of multilateral and bilateral security alliances Washington has progressively established. Since the Cold War, from an American perspective, the international security order has been based on two main pillars. First, Washington's exercise of leadership within its military alliances. Second, the very existence of such alliances in the face of external enemies capable of threatening the survival and promotion of the universal principles underlying the US-led liberal international order. The trade-off between allies was essentially clear. On the one hand, Washington would exercise hegemonic power, largely shouldering the necessary costs and providing an umbrella of security to its partners, which in turn should partially share the burden by accepting the role of supporting actors. On the other hand, the United States would reap the rewards of leadership by expanding its influence overseas, intrinsically linked to promoting globalization - 'Americanization' or 'Westernization'? (Yu 2003) - with positive spillovers within US borders. Especially in the post-Cold War period, this approach has been defended by the various US administrations, primarily in rhetoric, not always in practice.

One of the major historical goals for US foreign policy has been preventing the rise of a hegemonic power in Eurasia: Germany in the two World Wars, the Soviet Union – allied to the People's Republic of China (PRC) – in the early Cold War, and the PRC – supported by Russia – in the 21st century. Eurasia under the control of one or more hostile powers would be perceived as a direct threat to the American mainland and its overseas interests. In this framework, the US security alliance system built after the Second World War – ranging from formal agreements such as the Atlantic Alliance in Europe to more recent informal partnerships like the Quad in the Indo-Pacific region – has played a prominent role in US leadership and the preservation of the global balance of power under the American (and Western) leading influence. The US National Security Strategy published by the Donald J. Trump Administration in 2017 maintained that 'a central continuity in history is the contest for power. The present time period is no different' because the 'revisionist powers of China and Russia' were trying to 'challenge American power, influence, and interests, attempting to erode American security and prosperity'. As a consequence, alliances like NATO and other security partnerships 'increase our strategic reach and provide access to forward basing and overflight rights for global operations', thus preserving the US world role.

Ideology often overlaps with realpolitik on this path. In an op-ed published in November 2022, the Financial Times Editorial Board stressed that today 'There are echoes of the 1950s in America's efforts to assemble a coalition of democracies for a new cold war, where it confronts not just a belligerent Russia but an ever more assertive China'. In the last two decades, the rise of two revisionist powers, governed by authoritarian regimes, raised the (mis?)perception that their common goal is to revert the current balance of power by promoting illiberal values. The US National Security Strategy signed by American President Joe Biden in October 2022 stressed that 'the most pressing strategic challenge' facing the United States is 'from powers that layer authoritarian governance with a revisionist foreign policy'. It continues: 'It is their behavior that poses a challenge to international peace and stability—especially waging or preparing for wars of aggression, actively undermining the democratic political processes of other countries, leveraging technology and supply chains for coercion and repression, and exporting an illiberal model of international order. Many non-democracies join the world's democracies in forswearing these behaviors. Unfortunately, Russia and the People's Republic of China (PRC) do not'.

According to the most recent NSSs, thus, the international system is approaching (or has already started) a new Cold War. Is this true? From a historical perspective, Soviet moves in 1947 and 1948 changed the threat nature in Europe, starting a process of Western integration in the security and political fields. For the world, it was the Communist victory in China in 1949 that deeply altered the global balance of power (see Mireno Berrettini's chapter 1). After all, Chinese leaning to one side, that is Mao Tse-tung's deliberate choice to come closer to the Soviet Union, implied the definitive dissolution of the strategic Grand Design conceived by the US President, Franklin D. Roosevelt, to build a post-war international order. In such a global picture, the apparent overreaction of the Euro-Atlantic players, led by Washington (despite some tactical disagreements with certain allies, mainly the United Kingdom), and the outbreak of the Korean war put the world on the brink of a major Eurasian conflict between the Western

States and the Communist bloc led by the Sino-Soviet axis. In the end, the West pursued a more muscular strategic positioning in the following years, despite occasional divergences among the Euro-Atlantic allies. The 1950s were a hot decade for the Cold War.

Perhaps, today we are experiencing a similar dynamic. The end of the Cold War brought a new era of strategic cooperation between the two Eurasian giants: the PRC and Russia. Since the 1990s, the two countries have established a strong military and economic partnership. This *rapprochement* has allowed China and Russia to become closer partners on the world stage, and has helped to improve the security and stability of both players. At the beginning of the 1990s, Beijing and Moscow had a relatively distant relationship due to a rivalry going back to the 1960s. However, during the so-called 'second decade of Illusions' (de Leonardis 2011), that is the idea that the world was now finally safe in (and for) democracy, their relationship began to strengthen as a result of converging interests and as a reaction to the choices made by Euro-Atlantic players in terms of security policy. The Eastward expansion of NATO and the Kosovo campaign in 1999 were key moments in defining the future course of the relationship between the Western world and the Sino-Russian partnership.

By the end of the 20th century, thus, Beijing and Moscow came much closer and the strategic linkage between them had become much more substantial. In the 2000s, the Sino-Russian axis passed many tests, increasing its resistance. In 2001, the two countries signed the Treaty of Good-Neighborliness and Friendly Cooperation (the so-called 'Great Treaty'), establishing the framework for deeper cooperation. In this document, Beijing and Moscow defined the (vague) limits of their military collaboration and strategic partnership. Accordingly, on the basis of 'mutual respect of State sovereignty and territorial integrity, mutual non-aggression, mutual non-interference in each other's internal affairs, equality and mutual benefit and peaceful co-existence', China and Russia decided to 'develop the strategic cooperative partnership of good-neighborliness, friendship and cooperation and equality and trust between the two countries from a long-term view and in a comprehensive manner'. Moreover, they pointed out 'with satisfaction that each has no territorial claim on the other'. Thanks to this new level of cooperation, the PRC and Russia have increased their military and economic power in Eurasia and the world, while also improving their security and stability. In addition, this strategic partnership has allowed the two countries to become more influential in confronting the West.

However, compared with the scenario following the Second World War, there is no doubt that the current structural conditions of the international system have profoundly changed. In this sense, the end of the Cold War marked a new era of global politics. The collapse of the Soviet Union in 1991 signalled the beginning of the PRC's rise. Actually, on the world stage, no nation saw a greater shift in its standing than Beijing. In the decades since, the country has undergone rapid changes, becoming one of the most powerful nations in the world. The Chinese economy is now larger than the entire European Union and is on track to overtake the United States as the world's largest economy by the end of the decade. The essay by Barbara Onnis (chapter 3) underlines the transformation of Beijing position in the field of foreign policy since 1991. PRC gave up permanently the old 'victim mentality' (*shouhaizhe taidu* 受害者态度) and shaped a new 'great power mentality' (*daguo xintai* 大国心态), aimed at putting a definitive end to the narrative of the notorious 'century of humiliation', while fostering instead a new narrative focused on the importance for China to forge its own role. The Dragon has become increasingly influential in global affairs, playing a key role in international negotiations over issues such as climate change, trade, and even human rights. The PRC is also expanding its military capabilities, investing heavily in advanced weaponry, including nuclear and space arms, and becoming a major (trans)regional power. The rise of China as a relevant global player has profoundly impacted the international order. The country has become a major economic and political rival to the United States, and its growing influence has challenged the traditional Western-led order and its system of alliances. China's rise has also led to a shift in global power dynamics, as other countries adjust to a new multipolar world.

Over the years, these dynamics have brought analysts and practitioners to discuss the rise of a new spatial category of international politics: Eurasia, as a geopolitical entity. Indeed, Eurasian geopolitics has been gaining increasing attention from the international community, while its conceptual roots come back to the 1920s and Soviet thinking (Ferrari 2012). The post-Cold War renewed interest is due to a variety of factors, including the return of Russia, the spread of Chinese influence, and the emergence of a new geopolitical and economic order in the region. Eurasia, thus, is not only a geographical expression referring to the former Soviet space, as some authors argue. It is mostly a geopolitical concept of a large competing space ranging from the European peninsula to the Eastern coasts of Asia. Eurasia goes beyond geographical boundaries, involving the wider relationship between - in Halford J. Mackinder's and Nicholas J. Spykman's words - the Heartland and the Rimland, the World Island and the Offshore\ Outlying Islands (Petersen 2011). This is particularly important when we look at globalization and the challenge to the structural fundamentals of the US-led international order, including in the field of economy.

Globalization has indeed meant a relocation of this immense space in the circuits of the international division of labor and in global value chains. Over the past decades, there has been a significant increase in trade, investments, and other forms of economic cooperation within the region, facilitated by the opening up of markets and the removal of barriers such as tariffs. Concretization of these processes has been, since 2013, the Belt and Road Initiative (BRI), a large-scale infrastructure project connecting the PRC to the European Union via Central Asia. Although the years following the advent of COVID-19 marked a slowdown in the infrastructural construction project, BRI has allowed countries in Eurasia to become more interconnected and interdependent, creating an apparent more unified economic alignment (see Gianluca Pastori's chapter 8).

Meanwhile, since 2014, due to the cooling between the West and Russia because of the beginning of the Ukrainian crisis, the cooperation between Moscow and Beijing has become increasingly crucial for the Kremlin, which has sought an outlet to circumvent the Euro-Atlantic economic sanctions. In 2015, the Russian President, Vladimir Putin, and the Chinese President, Xi Jinping, referring to the principles of the 'Great Treaty', signed an important declaration reaffirming the centrality of Eurasian cooperation between the two countries in the name of their 'co-development' (Lukin 2020). In this context, Moscow and Beijing have shown interest in coordinating their two main multi-regional integration projects: the Russian-led Eurasian Economic Union and the Chinese-led BRI. At the moment, the Ukrainian war began in February 2022 has left many questions unanswered concerning economic integration in Eurasia. Nevertheless, from a long-term perspective, it seems that the Sino-Russian 'friendship without limits' is destined to increase its relevance, both economically and strategically. And, for sure, the concept of the 'rise of China' has become history (Womack 2010). What we are assisting these days is its claim to be recognized as a powerful Eurasian player with global ambitions.

The Trump years represented the turning moment in which the US public opinion and political class gained full awareness of these new dynamics. China's economic and political weight began being viewed as a threatening challenge in terms of international and national security. Lorenzo Medici and Valentina Sommella's article (chapter 7) highlights the dynamic of the Sino-US confrontation in those years within the World Health Organization (WHO), relating to the genesis of the COVID-19 and, later, in fighting against virus. 'In the current pandemic' they write 'the Chinese state media have emphasized how the PRC system has been able to guarantee effective application of lockdowns and procedures to control violations of government prescriptions', while 'at the same time this has sparked criticism in Western liberal societies and helped rekindle the debate on China's lack of democracy and its authoritarian methods'. Such a clash of narratives and exchange of accusations fueled previous strategic and economic tensions between the two countries.

The change of presidency in the White House did not alter how China is perceived strategically. The above-mentioned US National Security Strategy, issued by the Biden administration, clearly stated, with an unprecedented phraseology, that Beijing 'harbors the intention and, increasingly, the capacity to reshape the international order', while Moscow 'has shattered peace in Europe and impacted stability everywhere'. The unknowns about the Western reaction to what the NSSs view as a sort of 'axis of the revisionists', and the countermoves of this heterogeneous set of players, let us glimpse a very uncertain future for the international system.

Over the last few years, the entire post-Soviet space, especially Russian borders, experienced turmoil and instability: from Kazakhstan to Belarus passing through the conflict between Armenia and Azerbaijan over Nagorno-Karabakh. Undoubtedly, the dramatic US withdrawal from Afghanistan in 2021 and the never-ending situation in Xinjiang contributed to this new arc of instability. Finally, the Russian large-scale invasion of Ukraine furtherly ignited an already burning fire, placing a huge question mark on the future of Eurasia and the struggle for power there. On the Western side, the historic US security alliance system is going through a highly needed phase of renewal. New international factors, challenges, dynamics and players call for the US and its Western allies to redefine outdated Cold War security agreements. On the one hand, the US moved away from the practices of multilateralism under the Trump presidency, exerting strong pressure on long-standing allies and ringing them a loud wake-up call to confront Russia and China. On the other hand, the Biden presidency opened up with new perspectives, pledging to relaunch traditional alliances and create new partnerships if possible with the same goal of contrasting Moscow and Beijing.

At the moment, it is in the Asia-Pacific region, particularly in the maritime domain, that the Chinese quest for influence has played out more vividly. As Francesca Frassineti stresses (chapter 5), 'By embracing maritime power as an essential element of the 'China dream' of achieving national rejuvenation by 2049, President Xi Jinping has doubled down on his predecessor's pledge to build a 'great maritime power'. On the one hand, growing amounts of resources are being devoted to enable the PLAN to conduct long-distance operations. On the other, a large share of the official defence budget has been justified by the necessity to deploy new platforms and weapon systems that could potentially allow China to prevent third parties from accessing contested areas and thus deter them from being involved'. This in turn has raised new considerations about the nature and development of the US Cold War security arrangements with Japan and South Korea as well as the trilateral alliance with Australia and New Zealand (ANZUS). Their relaunch is key in US strategic vision.

The influential partnership between the US and India enlisted in the Quad adds a further counterweight to Chinese ambitions. In Raimondo Neironi's words (chapter 4), 'The Quad will continue to make sense as long as India, a nuclear power, is part of this initiative. It is a known fact that it constitutes the linchpin of the US grand strategy in the Indo-Pacific for three main reasons. First, New Delhi's recognition of freedom and democratic values, in international relations as well as domestic policy, demonstrates the existence of a credible and lingering alternative to authoritarianism in Asia. Second, engaging Indian Navy means that the US INDOPACOM could conduct a large number of maritime special operations in the Indian Ocean to secure the most important chokepoints of the region. Third, Modi's commitment to manufacturing and donating COVID-19 vaccines across the small- and medium-income countries is due to yield concrete results against the pandemic and China's vaccine diplomacy in Asia'.

Nevertheless, Beijing's increasing assertiveness goes beyond the Far East, affecting the European theater too. Once again, the two sides of Eurasia seem strictly intertwined, and Russia is the main transition belt. The Atlantic Alliance was born in 1949 to confront the Soviet Union and, through a progressive strategic renewal in the post-Cold War era, it still represents the cornerstone of Euro-Atlantic security. In the past decade, Russia's resurgence as a great power, the American 'Pivot to Asia' and Brexit made the European strategic framework much more uncertain, apparently questioning the role of Europe as the closest US ally. Recently, the European Union and the US put China on their priority list as a strategic competitor, while NATO began to look at Chinese power as a potential threat to transatlantic security. In this fluid overlapping picture, the changing positioning of the post-Brexit United Kingdom sheds new light on the usefulness of the so-called Anglosphere, that is the informal alliance between the United Kingdom, the US and the past British Dominions of Canada, Australia, and New Zealand, which cooperate military in several regions and share intelligence information at the highest level. The historical 'special relationship' between Washington and London, which is the core of the Anglosphere, still can play a relevant role in the longer term, despite the change in British international status after Brexit. According to Simone Zuccarelli (chapter 6), 'The relative decline of the United States and the rise of China as a peer competitor will force Washington to bolster its partnerships, especially with close allies. It is therefore likely that the Special Relationship will be further strengthened in the coming years. And for the first time in history, maintaining this relationship will be as important to Washington as it already is for London. Consequently, the Anglosphere will gradually evolve into a more structured system of alliance'. The newly formed partnership between the United States, Britain and Australia (AUKUS) could be a first step in this process.

The events that happened in recent years seem to have accelerated the redefinition of global dynamics, where Eurasia plays the central role in the struggle for power. So, what is next? As Davide Borsani stresses (chapter 2), 'There is no crystal ball to foresee the future, but it seems fair to state that Western political leaders should be aware of historical complexities in framing new policies for the future. Does the current global order architecture reflect the real balance of power? Do Beijing and Moscow really share the same long-term interests? Could a timely diplomatic action by the US and its Western allies help weaken what now seems to be an authoritarian monolith to many? These questions appear among the most crucial for the evolution of the international system'.

In light of multidisciplinary historiographical and political analysis, this collection of essays aims to reflect on these questions and, mostly, the ongoing Eurasian shift of power, its consequences and the concrete possibilities of the affirmation of Eurasia as a geopolitical cooperative\competing space in the international arena. Moreover, the essays will try to measure the actions (and reactions) of the United States and its system of alliances to the strengthening of the Sino-Russian strategic partnership.

The editors thank Pier Paolo Alfei and Simone Zuccarelli for contributing to the formal editing of this volume.

Bibliography

de Leonardis M. (2011). *Alla ricerca della rotta transatlantica dopo l'11 settembre 2001. Le relazioni tra Europa e Stati Uniti durante la presidenza di George W. Bush.* Milan: Educatt.

Ferrari A. (2012). *La foresta e la steppa. Il mito dell'Eurasia nella cultura russa.* Milan: Schwiller.

Lukin A. (2020). *The 'Roads' and 'Belts' of Eurasia.* Singapore: Palgrave Macmillan.

Petersen A. (2011). *The World Island. Eurasian Geopolitics and the Fate of the West.* Santa Barbara, CA: Prager.

'Joint Statement of the Russian Federation and the People's Republic of China on the International Relations Entering a New Era and the Global Sustainable Development', 4 February 2022, <http://www.en.kremlin.ru/supplement/5770>, accessed 2 November 2022

'*National Security Strategy of the United States of America*', December 2017, <https://trumpwhitehouse.archives.gov/wp-content/uploads/2017/12/NSS-Final-12-18-2017-0905.pdf> accessed 2 November 2022

'*National Security Strategy of the United States of America*', December 2017, <https://www.whitehouse.gov/wp-content/uploads/2022/10/Biden-Har ris-Administrations-National-Security-Strategy-10.2022.pdf> accessed 2 November 2022

The Financial Times, *US trade moves sour the transatlantic relationship*, 28 November 2022, <https://www.ft.com/myft/saved-articles/c7745417-28bf-4c2b-85e3-96732fed8291>, accessed 28 November 2022

'*Treaty of Good-Neighborliness and Friendly Cooperation Between the People's Republic of China and the Russian Federation*', 24 July 2001, <https://www.fmprc.gov.cn/mfa_eng/wjdt_665385/2649_665393/200107/t20010724_679 026.html>, accessed 14 November 2022

Womack B. (2010). *China's Rise in Historical Perspective*. Lanham, MD: Rowman Littlefield.

Yu K. (2003). 'Americanization, Westernization, Sinification: Modernization or Globalization in China?'. In N. Sznaider (ed), *Global America? The Cultural Consequences of Globalization*, pp. 134–152. Liverpool: Liverpool University Press.

Mireno Berrettini

The Eurasian Heartland and the Atlantic Alliance: An Interpretative Essay

During a speech given at the Munich Security Conference in February 2019, NATO Secretary-General Jens Stoltenberg underlined how, alongside the enormous possibilities of collaboration and dialogue with the People's Republic of China, Beijing's 'rise also presents a challenge' for Western Countries and for the same Atlantic Alliance. This is not the first time Asian strategic dynamics had deep repercussions on the evolution of the Atlantic Alliance itself. The essay aims at retracing these historical moments and reflecting on NATO nowadays, if it still can be considered an appropriate security tool for the Westerners in their relations with an increasingly dynamic Beijing or is becoming the place where tensions between the two shores of the Atlantic, regarding the different approaches to the 'Chinese question', are released.

Introduction

During a speech given at the Munich Security Conference in February 2019, NATO Secretary General Jens Stoltenberg underlined how, alongside the enormous possibilities of collaboration and dialogue with the People's Republic of China (PRC), Beijing's 'rise also presents a challenge' for Western countries and for the Atlantic Alliance[1].

Stating that the Asia-Pacific balance of power has repercussions for Europe seems obvious, even if it has long been considered a hyperbole. Indeed, it could not be otherwise. After all, the Atlantic Pact and the military structure of NATO arose as a Western organisation in reaction to the Soviet Union threat in continental Europe. In much of the history of the Atlantic Alliance it may appear that the events in East Asia have been of little relevance to understanding its dynamics and strategies. However, upon closer inspection, it seems clear that they actually had a great impact on the international choices made by the Western players, albeit indirectly and with regard to global strategic interactions.

The Eastern Asian – and especially Chinese – question within the Atlantic Alliance is progressively gaining the attention of analysts, commentators, and

---

1 Stoltenberg, J. (2019). 'Speech at the Munich Security Conference', 15 February. <https://www.nato.int/cps/en/natohq/opinions_163791.htm>.

scholars (Bechná and Thayer 2016; Pothier 2019; Brzezinski 2020; Speranza 2020; Nouwens and Legarda 2020; Bērziņa-Čerenkova 2021). This essay is a brief contribution to this debate, adopting a mixed analytical approach, where historical documentation is in dialogue with an IR interpretative theoretical frame. The aim is to examine the NATO of today and analyse whether it can still be considered a valid security tool for a West that relates to an increasingly dynamic People's Republic of China, or whether it is becoming the arena in which tensions between the two shores of the Atlantic resulting from the different approaches to the Chinese question are released.

The Place of China in the Twentieth Century International System: Structural Constraints and Historical Perceptions

As is well known thanks to modern world history studies, Asia has been connected, albeit in a karstic way, to Europe for a very long time. For centuries some of its countries, such as China, have represented an ideal to aim for in the imagination of European culture in terms of refinement and culture. Certainly, on the cusp between the nineteenth century and the beginning of the twentieth, the political balance and dynamics of the two extremes of Eurasia became tirelessly interconnected. On the one hand, the expansion of the European system of States, on the other, the encounters and clashes between the other players in that area, marked a profound transformation in international relations. Regional issues became problems of global importance, and each single issue began to be perceived as a segment of a confrontation between Empires, making it structurally impossible for the Great Powers to restrain their partners for fear of weakening them and thus weakening the alliance in the event of war (Schroeder 1978). In those years it was certainly very difficult to think about the Asian players, and in particular the Qing Empire, as active participants in international relations. Much more fitting was to consider China as the prey in a competition between Great Powers.

The Second World War radically changed everything, or rather it accelerated the processes that had begun in the 1930s. Informally, China joined the Big Four for the first time on 29 May 1942, when President Franklin D. Roosevelt recommended it became one of the 'Four Policemen' of the world during a meeting with Vjačeslav M. Molotov and Harry L. Hopkins. The unprecedented new status hypothesized for China both during the war and in the future post-war order, raised questions for the British Prime Minister Winston Churchill. Nonetheless, London finally acquiesced, and the Chinese were slowly but progressively incorporated into the decision-making circuit of the Grand Alliance. At the insistence of the US, China was included among the signatory powers of the Declaration of Four Nations on General Security (30 October 1943). Alongside Roosevelt and Churchill, the leader of China, Generalissimo Jiang Jieshi, was invited to join the Cairo conference (22–26 November 1943) and participated in the drafting of the Cairo Declaration (1 December 1943). At the same time, the internal fractures within the Chinese political world were settled, albeit in a fragile way. The Kuomintang (KMT) and the Chinese Communist Party (CCP) agreed on a common policy of fighting the Japanese invaders and the resumption of the civil war that had begun in 1927 was theoretically averted when, on the 10 October 1945, the signing of the Double Tenth Agreement seemed to neutralise China's possible internal explosion by enabling it to join the winners' group, the Big Four. Theoretically, the Big Four venture was by now in full force and globally it became the schema for the new architecture of international relations.

Certainly, as after every hegemonic war (Gilpin 1981), the scenario following the defeat of the Japanese Empire in 1945 led to friction within the victorious Great Powers. Historiography has traditionally focused on the disagreements between the Anglo-Americans and the Soviets. Seen from a global perspective, however, in the aftermath of the end of the Second World War, the frictions within the Grand Alliance did not undergo an ontological change, rather they continued to be part of the aggressive negotiation between the former allies. In fact, they were frictions which, even if some were serious, nevertheless concerned specific issues, incapable, *per se*, of changing the global balance of power or the status of the winners' relations.

Unexpectedly, it was not the tensions in Central-Eastern Europe that brought down the Rooseveltian design for the Big Four, but the new Chinese positioning matured with the beginning of a new phase of its civil war, continued with the Maoist victory of 1949 and culminating in the Sino-Soviet Treaty of Friendship, Alliance and Mutual Assistance, signed on 14 February 1950. From 1945 China as a whole, and then Communist China, took the first revisionist action against the global order shaped directly or indirectly by the other victorious Great Powers. This rebellion became clear after 1949 and 1950 with the so-called 'leaning to one side', that is Beijing's choice to approach the Soviet Union. The alliance of the heartland (the Soviet Union) with part of the Asian rimland (the PRC) destabilized the international economic system by depriving the Euro-Atlantic economies – which were still struggling to stabilize after the 1947 Dollar gap crisis – of access to material resources and commercial outlets. From the strategic point of view, the Sino-Soviet alliance gave geopolitical import to the maintenance of Western control over Korea and Indochina. The fact that both conflicts were major wars fought by Westerners in the second half of the twentieth century was not a coincidence. At stake was the danger of the entire Asian-Pacific continental shore being transformed into a socialist bloc. In addition, the consolidation of the Sino-Soviet axis hampered the possibility of continuing to operate those mechanisms for localising confrontation that had worked imperfectly until 1949 (not least during the Berlin blockade). From that moment on every crisis was read through the interpretative prism of the Cold War and its all-encompassing perspective (Berrettini 2016).

Politicians and analysts at the time were fully aware of the new scenario. This was the geostrategic reason for the militarization of the North Atlantic system and for the construction of a Western defensive mechanism which, together with other regional alliances, would surround the Sino-Soviet perimeter. According to various documents included in a long US Department of Defense dossier issued in September 1949, a Communist China would mean that 'the whole Asian continent and the islands [would] inevitably become communist'. It declared that it would be 'a disaster of unprecedented magnitude', which would seriously jeopardize the 'fruits of [US] victory in the Second World War'[2]. Some days earlier, a high-profile meeting had considered that the victory of the Chinese Communist Party in the civil war would facilitate Soviet penetration into the Indian Ocean, a scenario that would hand Moscow 'all of Asia and the entire Mediterranean, while the continents of Europe and Africa [would be] threatened. All this [would leave] North and South America completely isolated'[3]. In the same month a document of the joint US, Canadian and British Intelligence indicated that, in the event of a Sino-Soviet treaty, they anticipated a possible attack by Moscow on Western Europe from 1957 to 1950. Beijing would support the USSR, diplomatically or 'in the event of war', which would follow a path 'of further expansion' using a policy of pressure on the Mediterranean straits and in Central Asia, launching simultaneous operations 'to ensure that the Allies did not [control] positions from which to launch attacks on areas of vital Soviet

---

2   National Archives and Record Administration (Washington). RG 218. Sec. 7 Pt. 4–7 Box 15. Secretary of Defense to the Joint Chief of Staff, *Military Aid to China* (8 September 1949) and *Summary of Present Communist Crises in Asia* (10 May 1949).

3   National Archives and Record Administration (Washington). RG 218. Sec. 7 Pt. 4–7 Box 15. *Memorandum of Conversation. General MacArthur's Briefing of Huber Subcommittee* (5 September 1949).

interest'[4]. Strategic anxieties and geopolitical fears materialized as the alliance treaty between Moscow and Beijing took shape. In a letter dated 2 February 1950 written by Sir Esler M. Dening, Assistant Under-Secretary of State in the British Foreign Office, to Sir Charles H. Bateman, officer of the Northern Department, the former considered the Sino-Soviet axis 'as the equivalent of the Atlantic Pact, [...] a diplomatic victory for the Russians which [would have] destabilizing effects in Europe and Asia'[5].

The centrality of Asian events in defining the architecture of Cold War international system is confirmed by the fact that the militarization of the Atlantic Alliance, created in 1949 as a security system and, above all, as a political organisation of the West, occurred as a consequence of including the Federal Republic of Germany in the Western security perimeter in reaction to the Korean War, indirectly a strategic consequence of what Carl Schmitt (1942) would have called a geopolitical Behemoth: the Sino-Soviet communist bloc.

From History to the Present: Asia and the Future of the Atlantic Alliance

In the previous paragraph I made a brief historical journey that is anomalous to the master-narratives relating the history of international relations in the second half of the twentieth century. It is an unusual proposal, but it acts as a logical support to my discourse on the importance of Asia (and China) in understanding the history, current events, and future of transatlantic relations.

Whether or not we share these historical premises, it has become clear that Asia has assumed a systemic centrality such as to have repercussions on the policies of the West. The world leaders and commentators have slowly become aware of this. By the end of the Obama Administration, Washington started to pay more strategic attention to Asia, especially to the rise of China. From a cultural point of view, probably the zenith of this process was the publication of Graham Allison's book entitled *Destined for War: Can America and China Escape Thucydides's Trap*, in 2017. And actually, for the United States, 2017 was a turning point: the formalisation of the threat represented by Beijing and the awareness of the strategic value of economic relations with the PRC. Scholars and commentators have spoken about a new 1947, referring to the tensions

---

4 The National Archives (London). DEFE 4/29. *Minutes of meeting held on Wednesday, 8th March, 1950* (8 March 1950).
5 The National Archives (London). FO 371/83313 Sino-Soviet relations. Esler Dening to Charles Bateman (2 February 1950).

between Washington and Beijing as a new cold war (Kaplan 2019; Wertheim 2019; Nye 2020; Rachman 2020). For Europeans, this process has been slower, also because for the Old Continent players the Chinese challenge is not systemic. The two sides of the Atlantic eventually came to agree on the problem but have different solutions on how to deal with it.

Since 2018, all the most important public documents in the US related to international politics have listed Beijing as one of the most relevant 'competitors' or as a 'revisionist power'[6] aiming at 'undermining the international order from within the system by exploiting its benefits while simultaneously undercutting its principles and "rules of the road"'[7]. On the other side of the Atlantic, the formulation of a Chinese policy has been more complicated, just as its implementation is more articulated. In March 2019, the EU Commission designated the PRC as a 'strategic competitor' and 'systemic rival'[8], but not all Europeans are ready to take the confrontational positions that Washington clearly took during the Trump administration. The US President did not share his commercial strategy with Europe before unleashing his trade war against the RPC. Furthermore, while even the Old Continent has been hit by US protectionist manoeuvres, Europe considers Beijing its second trading partner and the COVID crisis has highlighted the extent of EU dependence on Chinese products. Indeed, for some European players there are no advantages, only disadvantages, to demonizing Beijing, or to raising the confrontation to a level that could eventually lead to economic friction or an armed conflict.

So, given such different perspectives, what does that mean for NATO? The Alliance is not new to paying attention to and operating in areas beyond its traditional borders. I am not referring to the well-investigated involvement in Afghanistan, the Alliance's largest foreign operation, but to Eastern Asia. NATO turned its attention to the area after the breakup of the Soviet Union and the end of the Cold War, but since 2009 its diplomatic projection has become more structured. In fact, in 2010, after the Lisbon Summit, the new Strategic Concept

---

6   White House Office (2017). 'National Security Strategy of the United States of America', 18 December, <https://www.whitehouse.gov/wp-content/uploads/2017/12/NSS-Final-12-18-2017-0905-2.pdf>.

7   Department of Defense (2018). 'National Defense Strategy, Sharpening the American Military's Competitive Edge', 19 January, <https://dod.defense.gov/Portals/1/Documents/pubs/2018-National-Defense-Strategy-Summary.pdf>.

8   European Commission (2019). 'EU-China: A Strategic Outlook', 12 March, <https://ec.europa.eu/commission/sites/beta-political/files/communication-eu-china-a-strategic-outlook.pdf>.

underlined the importance of cooperation across the globe, a first step towards the consolidation of a new general role for the Atlantic Alliance in the present international system. During the years of Anders Fogh Rasmussen's secretariat, NATO focused on Asia as a sector of great importance in the global balance of power and for the interests of its member countries. NATO established partnerships with relevant key Asia-Pacific players, including Korea, New Zealand, Mongolia (2012), Australia and Japan (2013). Such a policy triangulated with the 'Pivot to Asia' of the US Administration led by Barack H. Obama, announced and developed during those years.

In the Alliance's public narrative, the main concern was the stabilisation of the Asian theatre. Potentially very complicated, some of the biggest issues were the military build-up of the Chinese People's Liberation Army (PLA), the renewed international assertiveness of the PRC, especially in the East and the South China Sea, and the question mark about Pyongyang's regime. In particular, Beijing was realizing its project to modernize its army by 2027 and to create a first-class armed force by 2049.

Another issue has been China's economic, financial, and technological presence in the West, and Beijing's growing capacity for power projection. Even before 2009, of great concern to the Atlantic Alliance was the PRC's interest in key areas, from the Mediterranean Sea to the Middle East, and within Europe itself. The Belt and Road Initiative and the relations between the PRC and the 17+1 Group consolidated the Chinese economic and infrastructural presence in Europe: from Piraeus in Greece to Zeebrugge and Antwerp in Belgium, passing through Valencia and Bilbao in Spain. Moreover, Beijing established strategic partnerships with Egypt, Algeria (Matallah 2018), Tunisia and Morocco (Zoubir 2020). From a strategic point of view, the PLA Navy has been able to send military patrols to Mediterranean ports since 2013, while in 2017 the PRC established a Support Base in Djibouti, demonstrating Chinese projection capabilities in an area of high interest to the countries of the southern flank of the Atlantic Alliance.

Summing up, for many years NATO was engaged on a global level and in extra-European areas, but still the Atlantic Alliance was not moving towards an Asia-Pacific projection, despite the former Commander of US and NATO military forces in Afghanistan, General John Allen, raising a provocative question in 2017 about the application of Article 5 in the event of a new Korean war (Gady 2017). For an official position regarding the PRC, we had to wait even longer: the turning point was Donald J. Trump's administration. NATO conducted the first China Review in 2018, and in August 2019, during a visit to Australia, Secretary General Jens Stoltenberg renewed the Atlantic Alliance's interest in the PRC, stating that Beijing was 'investing heavily in critical infrastructure in Europe, [had an] increased presence in the Arctic and also [an] increased presence in Africa, and in cyberspace'[9]. Some months later, in December 2019, the London Declaration issued during the North Atlantic Council for the first time officially considered the PRC's 'growing influence and international policies' both as 'opportunities and challenges'[10]. The COVID-19 pandemic and health system crisis renewed the Secretary General's criticism of Beijing[11]. That was why in June 2020 he twice spoke officially about the PRC, first stating that the Atlantic Alliance needed 'a more global approach'[12], and secondly affirming that 'China is high on the NATO agenda'[13].

The first concrete step taken in that direction was in December 2020, when a document entitled NATO 2030: United For a New Era was presented. Compiled by a group of experts assembled by Stoltenberg, it represented an unprecedented scenario, charting a future of great change for NATO. As had been anticipated by the Secretary General's previous statements, the memorandum did not suggest a build-up of the Atlantic Alliance in the Asia-Pacific, it simply recognized the multidimensional threat of Beijing to some (European) players, and their permeability regarding Chinese presence, especially in the field of high technology and cybersecurity. Ten years after the drafting of the last Strategic Concept, this document represents a possible passage for the future positioning of the Alliance. Indeed, it records, for the first time in a formal way, the challenge brought by Beijing: 'the scale of Chinese power and global reach poses acute challenges to

---

9   Mair, J., and Packham, C. (2019). 'NATO needs to address China's rise, says Stoltenberg', *Reuters*, 8 August, <https://www.reuters.com/article/us-australia-nato/nato-needs-to-address-chinas-rise-says-stoltenberg-idUSKCN1UX0YX>.

10   North Atlantic Council (2019). 'London Declaration. Press Release', 4 December, <https://www.nato.int/cps/en/natohq/official_texts_171584.htm>.

11   See the interview in Gramer, R. (2020). 'NATO Chief Rebukes China Over Coronavirus Disinformation' *Foreign Policy*, 17 April, <https://foreignpolicy.com/2020/04/17/nato-cheif-rebukes-china-coronavirus-disinformation/>.

12   Stoltenberg, J. (2020). 'Remarks on launching #NATO2030 – Strengthening the Alliance in an increasingly competitive world', 8 June, <https://www.nato.int/cps/en/natohq/opinions_176197.htm>.

13   Stoltenberg, J. (2020). 'Press conference following the meeting of Nato Defense Ministers', 17 June, <https://www.nato.int/cps/en/natohq/opinions_176520.htm?selectedLocale=fr>.

open and democratic societies, particularly because of that country's trajectory to greater authoritarianism and an expansion of its territorial ambitions'[14].

The document was published at the end of Donald J. Trump's presidential term, which, as is well known, subjected the transatlantic relationship to strong tensions. The so-called 'China threat' exacerbated the relations between the members of the Alliance, dividing them into the two sides of the Atlantic. That is why the document must be read, not in isolation, but as a stage in the process of defining the next Strategic Concept, and as a mediation between the two different positions of the Euro-American counterparts. United For a New Era represents a partial response to the denunciation made in November 2019 by French President Manuel Macron regarding the 'brain death' state of the Atlantic Alliance[15], but also a response to the US Trumpist international isolation, the possible break-up with Turkey and the other big issue, the US request for burden-sharing, that is that 2 per cent of European GDP be allocated to defence.

It was a short-lived stage, because a few days later Beijing was the protagonist of two very successful diplomatic initiatives: the Regional Comprehensive Economic Partnership (RCEP) and the Comprehensive Agreement on Investment (CAI). Thanks to the former, Beijing was included in the geoeconomics area producing 30 per cent and 27.4 per cent of global GDP and trade respectively. RCEP created the world's largest free-trade agreement which includes democracies such as Australia, New Zealand, South Korea and Japan. The second Chinese goal was the CAI, which represents the final stage of more than 35 rounds of negotiations with the European Union, the most important strategic and economic partner of the US and Washington's counterpart within the Atlantic Alliance.

Conclusion: Europe between Eurasian and Transatlantic relations

In 1928, a young historian named Philip Joseph concluded in his doctoral research that, at least by the end of the nineteenth century, 'China and Europe were fused into one political system. Henceforth European politics could not be divorced from Chinese affairs' (Joseph 1928). It was a view that historiographically certainly does not appear exaggerated. In Manchuria, during the Russo-Japanese

---

14 Reflection Group Appointed by the NATO Secretary General (2020). 'NATO 2030: United For a New Era', 25 November, <https://www.nato.int/nato_static_fl2014/assets/pdf/2020/12/pdf/201201-Reflection-Group-Final-Report-Uni.pdf>.

15 'Emmanuel Macron in his own words' (2019). The Economist, 7 November, <https://www.economist.com/europe/2019/11/07/emmanuel-macron-in-his-own-words-english>.

war of 1904–1905, the chain of crises that resulted in the Great War began (Kowner et al. 2010). In the 1930s, the Japanese invasion of China started the slow collapse of the Paris order of 1919 (Lamb and Tarling 2001). Similarly, in this short essay I propose that the refusal of the PRC to participate in the new post-war order, together with the Maoist victory in the 1949 civil war and the 1950 Sino-Soviet alliance, contributed to determining the architecture of the Cold War international system. They transformed the competitive relationship between the winners of the Second World War into a zero-sum game and created the structural conditions leading to the construction of the Western military system.

We cannot know yet if the beginning of the pandemic in the PRC is another turning point (Kissinger 2020), a changing in the tide of the global international system coming from Asia, or not (Ferguson 2020). For sure, today we are in a scenario that has similar but also profoundly different traits to the Cold War one. According to some analysts, the conflict began on 24 February is confirming the return to a polarizing logic of the geostrategic confrontation among two worlds, values, and visions of politics. On the one hand, we are witnessing a consolidation of the axis between Beijing and Moscow, which was partly the result of Western policies of diplomatic and military pressure (Russett and Stam 1998). Of course, there are frictions and different views, but within and outside the framework of the Shanghai Cooperation Organization (SCO), these two players are recreating a possible geopolitical block opposed to the West (Brzezinski 1997). In 2017, the PRC and Russia held joint military exercises in Asia, the Mediterranean and the Baltic Seas (Zhang 2017). The axis has been confirmed during 2022, despite the shyness and acrobatics with which Beijing has moved in this phase of the war in Ukraine. On the other hand, even if the Russian global threat is not as alarming as the Soviet one was, the US is likewise not in the same position as it was in the 1950s: the system is on the cusp of a hegemonic transition where Washington's attractiveness and leadership are being eroded. Beijing's defence budget is the second largest in the world, but economic forecasts estimate that Chinese GDP will overtake the US in 2028. Washington itself seems to be undermining the foundations of the global architecture it helped shape in 1945, with the more or less reticent collaboration of the other winners of the Second World War and reshaped from 1991 onwards. Such a process is a reaction to the fears about Washington's decline as the systemic centre and world hegemonic power. It symbolically began in 1971 with the dismantling of Bretton Woods, resurfaced in the following years leading up to the Trump era and then accelerated with the COVID-19 health crisis.

Joe Biden's presidency is unlikely to change the US position towards the PRC, though it will likely be without the harsh Trumpist rhetoric (Campbell and Doshi 2021). At the same time, it should be emphasized that the centrifugal diplomatic movements of Europe from the United States have stopped. It is well known that the Bruxelles prefer normative and diplomatic pressures to Washington's muscular manoeuvres. However, the Russian aggression in Ukraine is triggering the EU rearmament and a decisive compromise of the major European Countries, including Germany, to raise military spending to the 2 per cent of their own GDP, responding in the affirmative to US wishes. In this new context, the European NATO members cannot shirk facing up to the new Asian repositioning of Washington's priorities and the friction with Beijing.

The United States is turning from the Atlantic to the Pacific, and the Europeans are doing the same, as we can see from their increased commitment in recent years. France, due to its historical presence in the South-Eastern flank, was the first European power that formulated its Indo-Pacific strategy[16], followed in 2020 by Germany and the Netherlands, tightening cooperation with India, Indonesia, Japan and Malaysia. However, Old Continent countries are moving in a strategically autonomous way, often outside the multilateral framework of the EU projection, and often pushing the priorities of the Atlantic Alliance itself to the side-lines or showing reluctance to align with the US. In talking about the Sino-US frictions the official German policy guidelines for the Indo-Pacific stated 'no country should [...] be forced to choose between two sides'[17]. European players are also having trouble deploying forces to Eastern Asia. The war in Ukraine is provoking a compaction of the Atlantic Alliance and the return of its focus on European issues, but it remains to understand how the new NATO, and the different NATO's members will deal with the PRC's question. In this sense, the relationship with the Quad will be central to the future of the Atlantic defence system in the Asia-Pacific, even if a welding between the two groups appears to be quite improbable for the reasonable future.

NATO probably is still the most successful alliance in Western history. First class European leaders stated that 'le temps de la naïveté européenne' [the

---

16 Ministère des Armées (2017). *Revue stratégique de défense et de sécurité nationale,* 12 October, <https://www.defense.gouv.fr/dgris/presentation/evenements-archives/revue-strategique-de-defense-et-de-securite-nationale-2017>.

17 Auswärtiges Amt (2020). '"Germany – Europe – Asia: shaping the 21st century together": The German Government adopts policy guidelines on the Indo-Pacific region', 1 September, <https://www.auswaertiges-amt.de/en/aussenpolitik/regionales chwerpunkte/asien/german-government-policy-guidelines-indo-pacific/2380510>.

time for European naivety] regarding Chinese issues is over (Macron 2019), underlying the importance of a 'new transatlantic agenda' (Von der Leyen 2020) and they called for a 'reunification of the so-called Western world [...] to face this challenge of China' (Weber 2020). However, we cannot fail to observe two dynamics: fractures within the Alliance and transatlantic cleavages, directly or indirectly linked to the PRC. The latest one is probably the pandemic crisis management both in the Old and in the New Continents which represents a challenge for the resilience of the Atlantic Alliance. Other challenges include Turkish dynamism in the Mediterranean, on a direct collision course with some NATO fellow members; Brexit and the crisis of the European integration process; and growing Russian indirect muscle-flexing and direct assertiveness in Central and Eastern Europe. The undoing of the Asian (Chinese) knot is therefore central to the definition of the new Strategic Concept: NATO's future is still foggy but its new identity in this era of hegemonic transition will depend on it.

Bibliography

Allison, G. (2017). *Destined for War: Can America and China Escape Thucydides's Trap*. Boston, MA: Houghton Mifflin Harcourt.

Auswärtiges Amt (2020). ' "Germany – Europe – Asia: shaping the 21st century together": The German Government adopts policy guidelines on the Indo-Pacific region', 1 September, <https://www.auswaertiges-amt.de/en/aussen politik/regionaleschwerpunkte/asien/german-government-policy-guideli nes-indo-pacific/2380510>.

Berrettini, M. (2016). ' "Neither War, Nor Peace": una genealogia etimologica della Guerra Fredda', *Nuova Storia Contemporanea*, 5–6, 129–142.

Bērziṇa-Čerenkova, U.A. (2021). 'Towards a NATO China Strategy', *Rahvusvaheline Kaitseuuringute Keskus*, January, <https://icds.ee/wp-content/uploads/2021/01/ICDS_Brief_NATO2030_Series_2_Aleksandra_Berzina-Cerenkova_January_2021.pdf>.

Brzezinski, Z. (1997). *The Grand Chessboard: American Primacy and Its Geostrategic Imperatives*. New York, NY: Basic Books.

Brzezinski, I. (2020). 'NATO's role in a transatlantic strategy on China', *Atlantic Council*, 1 June, <https://www.atlanticcouncil.org/blogs/new-atlanticist/natos-role-in-a-transatlantic-strategy-on-china/>.

Campbell, K.M, and Doshi, R. (2021). 'How America Can Shore Up Asian Order', *Foreign Affairs*, 12 January, <https://www.foreignaffairs.com/articles/united-states/2021-01-12/how-america-can-shore-asian-order>.

Department of Defense (2018). 'National Defense Strategy, Sharpening the American Military's Competitive Edge', 19 January, <https://dod.defense.gov/Portals/1/Documents/pubs/2018-National-Defense-Strategy-Summary.pdf>.

'Emmanuel Macron in his own words' (2019). *The Economist*, 7 November, <https://www.economist.com/europe/2019/11/07/emmanuel-macron-in-his-own-words-english>.

European Commission (2019). 'EU-China: A Strategic Outlook', 12 March, <https://ec.europa.eu/commission/sites/beta-political/files/communication-eu-china-a-strategic-outlook.pdf>.

Ferguson, N. (2020). 'Why Trump and Xi might both lose the corona wars', *The Spectator*, 18 April, <https://www.spectator.co.uk/article/corona-wars>.

Gady, F.S. (2017). 'Second Korean War: Would NATO Invoke Article 5?'. *The Diplomat*, 29 May, <https://thediplomat.com/2017/05/second-korean-war-would-nato-invoke-article-5/>.

Gramer, R. (2020). 'NATO Chief Rebukes China Over Coronavirus Disinformation' *Foreign Policy*, 17 April, <https://foreignpolicy.com/2020/04/17/nato-cheif-rebukes-china-coronavirus-disinformation/>.

Joseph, P. (1928). *Foreign Diplomacy in China 1894–1900: A Study in Political and Economic Relations with China*. London: George Allan & Unwin.

Kaplan, R.S. (2019). 'A New Cold War Has Begun', *Foreign Policy*, 7 January, <https://foreignpolicy.com/2019/01/07/a-new-cold-war-has-begun/>.

Kissinger, H.A. (2020). 'The Coronavirus Pandemic Will Forever Alter the World Order', *Wall Street Journal*, 3 April, <https://www.wsj.com/articles/the-coronavirus-pandemic-will-forever-alter-the-world-order-11585953005>.

Kowner, R. (ed.) (2010). *The Impact of the Russo-Japanese War*. London-New York, NY: Routledge.

Lamb, M., and Nicholas, T. (2001). *From Versailles to Pearl Harbor: The Origins of the Second World War in Europe and Asia*. London: Palgrave Macmillan.

Mair, J., and Packham, C. (2019). 'NATO needs to address China's rise, says Stoltenberg', *Reuters*, 8 August, <https://www.reuters.com/article/us-australia-nato/nato-needs-to-address-chinas-rise-says-stoltenberg-idUSKCN1UX0YX>.

Matallah, S. (2018). 'Sino-Algerian Strategic Cooperation: Towards a New Stage of Development', *China and the World*, 1(3), 1–18.

Ministère des Armées (2017). *Revue stratégique de défense et de sécurité nationale*, 12 October, <https://www.defense.gouv.fr/dgris/presentation/evenements-archives/revue-strategique-de-defense-et-de-securite-nationale-2017>.

North Atlantic Council (2019). 'London Declaration. Press Release', 4 December, <https://www.nato.int/cps/en/natohq/official_texts_171584.htm>.

Nouwens, M., and Legarda, H. (2020). *China's rise as a global security actor: implications for NATO*. London: The International Institute for Strategic Studies.

Nye, J.S. (2020). 'Cold War With China Is Avoidable', *Wall Street Journal*, 20 December, <https://www.wsj.com/articles/cold-war-with-china-is-avoida ble-11609347643>.

Pothier, F. (2019). 'How should NATO respond to China's growing power?', *The International Institute for Strategic Studies*, 12 September, <https://www.iiss. org/blogs/analysis/2019/09/nato-respond-china-power>.

Rachman, G. (2020). 'A new cold war: Trump, Xi and the escalating US-China confrontation'. *Financial Times*, 5 October, <https://www.ft.com/content/ 7b809c6a-f733-46f5-a312-9152aed28172>.

Reflection Group Appointed by the NATO Secretary General (2020). 'NATO 2030: United For a New Era', 25 November, <https://www.nato.int/nato_st atic_fl2014/assets/pdf/2020/12/pdf/201201-Reflection-Group-Final-Report-Uni.pdf>.

Robert, G. (1981). *War and change in world politics*. Cambridge: Cambridge University Press.

Russett, B., and Stam, A.C. (1998). 'Courting Disaster: An Expanded NATO vs. Russia and China', *Political Science Quarterly*, 113 (3), 361–382.

Schmitt, C. (1942). *Land und Meer. Eine weltgeschichtliche Betrachtung*. Leipzig: Reclam.

Schroeder, P.W. (1976). 'Alliances, 1815–1945: Weapons of Power and Tools of Management'. In Knorr, K. (ed.), *Historical Dimensions of National Security Problems*, pp. 247–286. Lawrence: University Press of Kansas.

Speranza, L. (2020). *A strategic concept for countering Russian and Chinese hybrid threats*. Washington, DC: Atlantic Council.

Stoltenberg, J. (2019). 'Speech at the Munich Security Conference', 15 February. <https://www.nato.int/cps/en/natohq/opinions_163791.htm>.

–––– (2020). 'Remarks on launching #NATO2030 – Strengthening the Alliance in an increasingly competitive world', 8 June, <https://www.nato.int/cps/en/ natohq/opinions_176197.htm>.

–––– (2020). 'Press conference following the meeting of Nato Defense Ministers', 17 June, <https://www.nato.int/cps/en/natohq/opinions_176520.htm?selecte dLocale=fr>.

Wertheim, S. (2019). 'Is It Too Late to Stop a New Cold War with China?', *The New York Times*, 8 June, <https://www.nytimes.com/2019/06/08/opinion/sunday/trump-china-cold-war.html>.

White House Office, The (2017). 'National Security Strategy of the United States of America', 18 December, <https://www.whitehouse.gov/wp-content/uploads/2017/12/NSS-Final-12-18-2017-0905-2.pdf>.

Zhang, T. (2017). 'Navy conducts live-fire drill en route to Baltic', *China Daily*, 12 July, <http://eng.mod.gov.cn/news/2017-07/12/content_4785302.htm>.

Zinaida, B., and Bradley, A. T. (2016). 'NATO's New Role: The Alliance's Response to a Rising China', *Naval War College Review*, 69 (3), 1–17.

Zoubir, Y.H. (2020). 'Expanding Sino–Maghreb Relations. Morocco and Tunisia', *Chatham House*, 26 February, <https://www.chathamhouse.org/2020/02/expanding-sino-maghreb-relations>.

Davide Borsani

Eurasian Monolith?: The United States, NATO and the Sino-Russian Strategic Relationship

In 1950, the Sino-Soviet military alliance was a game-changer for the global balance of power. The two countries joined together to pursue their national interests. The West misread the Sino-Soviet relationship in the 1950s. The Allies overstated the political linkage between Moscow and Beijing by largely interpreting it through an ideological lens. The current Western political climate tends to read the Sino-Russian relationship through a similar view, maintaining that the two authoritarian powers threaten democracy. As a result of overlapping factors over the years, the Eurasian alignment between Moscow and Beijing has actually arisen as the greatest threat for the Western-led international order. This essay intends to highlight the difficulties that the PRC and Russia incurred in trying to develop a long-standing diplomatic and strategic front against the 'free world'. It also focuses on how the West, mainly NATO, perceived – and still perceives – the Sino-Russian relationship.

Introduction

In 1950, the Union of Soviet Socialist Republics (USSR) and the newly born People's Republic of China (PRC) signed the Treaty of Friendship, Alliance and Mutual Aid. The Treaty marked 'one of the turning points in the history of the twentieth century', and was 'a geopolitical earthquake of the highest magnitude' for the international balance of power (Radchenko 2017: 243). The alliance between Moscow and Beijing opened a window of opportunity for North Korea to invade the US-supported southern neighbour a few months later. The Sino-Soviet alliance plus the Korean conflict dramatically increased the fear of Communism in the Western world, pushing the Atlantic Alliance to transform itself into a full-fledged organization with an integrated military structure. The European and Asian-Pacific strategic theatres united. The possible opening of multiple fronts in containing the world expansion of Communism became a reality for the West. The Sino-Soviet alliance turned out to be a strategic nightmare for the US and 'free world' countries.

The Sino-Soviet alliance did not last long. The Treaty stated that it should remain in force for thirty years. In fact, it was a dead letter in the late 1950s. In 1980, China decided not to renew the alliance. Nevertheless, the idea that an alignment between Moscow and Beijing could be a strategic obstacle for the West survived in the geopolitical thinking, re-emerging in the twenty-first century. Meanwhile, NATO had started expanding eastward to the detriment of the Russian strategic positioning. Perceived pressure from the West made the Kremlin turn its sight toward the East. As a result, Beijing and Moscow came closer, solidifying their relationship not in the form of an alliance but as a partnership. After a number of joint declarations, the bilateral Treaty of Friendship signed in July 2001 laid the new foundations for solid cooperation between the two countries. It became the bedrock of a transregional security system ranging from Kaliningrad to Shanghai. The Ukrainian crisis that erupted in 2014 helped strengthen the Sino-Russian cooperation, pushing NATO and the US to look at both powers as an increasing security threat for the Western-led international system.

This chapter aims at surveying how the strategic relationship between Moscow and Beijing developed in the 1950s and over the three decades after the collapse of the Soviet Union. It does not imply that the Sino-Russian connection was – or it is – a monolithic axis. On the contrary, this essay intends to highlight the difficulties the two powers incurred in trying to develop a long-standing diplomatic and strategic front against the 'free world'. But this is only a part of the story. On the other hand, the chapter focuses on how the West, mainly NATO, perceived – and still perceives – the Sino-Russian relationship. Can the fear of Communism in the 1950s be mirrored in the newly proclaimed struggle between democracy and authoritarianism? Are we witnessing a new Cold War? The dynamics of the multipolar world do seem much more complex.

The method sets out to draw a preliminary comparison between the 1950s and current dynamics through a historical lens. Archival resources concerning the Sino-Soviet alliance and Western attitude, particularly NATO, in the 1950s are available, while those regarding more recent events are not. Nevertheless, statements, strategic guidelines, communiqués, etc., that can underpin the historical investigation of current affairs have been published. Finally, the essay argues that the diplomatic reality and its nuances do not necessarily reflect political perceptions. Western governments should be careful in dealing with the today's strategic scenario without considering diplomatic history.

The Sino-Soviet alliance and the West

The Sino-Soviet alliance treaty was signed in 1950 by the USSR Minister of Foreign Affairs, Andrei Vyshinskii, and the PRC Prime Minister, Zhou Enlai. It was negotiated over two months during Mao Zedong's first trip to Moscow. The visit of the Chinese Communist leader to the Soviet Union had considerable importance. After the end of the Chinese Civil War and the defeat of Nationalist forces, Soviet leader Joseph Stalin was confronted with the new political situation in the Far East. It gradually became impossible for him to defend the status quo and those imperial concessions granted by Chinese Nationalist leader Chiang Kai-shek in 1945 as a result of the consensus reached among the Big Three at the Yalta Conference. Stalin cannot ignore that Mao kept labelling himself as his pupil, asking for Soviet political advice and economic-military help to strengthen the Communist grip over China. According to Mao, Beijing was ready to strategically subordinate itself to the Soviet line, even if the Chinese regime would tactically disagree on some issues. The vassalage was a clear opportunity for the USSR to legitimize Communism as the world-leading political force vis-à-vis the US-led Western 'imperialist' bloc. In Stalin's eyes, the eventual reframing of the Sino-Soviet relationship should not happen in the name of ideological comradery. The national interest was the main rationale – that is, to empower the Soviet Union as a superpower (Heinzig 2015).

In the first meeting between Stalin and Mao on 16 December 1949, the Chinese leader stressed that 'China needs a period of 3–5 years of peace, which would be used to bring the economy back to pre-war levels and to stabilize the country in general'. Peace, in his opinion, could be reached under the Soviet security umbrella only. Stalin answered that 'we can discuss and decide', but with no modification of 'any of the points' of the already-existing Chinese-Soviet agreement. Mostly, Stalin needed to be sure that a revision of the former treaty did not compromise the right for Soviet troops to station in the Chinese mainland, notably Port Arthur. Mao told him that he favoured keeping them there.[1]

A month later, on 22 January 1950, Mao reiterated that 'we should strengthen our existing friendship using the help of treaties and agreements. This would resonate well both in China and in the international arena' to prevent that 'the imperialist countries will attempt to hinder us'. He continued: 'The new treaty must include the questions of political, economic, cultural and military cooperation', including 'a paragraph on consultation regarding international concerns'. As for the Soviet troops in China, they 'could serve as a base for our

---

1   Record of Conversation between I.V. Stalin and Chairman of the Central People's Government of the People's Republic of China Mao Zedong, 16 December 1949, *The Cold War International History Project,* Woodrow Wilson Center Digital Archive, <https://digitalarchive.wilsoncenter.org/document/111240> accessed 21 March 2022.

military collaboration'. After all, Chinese soldiers and political élite could draw 'on the experience of our Soviet comrades'. Stalin was convinced that the Chinese subordination was authentic and, most importantly, in harmony with the Soviet leadership and interests. The Kremlin, thus, agreed to start drafting the security alliance.[2]

On 14 February 1950, Vyshinskii and Zhou Enlai signed the Treaty of Friendship, Alliance and Mutual Assistance. The two powers stated in the preamble that their goal was to strengthen their 'friendship and cooperation' in order 'to prevent the revival of Japanese imperialism and the repetition of aggression on the part of Japan or of any other State that might in any way join with Japan in acts of aggression'. The first article affirmed: 'Should either of the Contracting Parties be attacked by Japan or by States allied with Japan and thus find itself in a state of war, the other Contracting Party shall immediately extend military and other assistance with all the means at its disposal'. The alliance was defensive and directed against Japan, while the *casus foederis* clearly concerned the Americans, who were occupying the Japanese territory. Furthermore, Moscow and Beijing accepted not to 'enter into any alliance directed against the other Party', or participate in any coalition or in any action or measures directed against the other Party', and to 'consult together on all important international questions involving the common interests'.[3] The Treaty entered into force on 11 April 1950.

Hence, Stalin stabilized the Soviet presence and influence in the Far East and China, while enlarging Communist control over the Eurasian landmass. It was a game-changer in both diplomatic and military fields in the already-existing Cold War. On his part, Mao obtained political legitimacy from the Soviet elder comrade. The Communist regime in the PRC was finally awarded the security umbrella that it strongly needed from the senior party of the alliance. After all, from the Chinese point of view, what was happening in the US was particularly

---

2   Record of Talks between I.V. Stalin and Chairman of the Central People's Government of the People's Republic of China Mao Zedong, 22 January 1950, *The Cold War International History Project,* Woodrow Wilson Center Digital Archive, <https://digitalarchive.wilsoncenter.org/document/111245> accessed 21 March 2022.

3   Treaty of Friendship, Alliance and Mutual Assistance between the Union of Soviet Socialist Republics and the People's Republic of China, 14 February 1950, *The World and Japan Database,* Contemporary International Relations – Basic Documents, <https://worldjpn.grips.ac.jp/documents/texts/docs/19500214.T1E.html> accessed 21 March 2022.

worrying at that time. Mao's government had become convinced that the American 'imperialist' goal was to ruin the new regime.

One of the myths concerning Sino-American relations is that the United States owned China in the mid-1940s. According to this perspective, the Communist victory in 1949 led to the infamous 'loss of China'. It is hard to argue that the US grip on Chiang Kai-Shek's Nationalist Forces was enough to own China at that time (Chi-kwan 2012). Nevertheless, the 'China lobby' in the US Congress disagreed. Henry R. Luce and Joseph R. McCarthy were among its most notable members. The lobby was a powerful force in influencing the Truman administration confronting Communist China and outlining security strategies and defence perimetries across Eurasia. Also, American public opinion played an important role in shaping the government's policy. The release of the 'China White Paper' in August 1949 inflamed the domestic debate, feeding the perception that President Harry Truman did not make enough to defend the US positioning in the Far East. Meanwhile, influential magazines such as *Time* or *Life* published maps to show how over 40 per cent of the global population and roughly the entire landmass of Eurasia went under Stalin's control due to Communist victory in China. It is true that in the late 1940s some US diplomats tried to approach Mao's inner circle to avoid an alliance between Moscow and Beijing. Between 1949 and 1950, however, domestic pressures largely contributed to making the Truman Administration overtly tilt towards diplomatic hostility (Mayers 1986).

The Secretary of State, Dean Acheson, believed that China was only a temporary satellite of the Soviet Union, and it would reject the junior ally status in the longer term. In his opinion, the US had to be careful in differentiating Soviet interests from Chinese ones (Bartley 2020). McCarthy's anti-Communist lobbying was crucial in reverting the debate. Not only he publicly declared that many Communist sympathisers were working at the Department of State, but he also alleged their betrayal for the 'loss of China', asking for an investigation. Acheson felt compelled to undertake a tour across the US to convince the public opinion that he was not a traitor. His diplomatic line, thus, could not be defended. Furthermore, President Truman was very sensitive to the domestic mood. Like him, many administration officials saw the Sino-Soviet alliance as a totalitarian conspiracy toward the 'free world'. The US, hence, chose to oppose the Communist 'monolith' in Eurasia in the broader framework of the strategy of containment.

The National Security Council Report 68 (NSC\68) adopted in April 1950 stated that 'Soviet efforts are now directed toward the domination of the Eurasian land mass'. Although the new strategy acknowledged some national differences among Communist countries, it maintained that the 'free world' and the US had the fundamental task to avoid 'a Soviet Empire compromising all or most of Eurasia'. The victory of Communism in China was a critical piece in the Soviet attempt to rule the most crucial world area and the world itself. However, the NSC\68 Report stressed that Europe still had to be prioritised over Asia in the American strategy.[4]

The Western unity was required to tackle Communist ambitions across Eurasia. But reality was more nuanced. Once Mao proclaimed the creation of the PRC, the issue of diplomatic recognition came to the front. The United States was adamantly opposed to recognizing the new regime. Europe was more ambivalent. France was involved in fighting Communism in Indochina, and the recognition of the revolutionary forces' victory in China was not an option. On the contrary, the United Kingdom swiftly recognized the PRC in January 1950. London had plans to retain Hong Kong as a colony, and it could not defend it without coming to terms with Mao. Moreover, the British had considerable investments in the Chinese mainland. The Americans told the British that this diplomatic concession was unwise, reducing strategic options for the West. The British response was that the American diplomatic hostility would only prolong and deepen Sino-Soviet cooperation (Lanxin 1995). Many non-Communist European countries followed in Britain's footsteps, including allies (the Netherlands and Norway) and neutral States (Switzerland and Sweden). The US leadership was not enough to rally the allies around the common Western flag. Nevertheless, Chinese moves helped solidify the Western bloc. After ordering the seizure of the US Consulate in Beijing and refusing the exchange of Ambassadors with the British, Mao and his 'volunteers' were a military factor against the United Nations (UN) forces in the Korean war.

From the Korean war to the split

The outbreak of the Korean War in June 1950 was a watershed for the Eurasian balance of power. On the one hand, it was the only 'hot' war fought by the United States during the Cold War against another great power – PRC (even if unofficially) – with crucial strategic consequences from the Far East to Europe. According to President Truman, the Korean war proved that China had finally

---

4   National Security Council Report, NSC\68, 'United States Objectives and Programs for National Security', 14 April 1950, *History and Public Policy Program Digital Archive*, U.S. National Archives, <https://digitalarchive.wilsoncenter.org/document/116191. pdf> accessed 21 March 2022.

accepted the role of 'Russian puppet' (Pearlman 2008: 269). On the other hand, it was a critical test for the newly born Sino-Soviet alliance. Once North Korea's leader Kim Il Sung received Stalin's approval to attack South Korea in January 1950, he pilgrimed to Beijing, where Mao granted him China's support. After the invasion, the Communist camp coordinated its diplomatic and military activities. The Sino-Soviet alliance represented a deterrent for the US-led UN military forces to enlarge the war. Stalin's support covered Mao's back, giving the PRC strategic immunity.

The USSR and the PRC cooperated as comrades-in-arms. Nevertheless, criticalities were present. Soviet military aid to China was not for free, and turned out to be technologically obsolete compared to the US. Moreover, joint military planning was absent, and even common drills were never conducted afterwards (Goncharenko 1998). Chinese military operations dramatically improved Beijing's political standing in its relationship with Moscow. On the one hand, the Korean war increased Chinese military dependence on the USSR. On the other hand, the junior ally fought the common 'imperialist' enemy alone on the field, shouldering the largest share of the war burden. Communist China entirely proved its worth to the elder Soviet brother. Now, Mao thought that the Kremlin must recognize the new political balance between the two countries. The PRC must be seen as an equal partner.

The Korean War was 'a turning point in the history' of the Atlantic Alliance (Kaplan 1984: 8–9). Washington was reluctant to be too long engaged in Korea since the risk to be bottled up was very high. Furthermore, both the US and Britain believed that a prolonged war against China would only help the Soviets by draining Western power. Nevertheless, a crucial question quickly came to the front. If Communist forces waged an offensive war in Asia, why cannot the same happen in Europe? A second Communist invasion against the 'free world' possibly seemed imminent, and the Eurasian nightmare described by the NSC\68 Report was concrete. The strategic linkage between the two sides of Eurasia was evident, and it promptly led to the evolution of the North Atlantic Pact into an organization through its institutionalization. The Secretariat General and an integrated military structure were created, and the North Atlantic Treaty Organization (NATO) was born. It was also time to increase military spending, and rearmament went top on the Western agenda.

NATO's overall perception of the threat posed by the Sino-Soviet alliance is shown in two documents prepared in 1952 by the NATO Working Group on Trends in Soviet Policy. The first report stated: 'it seems that, for the moment at least, the USSR is willing to entrust China with the main role' in fuelling Communist revolutionary activities in Asia. Korea was only the beginning.

Moscow would divert its sight toward Europe, while Beijing would concentrate in Asia. According to their territorial competence, thus, China and the Soviet Union had divided tasks in Eurasia between them with the common goal to expand Communism.[5] 'Soviet confidence has greatly increased since the inclusion of the [European] Satellites and China in the Soviet bloc', the second report maintained. 'Close harmonious relations between Moscow and Communist China are of fundamental and vital importance in the pursuit of common objectives. Although potential sources of friction are readily discernible [...] it is believed that the USSR and Communist China will continue for an indefinite period to present a united front to the rest of the world'.[6]

Perceptions slightly differed in the following years, particularly that of the United States. In October 1958, the American delegation to NATO was still worried about the Sino-Soviet alliance in the long term. Despite some 'meaningful differences', such as 'Peiping's emergence as a second ideological centre within the bloc, the two powers strong community of interests based upon their commonly shared ideology' would 'unlikely' lead to 'a major split between Moscow and Peiping in the foreseeable future and it seems equally likely that the dominant characteristic of the alliance will be one of solidarity and close co-operation'.[7] Nevertheless, in less than two years, the Sino-Soviet split was a fact.

Divisive political elements in the Sino-Soviet alliance were highly influential in shaping intra-Communist dynamics at the end of the 1950s. Ideology played a relevant role, not as a glue but as a wedge. In 1956, the process of 'destalinization' provided a crucial moment of conflict between Moscow and Beijing. The condemning speech of the new Soviet leader Nikita Khrushchev at the Twentieth Congress of the USSR Communist Party reverberated worldwide. Mao took up the opposite stance on Stalin, both as idealogue and political leader. In the Chinese view, Khrushchev's 'blasphemy' legitimated Mao as heir to the Marx-Lenin-Stalin succession. Hence, China – and not the Soviet Union – should

---

5   Projet de Rapport du Groupe de Travail Politique sur la Politique Étrangère Sovietique, D-D(51)285-REV2-ADD1 – Additif 1, 31 January 1952, *NATO Archives Online*, <https://archives.nato.int/additif-1-projet-de-rapport-du-groupe-de-travail-politi que-sur-la-politique-etrangere-sovietique> accessed 21 March 2022.

6   Working Group on Trends in Soviet Foreign Policy – Report AC/34-R/2(I), 28 October 1952, *NATO Archives Online*, <https://archives.nato.int/working-group-on-trends-in-soviet-foreign-policy-report-ac-34-r-2-i> accessed 21 March 2022.

7   Divisive and Cohesive Elements in the Sino-Soviet Alliance, AC/119-WP(58)76, 1 October 1958, *NATO Archives Online*, <https://archives.nato.int/divisive-and-cohes ive-elements-in-sino-soviet-alliance> accessed 21 March 2022.

be considered the ideological leader of the Communist bloc. Moscow would provide military tools, but Beijing would play the role of the doctrinal guide, increasing its international prestige in the struggle against the 'imperialist' West. However, this proved unacceptable to Khrushchev, who did not want to share Soviet leadership and power at any level. At the end of the 1950s, the Kremlin realized that it was neither possible to manipulate China in the name of Communist unity nor to maintain the father-son relationship at a minimal cost (Lüthi 2008). Despite this, the US delegation to NATO still believed in 1959 that 'there is no reason' to think that these differences would threaten 'the essential solidarity of the Sino-Soviet alliance'.[8]

The Sino-Soviet dispute also concerned the relationship with the 'free world'. Khrushchev's policy of 'peaceful coexistence' triggered increasing preoccupations in Beijing. Mao feared the Chinese marginalization in a bipolar world where the two superpowers would negotiate bilaterally. The Non-Aligned Movement started acquiring significant appeal in Mao's eyes, not by chance. Moreover, the Soviets were worried about Chinese bombardments during the two Taiwan crises (1954–1958). The shelling was waged without consultations with Moscow, and risked leading to a Sino-American war due to the US-Taiwan Mutual Defense Treaty. As a consequence, a general conflict involving the USSR seemed possible because of the Sino-Soviet alliance treaty. On his part, Mao was willing to increase PRC strategic power. He even asked the Kremlin for sharing the nuclear know-how. At the end of the day, Khrushchev denied such a technology transfer, terminated Soviet aid programs and withdrew military experts. The more the PRC claimed an equal status to the USSR, the more the bilateral rift increased in magnitude. China did not intend to play the role of the junior ally in the post-Stalin world anymore.

The Sino-Soviet split had consequences in Eastern Europe, too. In 1957, Zhou Enlai visited Warsaw and Budapest. Apparently, the goal was to embolden the Soviet prestige after two intra-bloc crises in Poland and Hungary at the end of 1956. In truth, the PRC government set out to show the existence of an alternative to the Kremlin even inside the Communist world by convincing the Soviet Union to 'abandon its hegemonic attitude in dealing with other countries' (Zhihua and Yafeng 2015: 182). A few years later, once Albania strengthened its

---

8   Soviet Bloc Reaction to Chinese Communes, AC/119-WP(59)5, 28 January 1959, *NATO Archives Online*, <https://archives.nato.int/soviet-bloc-reaction-to-chinese-communes> accessed 21 March 2022.

relationship with the PRC, Tirana left the Soviet sphere of influence, pleading allegiance to Beijing.

The Sino-Soviet alliance was still in force at the beginning of the 1960s, at least in principle. In fact, it was a dead letter. The PRC started building up its military and diplomatic strengths independently from the Soviets. Eventually, China developed its nuclear deterrent in the mid-1960s. In 1962, the USSR declared its neutrality during the Sino-Indian war. In 1969, Moscow and Beijing even fought a limited war on the Ussuri river, near Manchurian borders. The Eastern flank of the Soviet Union was now uncovered. The United States under the Nixon presidency wisely exploited the differences between the two former Communist allies. The famous 'triangular diplomacy' to drive a wedge between Moscow and Beijing was key in the Cold War. China was now recognized as a third prominent great power in the international system. In 1980, the Sino-Soviet alliance treaty officially came to an end.

The new Sino-Russian partnership

In the 1990s, after the dissolution of the Soviet Union, the Kremlin mainly focused on Russian-US relations and its inclusion in the Western-led global system. The pursue of democracy and a free-market economy guided Russian foreign policy. The collapse of the USSR also had consequences on its relationship with Beijing. In 1949, Mao went to Moscow to strengthen the ties. Now, the Russian President Boris Yeltsin made his trip to China.

In 1992, the two governments signed the Joint Statement on the Basis of Mutual Relations between the PRC and the Russian Federation. They saw themselves as friendly countries willing to cooperate in the longer term and formally ending hostilities. Two years later, in 1994, the two governments agreed on a new document – the Sino-Russian Joint Declaration. They pledged to build a constructive partnership, adding it would not be directed against any other State. Hereafter, high-level exchanges began to be held regularly, including in technological and military fields (Yu 2002). In April 1997, once US President Bill Clinton informed Yeltsin that NATO's membership would be expanded eastward, Russia and China signed a new Joint Declaration on a Multipolar World and the Establishment of a New International Order. Beijing and Moscow decided to upgrade their bilateral relationship to a 'a partnership based on equality and mutual trust for the purpose of strategic interaction in the twenty-first century'.[9] From that moment on, the relationship started being institutionalized.

---

9   See the translation included in the letter from the Permanent Representatives of China
    and the Russian Federation to the United Nations addressed to the Secretary-General,

Between 1996 and 1997, China and Russia signed two additional treaties on security and cooperation alongside the former Soviet republics of Kazakhstan, Kyrgyzstan and Tajikistan – the Treaty on Deepening Military Trust in Border Regions and the Treaty on Reduction of Military Forces in Border Regions. A new form of military collaboration in Central Asia was born. In 2001, these five countries plus Uzbekistan agreed on establishing a structured organization – the Shanghai Cooperation Organization (SCO). 'Against a background of the rapid development of the process of political multipolarization and information globalization in the 21st century', the document said, the signatories pledged to 'strengthen their consultations and coordination of activities in regional and international affairs, support and cooperate with each other closely on major international and regional issues, and jointly promote and consolidate peace and stability of the region and the world. In the current international situation, it is of particular significance to preserve global strategic balance and stability'. The Six did 'not seek unilateral military superiority in contiguous regions'.[10] In 2007, the SCO countries held their first military exercise. Two years earlier, Russia and China had teamed up for their first large-scale military drills. Since 2012, Beijing and Moscow have held joint military exercises on a regular basis, including in the SCO framework. India and Pakistan entered the organization in 2017. Soon, even Iran could join it.

Meanwhile, in December 1999, Vladimir Putin had replaced Yeltsin as the Russian President. Unlike his predecessor, Putin was less oriented toward the West by vocation. Russia, in his opinion, should not be considered a part of the Western world or let alone a European periphery. On the contrary, it was the pivot country of Eurasia, linking together the West and the East in the role of a great power. Accordingly, Russia was much more than a regional power in Putin's eyes. Moscow had interests in Europe, Asia and their Eurasian peripheries, and it must avoid choosing between them if not compelled to. Since 1999, Putin's starting goal had been to expand the Russian sphere of influence over the former republics of the USSR, including those countries in Central Asia where the Chinese rise could challenge it. In his view, the PRC and US-allied Europe can be both partners and rivals, depending on the strategic circumstances. Nevertheless, Beijing was a more attractive partner in confronting American

---

15 May 1997, *United Nations Digital Library*, <https://digitallibrary.un.org/record/234074> accessed 21 March 2022.

10 Declaration of Shanghai Cooperation Organization, 15 June 2001, <https://www.mfa.gov.cn/ce/cetur/eng/zt/shhzzz/t162011.htm> accessed 21 March 2022.

supremacy over the international system and its institutions in the twenty-first century diplomatic landscape. Still today, China and Russia appear as an 'axis of convenience', sharing the view that the United States is the main stumbling block in restructuring the global balance of power (Lo 2008). Hence, Putin quickly began to look to Beijing as a significant strategic asset in re-asserting the Russian role as a great power.

Russia and the PRC signed the Treaty of Good Neighborhood and Friendly Cooperation (the 'Great Treaty') in 2001, two years after the controversial NATO's intervention in the Kosovo war. It was not an alliance modelled on the 1950 security agreement, let alone on the 1949 North Atlantic Treaty. On the contrary, it sanctioned a less committing strategic partnership in which the two powers set out to deepen their military cooperation, contribute to the security of each other and preserve regional and international stability. Moscow and Beijing undertook not to enter into opposing alliances or blocs and not to take actions that would damage the partner's sovereignty, security, and territorial integrity. Accordingly, the two countries would build their 'strategic cooperative partnership of good-neighborliness, friendship and cooperation and equality and trust' upon the principles of 'mutual respect of state sovereignty and territorial integrity, mutual non-aggression, mutual non-interference in each other's internal affairs, equality and mutual benefit and peaceful co-existence'. They would 'neither resort to the use of force or the threat of force nor take economic and other means to bring pressure to bear against the other', and would 'adopt measures to increase trust between their militaries and reduce military forces in the border areas. The contracting parties shall expand and deepen confidence building measures in the military field so as to consolidate each other's security and strengthen regional and international stability'. In a situation in which their national security is threatened, the two governments 'immediately hold contacts and consultations in order to eliminate such threats'.[11] No binding *casus foederis* in case of armed attack was included. Strategic and diplomatic flexibility, thus, was key to the bilateral relationship.

The outbreak of the Ukrainian crisis in 2014 caused a sharp cooling in the relations between Russia and the West. According to the Russian National Security Strategy published in 2015, 'The strengthening of Russia is taking place

---

11 Treaty of Good-Neighborliness and Friendly Cooperation Between the People's Republic of China and the Russian Federation, 16 July 2001, <https://www.fmprc.gov.cn/mfa_eng/wjdt_665385/2649_665393/200107/t20010724_679026.html> accessed 21 March 2022.

against a backdrop of new threats to national security that are of a multifarious and interconnected nature. The Russian Federation's implementation of an independent foreign and domestic policy is giving rise to opposition from the United States and its allies, who are seeking to retain their dominance in world affairs. [...] The West's stance aimed at countering integration processes and creating seats of tension in the Eurasian region is exerting a negative influence on the realization of Russian national interests'.[12] Not by chance, the cooperation between Moscow and Beijing has become increasingly vital for the Kremlin from that moment on.

The Russian government has sought a flow into the East to bypass hostilities and economic sanctions applied by Western countries due to the annexation of Crimea. In 2015, Putin and Chinese President, Xi Jinping, recalled the 'Great Treaty' principles, signing a new joint declaration. They reaffirmed the centrality of Eurasian cooperation between the two countries in the name of their co-development and a 'new type of international relations'.[13] In this context, Russia and the PRC have shown interest in coordinating their two (multi)regional integration projects. On the one hand, the Russian-led Eurasian Economic Union – born in 2014, and bringing together Belarus, Kazakhstan, Russia, Armenia and Kyrgyzstan. On the other hand, the Chinese-led Belt and Road Initiative, aimed at connecting trade routes from Shanghai to Rotterdam, passing through Moscow.

Despite high-level cooperation, the formalization of a new military alliance between the two powers does not appear on their agenda at the time of writing. The Sino-Soviet alliance and its history still shadow the current strategic relationship. However, it remains a matter of debate. Scholars seem divided between the possibilists and critics. The formers consider the event (even the necessity) of signing a binding bilateral agreement to deepen the military integration between the two countries. Such an alliance would counterbalance the strategic presence of the United States in Eurasia with crucial political consequences on the current global order. The new Sino-Russian alliance would be supported by the SCO countries and possibly open to other members. On the contrary, critics believe that a binding strategic agreement is not in Russian or Chinese interests. Even

---

12 English translation of the 2015 Russian National Security Strategy, December 2015, *Russia Matters Project,* Harvard Kennedy School's Belfer Center for Science and International Affairs Archive, <https://russiamatters.org/node/21421> accessed 21 March 2022.

13 Press Statements Following Russian-Chinese Talks, 8 May 2015, <http://en.kremlin.ru/events/president/transcripts/49433> accessed 24 October 2021.

the partnership established by the 'Great Treaty' would be destined to crack down in the longer term due to a growing asymmetry between the two powers. Can Russia really decide to follow the Chinese leadership than to lead? Beijing is a rapidly (and steeply) rising power, while Moscow increasingly appears as a giant with clay feet. Because of the Kremlin's prestige and reluctance to be the junior partner, thus, the two countries would be destined to distance themselves in the future (Bekkevold and Lo 2019).

Democracy versus authoritarianism

Today the West seems quite worried that China and Russia could strengthen their strategic ties. The United States showed the most serious concern due to its international position. According to the National Security Strategy published in December 2017 by the Trump administration, the 'revisionist powers of China and Russia' are 'actively competing against the United States and our allies and partners'. More precisely, 'China and Russia want to shape a world antithetical to U.S. values and interests. China seeks to displace the United States in the Indo-Pacific region, expand the reaches of its state-driven economic model, and reorder the region in its favor. Russia seeks to restore its great power status and establish spheres of influence near its borders'. On the one hand, 'China gathers and exploits data on an unrivaled scale and spreads features of its authoritarian system', and is building 'the most capable and well-funded military in the world, after our own. Its nuclear arsenal is growing and diversifying'. On the other hand, 'Russia aims to weaken U.S. influence in the world and divide us from our allies and partners. Russia views the North Atlantic Treaty Organization (NATO) and European Union (EU) as threats. [...] The combination of Russian ambition and growing military capabilities creates an unstable frontier in Eurasia, where the risk of conflict due to Russian miscalculation is growing'. In sum, 'great power competition returned. China and Russia began to reassert their influence regionally and globally', and 'are contesting our geopolitical advantages and trying to change the international order in their favor'.[14]

The first strategic document published by the Biden administration – the 2021 Interim National Security Strategic Guidance – echoed the 2017 NSS. It stressed that China and Russia are geopolitical rivals. It also added that they are ideological competitors. The document maintained that the two 'antagonistic

---

14 National Security Strategy of the United States of America, December 2017, <https://trumpwhitehouse.archives.gov/wp-content/uploads/2017/12/NSS-Final-12-18-2017-0905.pdf> accessed 21 March 2022.

authoritarian powers' are 'increasingly' challenging the 'democratic nations'. Accordingly, 'Authoritarianism is on the global march, and we must join with likeminded allies and partners to revitalize democracy the world over. We will work alongside fellow democracies across the globe to deter and defend against aggression from hostile adversaries. We will stand with our allies and partners to combat new threats aimed at our democracies'. The PRC, in particular, 'has rapidly become more assertive', showing itself as the main rival. But 'Russia remains determined to enhance its global influence and play a disruptive role on the world stage'. Together, 'both Beijing and Moscow have invested heavily in efforts meant to check U.S. strengths and prevent us from defending our interests and allies around the world'. The only way to prevent an expansion of the Sino-Russian authoritarian influence across Eurasia and the world would be to strengthen the relationship with democratic allies in the name of a shared ideology. Indeed, 'Our democratic alliances enable us to present a common front, produce a unified vision, and pool our strength to promote high standards, establish effective international rules, and hold countries like China [and Russia] to account'.[15] The National Security Strategy published in October 2022 emphasised these arguments even more in light of the Russian invasion of Ukraine that occurred in the previous February.[16]

Western allies gradually adopted a similar perspective. The outbreak of the COVID-19 pandemic and the question of Hong Kong in 2020 have been apparently proof that China does not intend to act as a responsible stakeholder in the current international system. The Ukrainian crisis, which erupted into an open war in 2022, demonstrated that Russian revisionism has evolved into an open military threat to European stability and territorial integrity. In December 2020, the direction that NATO was about to follow was displayed by the report 'NATO 2030: United for a New Era'. This document has been prepared by a selected Reflection Group working alongside NATO Secretary General Jens Stoltenberg, who has been asked by the North Atlantic Council 'to undertake a Forward-Looking Reflection Process to assess ways to strengthen the political dimension of the NATO Alliance'. According to the report, 'NATO must adapt to meet the needs of a more demanding strategic environment marked by the

---

15 Interim National Strategic Security Guidance, March 2021, <https://www.whitehouse.gov/wp-content/uploads/2021/03/NSC-1v2.pdf> accessed 21 March 2022.

16 National Security Strategy, October 2022, < https://www.whitehouse.gov/wp-content/uploads/2022/10/Biden-Harris-Administrations-National-Security-Strategy-10.2022.pdf> accessed 8 May 2023.

return of systemic rivalry, persistently aggressive Russia, the rise of China [...] NATO critically needs political convergence on first order questions because the sheer scale of threats, and in particular the simultaneous geopolitical and ideological challenge from Russia and China, portend consequences for the security and prosperity of us all'.[17]

The Final Communiqué issued by NATO Heads of State and Government in June 2021 highlighted that the Allies must confront challenges and threats posed by 'assertive and authoritarian powers'. 'Russia's aggressive actions constitute a threat to Euro-Atlantic security', while 'China's growing influence and international policies can present challenges that we need to address together as an Alliance'. Among the most worrying circumstances, the Allies stressed that Beijing was 'cooperating militarily with Russia, including through participation in Russian exercises in the Euro-Atlantic area'.[18]

Finally, the new NATO Strategic Concept adopted at the Madrid summit held in June 2022 stressed that 'Authoritarian actors challenge our interests, values and democratic way of life. They are investing in sophisticated conventional, nuclear and missile capabilities, with little transparency or regard for international norms and commitments'. Indeed, they are 'at the forefront of a deliberate effort to undermine multilateral norms and institutions and promote authoritarian models of governance'. Russia is considered as 'the most significant and direct threat to Allies' security and to peace and stability in the Euro-Atlantic area', while China's 'stated ambitions and coercive policies challenge our interests, security and values'. Mostly important, the Strategic Concept maintains that 'The deepening strategic partnership between the People's Republic of China and the Russian Federation and their mutually reinforcing attempts to undercut the rules-based international order run counter to our values and interests'.[19]

According to the Transatlantic Trends report published in 2021, the public opinions of most Euro-Atlantic countries consider China 'more a rival than a partner' (Bertelsmann Foundation and GMF 2021). A Gallup poll in March 2022

---

17 NATO 2030: United for a New Era. Analysis and Recommendations of the Reflection Group Appointed by the NATO Secretary General, 25 November 2020, <https://www.nato.int/nato_static_fl2014/assets/pdf/2020/12/pdf/201201-Reflection-Group-Final-Report-Uni.pdf> accessed 21 March 2022.

18 Brussels Summit Communiqué Issued by the Heads of State and Government Participating in the Meeting of the North Atlantic Council in Brussels, 14 June 2021, <https://www.nato.int/cps/ru/natohq/news_185000.htm> accessed 21 March 2022.

19 NATO 2022 Strategic Concept, 29 June 2022, <https://www.nato.int/nato_static_fl2014/assets/pdf/2022/6/pdf/290622-strategic-concept.pdf>, accessed 8 May 2023.

showed that 96 % of American citizens believe that China's military power is a critical or important threat to US security, while 94 % think that also Russia is a significant or relevant military issue (Jones 2022). A 2021 survey by the European Council on Foreign Relations observed that most Europeans maintained that a new Cold War waged by Beijing and Moscow against the West is underway. However, the same report also underlined the lack of consensus in the European public opinion that the world of tomorrow will face a growing competition between democracy and authoritarianism. On the contrary, it is European institutions rather than the public to view the international system through this lens (Krastev and Leonard 2021). This has been a significant U-turn compared to the political address in the 2000s and the 2010s. Before the COVID-19 pandemic and the Ukrainian war, European institutions mainly tended to look at both Russia and China as economic opportunities in the energy market and trade respectively. A sometimes-surfacing degree of suspicion did not stop business.

The Sino-Russian Joint Statement on the International Relations Entering a New Era and the Global Sustainable Development signed in February 2022 on the eve of the Russian invasion of Ukraine could have been a turning point in the long term. Beijing and Moscow pledged that the 'friendship' between them in the form of a 'bilateral strategic cooperation' had 'no limits, there are no forbidden areas of cooperation'. They condemned Western countries, mainly NATO, for their ideological approach to international politics. The document stated: 'The sides oppose further enlargement of NATO and call on the North Atlantic Alliance to abandon its ideologized cold war approaches, to respect the sovereignty, security and interests of other countries, the diversity of their civilizational, cultural and historical backgrounds, and to exercise a fair and objective attitude towards the peaceful development of other States'.[20] Has this Joint Declaration been a prelude to the Russian invasion of Ukraine with Chinese assent? Nowadays, the fog of war is still too thick, even in its diplomatic dimension, to reach a verdict. Nevertheless, the Ukrainian war has shown that the Sino-Russia friendship has limits indeed. At the time of writing, Beijing has been reluctant to help Moscow militarily, particularly in comparison with what the West is doing alongside Kyiv.

---

20 Joint Statement of the Russian Federation and the People's Republic of China on the International Relations Entering a New Era and the Global Sustainable Development, 4 February 2022, <http://en.kremlin.ru/supplement/5770> accessed 7 February 2022.

Conclusion

Today, the international system has profoundly changed compared to the Cold War era. In 1950, the Sino-Soviet military alliance was a game-changer for the global balance of power. The two countries joined together to pursue their national interests. China badly needed a security umbrella to rebuild the country under Communist rule and against any 'imperialist' threat. The only available option was asking Stalin for aid in Mao's view. The Soviets looked to pursue their presence in the Chinese mainland, their influence over the new regime and their supremacy against the 'free world'. Once Mao convinced Stalin that the PRC would be a loyal squire to the USSR, the Soviet leader agreed to sign the treaty of military alliance. Ideology was a background force between them, not the main push. The primary rationale concerned pragmatism and power politics.

As NATO documents show, the West – mostly the US – misread the Sino-Soviet relationship in the 1950s, overstating the political linkage between Moscow and Beijing by largely interpreting it through an ideological lens. The widespread opinion was that the ideological glue was enough to overcome the emerging strategic and diplomatic differences. But, as history demonstrated, the reality was quite the opposite. The struggle for Communist ideological victory over the Western democracy was not enough to close the increasing gap between the USSR and PRC. At the end of the decade, China looked for the international recognition as a great power, not just as a 'Russian puppet'. In hindsight, Acheson was not so wrong ten years earlier.

The current Western political climate tends to read the Sino-Russian relationship through a similar ideological lens, maintaining that the two authoritarian powers threaten democracy. For sure, the Chinese rise on the international stage and Russian comeback as a great power are shaking the global balance of power as we know it since the end of the Cold War. Their new role poses significant challenges for the Western world with no easy answer, and their diplomatic statements or military actions did have sometimes troublesome echoes. Moscow and Beijing came closer and closer in the last three decades under the perception that the West did not take into account their interests. In 2014, Russia believed that its westward geopolitical route was largely compromised. As a result, the Kremlin turned its head toward the East. The Dragon was particularly anxious to welcome the Bear into its nest. The long-term question is whether the Bear would be pleased to stay under the Dragon's wings.

The West should be careful in mixing ideological issues with strategic problems. As a result of overlapping factors over the years, the Eurasian alignment between Moscow and Beijing has actually arisen as the greatest threat to the Western-led international order. According to many US and European political leaders, the Sino-Russian revisionism must be rejected, and a new Cold War has begun. Even NATO is involved in addressing this threat, although China is out of its area of jurisdiction as sanctioned by the North Atlantic Treaty. The Russian invasion of Ukraine in 2022 has started a process of vast NATO rearmament as already happened due to the Korean war. Several forces that so many politicians and scholars considered to be buried with the end of the Cold War have finally re-emerged in contributory negligence with no winners at first glance.

There is no crystal ball to foresee the future, but it seems fair to state that Western political leaders should be aware of historical complexities in framing new policies for the future. Does the current global order architecture reflect the real balance of power? Do Beijing and Moscow really share the same long-term interests? Could a timely diplomatic action by the US and its Western allies help weaken what now seems to be an authoritarian monolith to many? These questions appear among the most crucial for the evolution of the international system.

Bibliography

Bartley, A. (2020). *Perceptions of China and White House Decision-Making, 1941–1963*. London-New York, NY: Routledge.

Bekkenvold, J.I., and Lo, B. (eds) (2019). *Sino-Russian Relations in the 21st Century*. London: Palgrave Macmillan.

Bertelsmann Foundation, and the German Marshall Fund (2021), *Transatlantic Trends 2021*, <https://www.gmfus.org/news/transatlantic-trends-2021> accessed 21 March 2022.

Chi-kwan M. (2012). *China and the World Since 1945. An International History*. London-New York, NY: Routledge.

Goncharenko, S. (1998). 'Sino-Soviet Military Cooperation'. In Westad, O. A. (ed), *Brothers in Arms: the Rise and Fall of the Sino-Soviet Alliance, 1945–1963*, pp. 141–164. Washington, DC: Woodrow Wilson Center Press.

Heinzig, D. (2015). *The Soviet Union and Communist China 1945–1950. The Arduous Road to the Alliance*. Armonk, NY: M. E. Sharp.

Jones J. M. (2022). 'Terrorism, Nuclear Weapons, China Viewed as Top U.S. Threats', *Gallup*, 7 March <https://news.gallup.com/poll/390494/terrorism-nuclear-weapons-china-viewed-top-threats.aspx>, accessed 21 March 2022.

Kaplan, L. S. (1984). *The United States and NATO. The Formative Years*. Lexington, KY: Kentucky University Press.

Krastev I., and Leonard M. (2021). 'What Europeans think about the US-China Cold War', *European Council on Foreign Relations Policy Brief*, September <https://ecfr.eu/publication/what-europeans-think-about-the-us-china-cold-war/> accessed 21 March 2022.

Lanxin X. (1995). *Recasting the Imperial Far East. Britain and America in China, 1945–1950*. London-Armonk, NY: M. E. Sharp.

Lo, B. (2008). *Axis of Convenience: Moscow, Beijing, and the New Geopolitics*. Baltimore, MD: Brookings Institute Press.

Lüthi L. M. (2008). *The Sino-Soviet Split: Cold War in the Communist World*. Oxford-Princeton, NJ: Princeton University Press.

Mayers, D. A. (1986). *Cracking the Monolith. U.S. Policy Against the Sino-Soviet Alliance, 1949–1955*. London-Baton Rouge, LA: Louisiana University Press.

Pearlman, M. D. (2008). *Truman and MacArthur. Policy, Politics, and the Hunger for Honor and Renown*. Bloomington, IN: Indiana University Press.

Radchenko, S. (2017). 'The Rise and the Fall of the Sino-Soviet Alliance 1949–1989'. In N. Naimark, S. Pons, S. Quinn-Judge (eds), *The Cambridge History of Communism. Vol. III: The Socialist Camp and World Power 1941–1960s*, pp. 243–268. Cambridge-New York, NY: Cambridge University Press.

Shen Z. and Xia Y. (2015). *Mao and the Sino-Soviet Partnership, 1945–1959: A New History*. New York, NY: Lexington Books.

Yu B. (2002). 'Historical Ironies, Dividing Ideologies and Accidental "Alliance": Russian-Chinese Relations into the 21st Century'. In C. W. Pumphrey (ed), *The Rise of China in Asia: Security Implications*, pp. 111–160. Carlisle, PA: Strategic Studies Institute.

Barbara Onnis

From Isolation to Global Cooperation. An Overview of China's Foreign Policy in the Post-Cold War Era

The aim of this article is to provide an overview of the transformation of Chinese foreign policy in the post-1989 era, with a special focus on the 'grand strategy' adopted by the communist leaders as a response both to the domestic political challenge and the end of the bipolar system. The new approach implied, among the others, the abandoning of the former aversion to multilateralism; the adoption of a less conflicting and more constructive approach to regional and global problems; a growing participation in international governance; a 'skillful' management of contingent political-economic crises, followed by the creation of new multilateral mechanisms. The turn to multilateralism is in fact considered one of the few real radical changes in the post-Tiananmen era and a key element in the 'diplomatic face of China's grand strategy' designed 'to engineer the country's rise to the status of a true great power that shapes, rather than simply responds to, the international system.'

Introduction

People's Republic of China (PRC)'s foreign policy has undergone a radical transformation in the transition between the revolutionary and post-revolutionary era,[1] and became even more marked in the aftermath of the Tiananmen square incident, when Beijing had to manage a twofold crisis, a domestic one, related to the loss of legitimation of the Chinese Communist Party (CCP), and an international one, related to the condemnation and isolation from the western international community, that risked to jeopardize the reform process initiated by Deng Xiaoping in the late 1970s and early 1980s. A process that played down ideology and gave great emphasis on pragmatism, while looking at the economic modernization and country's development as the new compelling mission for Chinese leadership (Jia 1999; Jing 2007). Moreover, the end of the Cold War bipolar system, following the implosion of the Soviet Union and the

---

1 The revolutionary era is identified with the Maoist era (1949–1976), while the post-revolutionary era refers to the new reformist course initiated by Deng Xiaoping at the turn of the late 1970s and early 1980s.

demise of marxist-leninist parties in the former USSR satellites of Central and Eastern Europe, profoundly impressed and even frightened Chinese communist leadership (Zhao 2004). The collapse of the old bipolar world order, indeed, 'left Chinese leaders without a definition of their place in the world' (Oksenberg 1991: 9). Consequently, they began to feel vulnerable and marginalized in world affairs, given the difficulty for their country to 'identify quickly a satisfactory niche in a transforming international system' (Zhao 2004: 143).

Based on these premises, the aim of this essay is to provide an overview of the transformation of Chinese foreign policy in the post-1989 era, with a special focus on the 'Grand Strategy' adopted by the communist leaders in the middle of the 1990s as a response both to the domestic political challenge and the end of the bipolar system, sanctioned by the serial collapse and partial disintegration of one-party communist states elsewhere in the world between 1989 and 1991, that elevated the relevance of unity and stability at home as an important security consideration. In this sense, it can be seen as an 'adaptation strategy' in the new post-Cold War international context dominated by the United States. The new approach implied, among the others, the abandoning of the previous aversion to multilateralism, being considered as a potential vehicle of external pressures; the adoption of a less conflicting and more constructive approach to regional and global problems; a growing participation in the international governance and a gradual contribution to global security through an increased involvement in the UN peacekeeping operations (UNPKOs); a skillful management of contingent political-economic crises, followed by the creation of new multilateral mechanisms.

After analysing the reasons for the strategic choices imposed to the leadership headed by Deng Xiaoping in the aftermath of the June 4th incident and the end of the Cold War, the essay focuses on the contents of China's 'Grand strategy' and the specificities of the country's turn to multilateralism, in a framework where bilateralism remained (and still remains) dominant. In the last part it reflects on the outcomes of both strategies in a context where PRC plays an increasingly leading role.

From isolation to global cooperation

After Tiananmen, improving the country's image was an imperative for the CCP. To credibly (re-)build the reputation of a peaceful and a constructive power, as Denghist China had appeared during the 1980s, PRC had to prove that it cared about its international standing and respected the rules of the system. As acknowledged by Pan Zhongying, one of the top Chinese experts in international relations, in fact, 'the reputation of a nation is as important as its economy and military power' (quoted in Shirk 2007: 107). Western scholars also agree on the sensitiveness of Chinese to their image (Rabinovitch 2008; d'Hooghe 2015; Hartig 2016). It is worth mentioning that in the Chinese language, the word *mianzi* (面子) literally means 'face' but it also refers to reputation and social status in terms of prestige. Therefore, in Chinese culture *diu mianzi* (丢面子) [losing face] is one of the worst experiences that can happen in everyone's life, while *wanhui yanmian* (挽回颜面) [saving face] is an aim to be preserved at all costs. This discourse can also be applied at the level of international politics (Onnis 2022).

In order to cope with the domestic crisis and to prevent the country from following the same fate as the Soviet Union, Deng Xiaoping formulated a kind of 'survival strategy' summarized in the so-called *ershiba zi fangzhen* (二十八字方针) [28-Character Strategy], according to which China had to *lengjing guancha* (冷静观察) [observe calmly]; *wen zhu zhenjiao* (稳住阵脚) [secure our position]; *chenzuo yingfu* (沉着应付) [cope with affairs calmly]; *taoguang yanghui* (沉着应付) [hide our capabilities and bide our time]; *shanyu cangzhuo* (善于藏拙) [be good at maintaining a low profile]; *jue bu dangtou* (决不当头) [never claim leadership]; *you suo zuowei* (有所作为) [make some contribution] (Deng 1993: 326). Put simply, in a contest where the country was condemned and isolated internationally, Deng's strategy suggested downplaying China's ambitions and capabilities in the short term to maximize its long-run options, providing the basic principles that indicated how China could protect its national interests while increasing its interactions with the rest of the world. Some of these dictums have been the object of speculations and criticism among Western observers. In particular, the *taoguang yanghui* concept has become a vital component of China's diplomatic strategy and one of the keywords for understanding and grasping Beijing's foreign policy in the post-Cold War era, but it has often been misinterpreted in the West to mean that PRC should 'keep a low profile, and bide its time, until it was ready to challenge US global dominance'. In fact, it is most closely associated with diplomatic strategy and is usually viewed by Chinese analysts as an admonition for the country to remain modest while (re-)building a positive image internationally and achieving specific gains, as to avoid suspicions, challenges, and commitments that might undermine its long-standing emphasis on domestic development (Swaine 2010: 7).

While the official line was set by the paramount leader, an interesting debate over the future of the country's foreign policy developed among International Relations' scholars, especially among hardliners, reformers, and tough internationalists (Harding 1990). While the first argued for slowing down the pace of domestic reforms and keeping a higher control over the scale of interaction with the outside world; the second, on the contrary, sought to promote further economic and political restructuring through close relations with the West. The tough internationalists, on their part, promoted the maintaining of extensive economic ties with the outside world, preferably on Chinese terms. Another debate revolved around the specificities of the new world order in a contest characterized by the presence of the US as the sole dominant superpower (Foot 1999: 238; Zhao 2004: 142–3).

Beijing took some important steps in the direction suggested by both reformers and hard internationalists, and one of the most visible manifestation of the new posture is represented by the rapid turnaround of China's attitude towards *duobian zhuyi* (多边主义) [multilateralism] evident in the country's growing participation in the international governance, and its contribution to global security by increasing its commitment to the UN Security Council, through a gradual involvement in peacekeeping operations (PKOs), which is generally considered a major breakthrough in the foreign policy of contemporary China. The turn towards multilateralism is in fact considered one of the few real radical changes in the post-Tiananmen era and represents a key element in the 'diplomatic face of China's grand strategy' (Goldstein 2001), being identified as an instrument to steer a strategy for transcending the traditional ways for great power to emerge. This strategic choice has indeed been regarded as a distinctively Chinese 'alternative path' to global power and explained as China's way for 'managing relations with the superpower' (the US) and work towards building the rules of a 'new international order through multilateral security dialogue and with cooperation of organizations' (Lanteigne 2005).

Equally important is the responsible attitude revealed during the management of contingent political-economic crises, and the creation of new multilateral mechanisms. Actually, since PRC replaced the ROC (Taiwan) as the legal representative of China at the United Nations, in October 1971, China has expanded its membership from participation in both intergovernmental organization and nongovernmental organizations and is currently member or observer of the majority of them.[2] PRC has also participated in numerous *ad-hoc* negotiations on topics ranging from public health (within the WHO) to arms control (non-proliferation treaty) and climate change.[3]

---

2   <https://www.indexmundi.com/china/international_organization_participation.html>.

3   PRC was one of the first developing countries to ratify the United Nations Framework Convention on Climate Change, in 1993; in 1998 it signed the Kyoto Protocol that was

China's Grand Strategy

According to Avery Goldstein – one of the few scholars who first dealt with the topic – China's 'Grand Strategy' was not defined and/or explained in any official document, nor has never been explicitly presented in any comprehensive manner by Chinese rulers,[4] but it is rather identifiable in the 'rough consensus on China's basic foreign policy that has been entrenched among party leaders around 1996 and has since provided a guide for the country's international behavior' (Goldstein 2005: 17). For the author, although some elements of that approach appeared in the early 1980s – PRC's attempts to resolve disputes with the West and Japan after the post-Tiananmen sanctions, the avoidance of strategic alignments or alliances – 'its content ultimately reflected new challenges that China faced following the end of the Cold War' (Goldstein 2005). Four main factors were instrumental in the rationale for China's strategic turnaround. The first factor was related to the US strength and the Chinese scholars' admission that the world was not quickly going to become multipolar, as they first believed when the implosion of the Soviet Union put an end to the Cold War. On the contrary, unipolarity would presumably last for a long time, with the US as the world's sole superpower. Consequently, for the foreseeable future, China would have to operate in a context where the US would have the ability to frustrate Beijing's international ambitions. Strictly related to the first, the second factor had to do with China's weakness. In fact, although the country's economic and military capabilities were growing as a result of the reformist policy in place since 1979, it still lagged far behind the world's leading states, especially the US. Given the extraordinary military power demonstrated by the Americans during the Gulf War, Chinese leaders had to admit how far they had to go before their armed forces could be considered in the same league as those of the US and its allies. The third factor was associated to the nervous international reaction to the Chinese rise that gave birth to the so-called *Zhongguo weixie lilun* (中国威胁理论) [China's threat theory]. While in the US the discourse was put in terms of a new 'Thucydides Trap' – as popularized by American political scientist Graham Allison (2017) – among China's immediate neighbors, especially those in Southeast Asia, there was new concern about China's assertive posture towards resolving maritime and territorial disputes, and some wondered

---

ratified in 2002; in 2016 China signed and ratified the Paris Agreement and after the withdrawal of the US, it took the leadership on the fight against climate change.

4   Later, Chinese started to refer to this strategy as a strategy of *heping jueqi* (和平崛起) [peaceful rise] or *heping fazhan* (和平发展) [peaceful development] (Zheng 2005).

what this might portend about the role an even more powerful China would play in coming decades. Against this background, Beijing's leaders were alarmed by Washington's efforts in the mid-1990s to update its Cold War-vintage alliances with Australia and Japan, as well as enhanced US military cooperation with the nations of Southeast Asia – trends that China worried might be the beginnings of an American-led regional effort to contain the country. The last factor, but certainly not in terms of importance, had to do with the Taiwan tensions that characterized the Straits in the mid-1990s. The specific reference is to the growth of Chinese military pressures on Taiwan during the so-called Third Taiwan Strait crisis,[5] between July 1995 and March 1996, firstly to send a strong signal to the ROC government under Lee Teng-hui which, in Beijing eyes, was moving away from *yige Zhongguo's yuanze* (一个中国原则)[One-China policy], and then to intimidate the Taiwanese electorate in the run-up to the 1996 presidential election – that actually ended with Lee Teng-hui's election. The crisis did not only lead to a deterioration in China-US relations, but at the same time contributed to further fuel the Chinese 'threat syndrome' in both its neighboring countries (starting from Japan) and in the US and Europe, thus favoring the 'realignment' of PRC's international policy. For Goldstein, the foreign policy consensus around the above-mentioned policies represented a 'Grand Strategy' for China – in the sense the term is generally used by international scholars – referring to 'the distinctive combination of military, political, and economic means by which a state seeks to ensure its national interests' (Goldstein 2005).

As it appears evident, by the mid-1990s the international situation was far from being rosy from China's perspective. Thus, the adoption of a 'Grand Strategy' was aimed to

> engineer China's rise to great power status within the constraints of a unipolar international system that the United States dominates. It is designed to sustain the conditions necessary for continuing China's program of economic and military modernization as well as to minimize the risks that others, most importantly the peerless United States, will view the ongoing increase in China's capabilities as an unacceptably dangerous threat that must be parried or perhaps even forestalled. […] in short it aims to increase the country's international clout without triggering a counterbalancing reaction (Goldstein 2005: 12).[6]

---

5   The First and the Second Taiwan Straits Crisis occurred in 1954–5 and in 1958.

6   In the words of Jia Qingguo (2005), China had to adapt and prepare the country to 'live with the hegemon'.

The strategy was especially forged to meet two broad purposes: on the one hand, to maintain the international conditions that would make it feasible for China to focus on the domestic development necessary if it was to increase its relative (not just absolute) capabilities; on the other, to reduce the likelihood that the US or other countries with its backing could exploit their current material advantage to abort China's ascent and frustrate its international aspirations (Goldstein 2001: 836). In this sense, some scholars have interpreted China's 'Grand Strategy' as a 'calculative' strategy, in consideration of the fact that PRC was facing a very tough challenge in trying to become a peer competitor of the dominant US (Swaine and Tellis 2000: XI).

The adoption of this strategy had some relevant implications for Beijing's foreign policy. First of all, the abandoning of the former aversion to multilateralism, considered as a potential vehicle of external pressure; secondly, the adoption of a less conflicting and more constructive approach to regional and global problems; thirdly a growing participation in the international governance, with special reference to global security by increasing its commitment to the UN; last but not least, a 'mature' management of contingent political-economic crises, and creation of new multilateral mechanisms. The output was that China earned in terms of 'reputation for power' (Gilpin 1983: 31).[7] Indeed, the turn to multilateralism can be considered as one of the few real radical changes in the foreign policy of contemporary China and represents a key element in the 'diplomatic face of China's grand strategy' (Goldstein 2001; Goldstein 2005).

A second relevant implication was the formulation of a *xin anquan guan* (新安全观) [New Security Concept], according to which in the post-Cold war era nations were able to increase their security through diplomatic and economic interaction, while abandoning the outdated Cold War mentality of competing and antagonistic blocs. The New Security Concept was primarily directed at China's relations with its Asian neighbours, not only Southeast Asian countries but also the new Central Asian republics emerged from the ashes of the Soviet Union. In fact, China's Foreign Minister Qian Qichen publicly proposed the New Security Concept for the first time at the Southeast Asian Nations Regional Forum (ARF) in 1996, but Chinese leaders have reiterated the policy at numerous bilateral and multilateral regional meetings in the late 1990s and early 2000s; it also was laid at the basis of the Shanghai Cooperation Organization (SCO), established in 2001

7　From then on, the concept of China as a 'responsible power' started to be adopted to describe the country's posture to global governance and China's self-perception of its rise (peaceful and advantageous for the rest of the international community).

on the initiative of PRC and Russia, together with four of the five Central Asian Republics (Kazakhstan, Kyrgyzstan, Tajikistan, and Uzbekistan).[8]

In Beijing's view, the core of such New Security Concept should include mutual trust, mutual benefit, equality, and coordination

> Mutual trust means that all countries should transcend differences in ideology and social system, discard the mentality of cold war and power politics and refrain from mutual suspicion and hostility. They should maintain frequent dialogue and mutual briefings on each other's security and defense policies and major operations. Mutual benefit means that all countries should meet the objective needs of social development in the era of globalization, respect each other's security interests and create conditions for others' security while ensuring their own security interests with a view to achieving common security. Equality means that all countries, big or small, are equal members of the international community and should respect each other, treat each other as equals, refrain from interfering in other countries' internal affairs and promote the democratization of international relations. Coordination means that all countries should seek peaceful settlement of their disputes through negotiation and carry out wide ranging and deep-going cooperation on security issues of mutual concern so as to remove any potential dangers and prevent the outbreak of wars and conflicts (China's Position Paper on the New Security Concept 2003).

Interestingly at the beginning of 2000s, this security policy seemed to merge with the foreign policy doctrine known as 'China's peaceful rise',[9] formulated by

---

8   The SCO was the successor to the so-called 'Shanghai Five' group, that emerged from a series of border demarcation and demilitarisation talks between China, Russia, and three of the five new Central Asian Republics, namely Kazakhstan, Kyrgyzstan, and Tajikistan. Since 1996, when the group held its first presidential summit meeting in Shanghai, the five-country group has held annual summits, but two treaties signed in 1996 and 1997, in Shanghai and Moscow respectively – the Treaty on Deepening Military Trust in Border Regions and the Treaty on Reduction of Military Forces in Border Regions – contributed to create a basis of trust and cooperation which proved to be fundamental for the building of the SCO which implied deeper political and economic cooperation.

9   The reference to *heping jueqi* (和平崛起) [peaceful rise] was soon replaced by the more neutral formula of *heping fazhan* (和平发展) [peaceful development], because of its aggressive impact, especially with regards to a foreign public opinion increasingly worried about China's rise. The term *jueqi* was seen as provocative rather than reassuring; in fact, the character *jue* (崛) in *jueqi* (崛起) contains the radical for mountain and carries the connotation of 'abruptness'. The use of that term could thus easily cause suspicion and wariness among other countries, especially those using Chinese characters (primarily Japan and Korea), which actually expressed concern about the phrase. On the ascension and demise of the theory of 'peaceful rise': (Glaser and Medeiros 2007).

Zheng Bijian – one of China's leading intellectuals at that time – which sought to assure the international community that PRC's growing political, economic, and military power would not pose a threat to international peace and security and that other nations would benefit from China's rise (Zheng 2005). Indeed, the New Security Concept had some positive effect on Chinese foreign policy in the late 1990s and early 2000s, including fostering better relations with the Association of Southeast Asian Nations (ASEAN), favoring the foundation of the already mentioned SCO, and promoting joint efforts with the United States to control nuclear proliferation in North Korea (Larus 2005: 219–20).

Chinese scholars consider the New Security Concept deeply rooted in Chinese traditional culture, based on *heping yu hexie* (和平与和谐) [peace and harmony], and perfectly in line with China's 'Five Principles of Peaceful Co-existence', according to which relations among nations should be established on the basis of mutual respect for territorial integrity and sovereignty, mutual non-aggression, non-interference in each other's internal affairs, equality and mutual benefit, and peaceful coexistence.[10] On the other hand, according to some Western scholars, the adoption of the New Security Concept was to be considered linked to the contingencies of the post-Cold War, in particular represented a kind of Chinese reaction to the policies and actions by the United States that Beijing perceived as threatening. In David Finkelstein's opinion (2003) it expressed Beijing's dissatisfaction with the post-Cold War international system in which the United States had evolved into the sole superpower, and a reaction to perceived security threats, particularly efforts by the United States to strengthen its military alliances. In line with Filkenstein's point of view, David Shambaugh (2002: 292) further argued that the New Security Concept illustrated Beijing's more proactive stance in international affairs and its aspirations to be treated as a world power.

China's turn to multilateralism

As stated above, the turn to multilateralism can be considered one of the most relevant implications of China's Grand Strategy and represents one of the most radical changes in Beijing's contemporary foreign policy.[11] Such a change

---

10 First articulated publicly in 1954, they continue to formally represent the main pillars of Beijing's foreign policy.
11 Indeed, the discourse on multilateralism made its official entry into Chinese political discourses as early as the mid-1980s, with the report on the government's work presented by the then Prime Minister Zhao Ziyang, when the VII five-year plan (1986–1990) was officially launched. That was the first time that a Chinese leader defined

did not happen overnight, but rather took place very gradually and has been characterized by an adaptable approach to international institutions and regimes. In other words, PRC did not adopt a 'one-size-fits-all' posture, but rather it has tailored its participation to the constraints and opportunities presented by different institutions and depending on the specific contingencies.

In a study dedicated to the specificities of China's gradual exercise of multilateralism, Joel Wuthnow, Li Xin and Qi Lingling (2012) identified four distinctive and consecutive strategies: watching, engaging, circumventing, and shaping. In their vision, China adopts a 'watching' strategy when it first joins an institution and lacks adequate technical knowledge of the issues being addressed therein or does not have a clear sense of its interests in a particular negotiation. This does not imply apathy since China is not necessarily indifferent to the institution in which it is operating. Rather, it is attentive and tries to learn about what the institution does, how power is exercised within it, and how its responsibilities and authority relate to the country's interests. This strategy was firstly adopted when PRC entered the UN in 1971. Indeed, at the beginning Chinese diplomats tended to 'say little', avoiding representatives of the major powers in the so-called 'corridor diplomacy', and relying on non-participation and abstentions to register its ideological disapproval of certain agenda items, especially those concerning PKO, rather than exercising its veto power or attempting to shape resolutions through diplomacy. An 'engaging' strategy implies instead that a state takes a more active and/or assertive role in negotiations, by forming coalitions, eventually exercising veto power, attempting to place items on (or keeping them off) the agenda, and using tactics such as persuasion and side-payments to convince opponents to accede to its goals. Such a tendency has been evident in China especially since 2000s, when Beijing has shifted 'from a passive response to active participation and even initiation' in specific realms, and it is clearly exemplified in the country's evolving activity within the UN Security Council. Indeed, China's passive approach in the 1970s gave way to a more active strategy in the 1980s, when it began to work more constructively, abandoning, for instance, its practice of regular abstentions in Security Council votes. A more robust engagement within the Security Council is instead evident in the post-Cold War era, through a gradual commitment of China in the PKOs. Traditionally reluctant to intervene, PRC has become a major contributor to this kind of operations. Like other great powers, China's decisions to deploy troops were motivated by

---

multilateral diplomacy as an integral part of Chinese foreign policy. See 'Rapport Sur le Septième Plan Quinquennal' (1986: XXV). *Beijing Information*, 16, supplément.

its desire to protect national interests, gain operational experience, and secure a positive reputation and high status. Many authors have analysed the reasons that accompanied Beijing's change in attitude towards this type of operations (Gowan 2020; Lanteigne 2018; He 2019) to the point of making China become the second largest financial contributor to UNPKOs and the largest provider of troops among the five UNSC's permanent members – it has recently begun to provide combat troops (so called 'security forces' in Chinese official language), marking a significant change in its deployment profile. 2020 marked the 30th year of China's participation in the UNPKO around the world and to celebrate the event, in September 2020, the State Council Information Office (SCIO) issued a White Paper specifically dedicated to its armed forces' participation in UN peacekeeping operations, titled China's Armed Forces: 30 Years of UN Peacekeeping Operations (SCIO 2020). At a press conference following the release of the document, the spokesman for the Ministry of National Defense, emphasized how over the past three decades China's armed forces had become a key force in UN peacekeeping operations, taking part to twenty-five missions in over twenty countries and regions (mainly in Africa, but also in Middle East and Asia), setting up a peacekeeping standby force of 8,000 troops, helping train foreign peacekeepers and providing free military aid to the African Union to support the establishment of an African standby force and to boost its capacity for crisis response.[12] As to the strategy of 'circumventing', Wuthnow, Li and Qi argue that it is adopted when an actor perceives that the current system does not provide a net benefit to its interests. When this occurs, it may pursue a course of 'circumventing', in which it chooses to operate outside the existing architecture and may indeed help to establish novel regimes with goals, rules and structures of their own, without necessarily posing a direct challenge to existing institutions or norms. That said, 'circumventing' the current order can be problematic as it raises the challenge of damaging relations with status-quo powers. A good example of China's exercise of this strategy is the role played by Beijing in the creation of the afore-mentioned Shanghai Cooperation Organization (SCO), aimed at collectively addressing regional security challenges, such as terrorism and narcotics trafficking. Interestingly, since its inception, the SCO was looked at with suspicion in the West, being perceived as a tentative to challenge the NATO – in fact it was renamed the 'NATO of the East' – and/or become a 'rival

---

12 'China Focus: China issues white paper on participation in UN peacekeeping operations' (2020). Xinhuanet, 18 September, <http://www.xinhuanet.com/english/2020-09/18/c_139378788_2.htm>.

OPEC' (Bhadrakumar 2007; Wrobel 2014). The last identified strategy is pursued in the attempt to shape the underlying rules and procedures of an existing body to better suit a country's interests. According to the three authors, this strategy emerged in China in the second half of 2010 and was initially pursued with great caution. Indeed, China is most likely to shape an existing institution if doing so would not threaten the core interests of the other key players; or when there is a broad support for reform. Good examples of this strategy are represented by the creation of the Asian Infrastructure Investment Bank (AIIB), intended as a financial arm of the Belt and Road Initiative (BRI), and the New Development Bank (NDB), formerly referred to as the BRICS Development Bank, established by the BRICS governments (Brazil, Russia, India, China, and South Africa) as a multilateral development bank. Both examples can be considered in fact a direct answer to the perceived partiality of Western financial institutions, such as the International Monetary Fund and the World Bank (Wang 2019). It appears evident how China has evolved into a sophisticated player, willing and able to use complex resources to mobilize other actors towards the pursuit of its 'Grand Strategy' centered on the transformation of the international system towards *duojihua* (多极化) [multipolarism], and a distribution of power more adequate to accommodate its emerging global role.

That said, while attaching a growing importance to multilateralism, China continues to prefer bilateral dealings, since it can leverage its economic and geopolitical clout and better serve its own interests. At this purpose, starting from the early 2000s, China has developed a so-called *huoban zhanlue zhengce* (伙伴战略政策) [strategic partnership diplomacy], establishing strong relations with about eighty countries and five international organizations covering all five continents (Li and Ye 2019). Such an engagement can be considered one of the main outputs of PRC's embrace of globalization and multidimensional diplomacy and reflects Beijing's adaptation to the world and its efforts to shape a favorable world order through the creation of a partnership network as an alternative to alliances (Feng and Huang 2014).

The 'strategic partnership' diplomacy

Strategic partnerships represent a significant feature of the current international system, as clearly demonstrated by their rapidly growing number over the past decades (Michalski 2019: 4). With over 130 such agreements US and PRC are revealed to be the two most prolific strategic partnership builders, while other important international actors such as the EU, Russia, Brazil, India, Japan, South Africa, and Australia count around fifty strategic partnerships among them (Michalski 2019). So, while apparently PRC is not unique with respect to using partnerships as an instrument to advance its national interests, what makes Beijing's approach unique is the fact that it places this kind of networks at the center of its foreign policy and that very few other countries have attached more significance to establish partnerships than China (Li and Ye 2019: 66; Strüver 2017).

Indeed since 1993, when PRC signed its first strategic partnership with Brazil, building partnerships has become one of the most notable dimensions of Chinese diplomacy. As stated by PRC's Foreign Minister, Wang Yi, in the speech delivered in December 2014 at the opening ceremony of the Symposium on the International Development and China's Diplomacy, co-hosted by China Institute of International Studies and China Foundation for International Studies: 'Building partnerships is a distinctive feature of China's diplomacy. After the end of the Cold War which was marked by the confrontation between alliances of nations, we have drawn on the experience and lessons of history in a timely way and succeeded in developing a new approach of forming partners instead of allies' (Wang 2014). In his speech, Wang also underlined the three basic features characterizing the partnerships China was building

> First, equality. Countries, regardless of their sizes or levels of development, should respect each other's sovereignty, independence and territorial integrity as well as each other's choice of development path and values, treat each other as equals, and show mutual understanding for and support each other. Second, peace. What makes such partnership different from military alliance is that it does not have any hypothetical enemy nor is it targeted at any third party, thus keeping relations between countries unaffected by military factors. It aims to handle state-to-state relations with a cooperative rather than confrontational, and a win-win rather than zero-sum approach. Third, inclusiveness. The partnership we have initiated seeks to go beyond differences in social systems and ideologies to maximize common interests and pursue a common goal (Wang 2014: 7).

Those features perfectly depicted what Chinese President Xi Jinping summarized as *jieban bu jiemeng* (结伴不结盟) [partnership without alignment], specifying however that the creation of a 'global network of partnerships' would not imply any break with the country's decades-old foreign policy of non-alignment (Huang 2014).[13]

---

13 It may be helpful to remember that during the Cold War, except for two ten-year periods (1950–1960, 1972–1982) when Beijing had a formal alliance with Moscow and a quasi-alliance with Washington, respectively, China has kept for the most part a non-alignment policy. A non-alliance policy was formally announced during the 12th Party Congress in 1982 and reiterated in 1992 and 1997 during the 14th and 15th Party

In fact, Feng Zhongping and Huang Jing (2014) consider the strategic partnership 'boom' emerged in the first half of 2010s as a product of the country's embrace of globalization and multidimensional diplomacy, that reflects China's adaptation to the world and its efforts to shape a favorable world order. Indeed, Beijing has been largely successful in employing strategic partnerships as a prominent instrument in its limited diplomatic toolkit as to guarantee a benign environment for its rise. Interestingly, China has developed various titles and mechanisms for different partnerships that reflect the distinct peculiarities of each partnership, and which can change over time, depending on their relevance in addressing Beijing's foreign policy priorities (Feng and Huang 2014: 17). Li Quan and Ye Min have identified twenty-four titles used by the Chinese government to define its partnerships and agree in considering that 'the sheer number of partnership titles is quite intriguing since they certainly reveal subtle differences across them' (Li and Ye 2019: 68). They distinguish especially three main groups: *quanmian zhanlüe huoban guanxi* (全面战略伙伴关系) [comprehensive strategic partnerships], *zhanlüe huoban guanxi* (战略伙伴关系) [strategic partnerships] and *huoban guanxi* (战略伙伴关) [regular partnerships].

The first group was authoritatively described by China's Prime Minister Wen Jiabao in the keynote speech delivered on 6 May 2004 at the "China-EU Investment and Trade Forum" in Brussels, a few months after the signing of the China-EU comprehensive strategic partnership.[14]

> By 'comprehensive', it means that the cooperation should be all-dimensional, wide-ranging and multi-layered. It covers economic, scientific, technological, political and cultural fields, contains both bilateral and multilateral levels, and is conducted by both

---

Congresses. In 2011, Beijing's adherence to this policy was confirmed in the White Paper entitled China's Peaceful Development, according to which China would not 'form alliance with any country or group of countries, nor does it use social systems or ideology as a yardstick to determine what kind of relations it would have with other countries'. 'China's Peaceful Development' (2014). *English.gov.cn*, 9 September, <http://english.www.gov.cn/archive/white_paper/2014/09/09/content_281474986284 646.htm>.

14 The China-EU Comprehensive Strategic Partnership undeniably constitutes one of the most relevant partnerships of this kind for China and can be considered one of the major political achievements between Beijing and Brussels to this day, at least on a theoretical level. In practice, on the contrary, it does not appear to have produced results of great relevance, much less of strategic importance, leading many scholars to question its real value (Onnis 2019).

governments and non-governmental groups. By 'strategic', it means that the cooperation should be long-term and stable, bearing on the larger picture of China-EU relations. It transcends the differences in ideology and social system and is not subjected to the impacts of individual events that occur from time to time. By 'partnership', it means that the cooperation should be equal-footed, mutually beneficial and win-win. The two sides should base themselves on mutual respect and mutual trust, endeavor to expand converging interests and seek common ground on the major issues while shelving differences on the minor ones (Wen 2004).

In addition to the one signed with the EU, China has established more than thirty-five comprehensive strategic partnerships with as many diversified countries (Russia, Pakistan, Saudi Arabia, Chile, Australia, New Zealand, Ecuador, Uzbekistan, Germany, Great Britain, Belarus, Italy, Greece, Serbia, South Africa), depending on both political and strategic factors that help creating 'an enabling environment for China's domestic environment' – mainly market size, (natural) resources and opportunities for investment (Li and Ye 2019: 79).

As regards the other two categories (strategic partnerships and regular partnerships), they do not appear to be subject to specific definition criteria, while China's choice of partnership types depends on a set of variables that are largely determined by three main factors: the necessity to counter the US pressure, the need of pacifying and stabilizing the country's borders and achieving the long-term goal of modernization (Li and Ye 2019).

Conclusions

Starting from the 1990s, multilateralism became a relevant part of China's foreign economic and security policy, and the country has become involved in the majority of global multilateral mechanisms. That said, as stated by Wang Hongying, 'multilateralism does not have a "taken for granted" quality in Chinese foreign policy' (Wang 2013: 485). In other words, Chinese attitudes toward multilateralism are quite instrumental and multilateralism remains relatively peripheral in the official foreign policy ideology, that continues to prefer a bilateral approach to foreign relations. For this purpose China has developed a sophisticated 'strategic partnership' diplomacy with different titles aimed at highlighting the specificities of each bilateral relationship and trying to make the best of each of them, in order to better serve its own interests. Such an approach is emblematic of Beijing's definitive abandoning of the old *shouhaizhe taidu* (受害者态度) [victim mentality] and the development of a new *daguo xintai* (大国心态) [great power mentality] (Fravel and Medeiros 2007: 30–33), aimed at putting a definitive end to the narrative of the notorious 'century of humiliation', while fostering instead a new narrative focused on the importance for China to forge its own role in the concert of nations dominated by the US.

Bibliography

Allison, G. (2017). *Destined for War: Can America and China Escape Thucydides's trap?*, Boston: Mifflin Harcourt.

Bhadrakumar, M.K. (2007). 'The New "NATO of the East" Takes Shape: The SCO and China, Russia and US Maneuvers', *The Asia-Pacific Journal*, 5(8), 1–9.

'China's Peaceful Development' (2014). *English.gov.cn*, 9 September, <http://engl ish.www.gov.cn/archive/white_paper/2014/09/09/content_281474986284 646.htm>.

'China Focus: China issues white paper on participation in UN peacekeeping operations' (2020). *Xinhuanet*, 18 September, <http://www.xinhuanet.com/ english/2020-09/18/c_139378788_2.htm>.

'China's Position Paper on the New Security Concept, 31 July 2002' (2003). *China Report*, 39 (1), 128–131.

Deng, X. (1993). *Deng Xiaoping Wenxuan*. Vol. III, Beijing: Renmin Chubanshe.

d'Hooghe, I. (2015). *China's Public Diplomacy*. Leiden: Brill.

Feng, Z., and Huang, J. (2014). 'China's strategic partnership diplomacy: engaging with a changing world', *ESPO Working Paper*, 8.

Finkelstein, D.M. (2003). 'China's New Concept of Security'. In S. J. Flanagan, and M.E. Marti (eds), *The People's Liberation Army and China in Transition*, pp. 197–209. Washington: National Defense University Press.

Foot, R. (1995). 'China's Foreign Policy in the Post-1989 Era'. In R. Benewick, and P. Wingrove (eds), *China in the 1990s*, pp. 234–244. New York: McMillan.

Glaser, B.S., and Medeiros, E.S. (2007). 'The Changing Ecology of Foreign Policy-Making in China: The Ascension and Demise of the Theory of "Peaceful Rise"', *The China Quarterly*, 190, 291–310.

Goldstein, A. (2001). 'The Diplomatic Face of China's Grand Strategy: A Rising Power's Emerging Choice', *The China Quarterly*, 168, 835–864.

Goldstein, A. (2005). *Rising to the Challenge. China's Grand Strategy and International Security*. Stanford: Stanford University Press.

Gowan, R. (2020). 'China's pragmatic approach to UN peacekeeping', *Brookings*, 14 September, <https://www.brookings.edu/articles/chinas-pragmatic-appro ach-to-un-peacekeeping/>.

Harding, H. (1990). 'The Impact of Tiananmen on China's Foreign Policy', *NBR Analysis* 1(3), 1 December.

Hartig, F. (2016). *Chinese Public Diplomacy. The Rise of the Confucius Institute.* London: Routledge.

He, Y. (2019).'China Rising and Its Changing Policy on UN Peacekeeping'.In C.de Coning, and M.Peter, (eds), *United Nations Peace Operations in a Changing Global Order,* pp.253– 276.London: MacMillan.

Hsiung, J.C. (1995). 'China's Omni-Directional Diplomacy: Realignment to Cope with Monopolar U.S. Power', *Asian Survey,* 35 (6), 573–586.

Huang, K.L. (2014). 'President Xi Jinping puts "network of partners" on foreign policy agenda', *South China Morning Post,* 30 November, <https://www.scmp.com/news/china/article/1652296/xi-jinping-says-china-will-protect-its-sovereign-territory-amid-disputes>.

Jia, Q. (1999). 'From Self-imposed Isolation to Global Cooperation: The Evolution of Chinese Foreign Policy Since the 1980s', *Internationale Politik und Gesellschaft,* 2, 168–78.

Jia, Q. (2005). 'Learning to Live with the Hegemon: Evolution of China's policy towards the US since the End of the Cold War', *Journal of Contemporary China,* 14(44), 395–407.

Jing, M. (2007). 'Changing Ideology in China and Its impact on Chinese Foreign Policy'. In S. Guo, and S. Hua (eds), *New Dimensions of Chinese Foreign Policy,* pp. 7–39. New York: Rowman & Littlefield Publishers.

Lanteigne, M. (2007). *China and International Institutions. Alternate Paths to Global Power.* London: Routledge.

Larus, E.F. (2005). 'China's New Security Concept and Peaceful Rise: Trustful Cooperation or Deceptive Diplomacy?', *American Journal of Chinese Studies,* 12 (2), 219–241.

Li Q., and Ye M. (2019). "China's emerging partnership network: what, who, where, when and why", in *International Trade, Politics and Development,* 3(2), 66–81.

Medeiros, E. S., and Taylor Fravel, M. (2003). "China's New Diplomacy", *Foreign Affairs,* 82 (6), 22–35.

Michalski, A. (2019). 'Diplomacy in a Changing World Order: The Role of Strategic Partnerships', The Swedish Institute of International Affairs (SIIA), September, <https://www.ui.se/globalassets/ui.se-eng/publications/ui-publications/2019/ui-paper-no.-10-2019.pd>.

Oksenberg, M. (1991). 'The China Problem', *Foreign Affairs,* 70 (3), 1–16.

Onnis, B. (2019). 'La Cina, l'Unione Europea e la prospettiva di un nuovo ordine internazionale', *Rivista italiana di storia internazionale,* 2, 265–294.

Onnis, B. (2022). 'COVID-19 and China's global image'. In G. Pugliese, A. Fischetti and M. Torri (eds), *US-China competition, COVID19, and democratic backsliding in Asia, Asia Maior* (special issue), 2, 73-87.

Rabinovitch, S. (2008). 'The Rise of an Image-Conscious China', *China Security*, 4 (3), 33–47.

'Rapport Sur le Septième Plan Quinquennal' (1986). *Beijing Information*, 16, supplément.

SCIO (2020). 'China's Armed Forces: 30 Years of UN Peacekeeping Operations', 18 September, <http://english.www.gov.cn/archive/whitepaper/202009/18/content_WS5f6449a8c6d0f7257693c323.html>.

Shambaugh, D. (2002). *Modernizing China's Military: Progress, Problems, and Prospects*. Berkeley: University of California Press.

Shirk, S. (2007). *China. Fragile Superpower*. New York: Oxford University Press.

Strüver, G. (2017). 'China's Partnership Diplomacy: International Alignment Based on Interests or Ideology', *The Chinese Journal of International Politics*, 10 (1), 31–65.

Swaine, M.D., and Tellis, A.J. (2000). *Interpreting China's Grand Strategy: Past, Present, and Future*. Santa Monica, CA: Rand.

Swaine, M.D. (2010). 'Perceptions of an Assertive China', *Chinese Leadership Monitor*, 32, <https://carnegieendowment.org/files/CLM32MS1.pdf>.

Wang, H. (2019). 'The New Development Bank and the Asian Infrastructure Investment Bank: China's Ambiguous Approach to Global Financial Governance', *Development and Change*, 50 (1), 221–244.

Wang, J. (2011). 'China's Search for a Grand Strategy: A Rising Great Power Finds Its Way', *Foreign Affairs*, 90 (2), 68–79.

Wang, Y. (2014). '2014 in Review: a successful year of China's diplomacy', <https://www.fmprc.gov.cn/eng/wjb_663304/zzjg_663340/xws_665282/xgxw_665284/201412/t20141225_600272.html>.

Wen, J. (2004). 'Vigorously Promoting Comprehensive Strategic Partnership Between China and the European Union. Speech at the China-EU Investment and Trade Forum', 6 May, <https://www.mfa.gov.cn/ce/cebe//eng/zt/t101949.htm>.

Wrobel, R. (2014). 'China's New Energy Geopolitics: The Shanghai Cooperation Organization and Central Asia', *ASIEN-The German Journal on Contemporary Asia*, 133, 24–51.

Wuthnow, J., et al. (2012). 'Diverse Multilateralism: Four Strategies in China's Multilateral Diplomacy', *Journal of Chinese Political Science*, 17, 269–290.

You, J., and Jiang, Q. (1998). 'China's Re-emergence and Its Foreign Policy Strategy', *China Review*, 125–156.

Zhao, S. (2004). 'China's Foreign Policy after Tiananmen'. In S. Zhao (ed), *Chinese Foreign Policy. Pragmatism and Strategic Behaviour*, pp.140–50. New York and London: M.E. Sharpe.

Zheng, B. (2005). *China's Peaceful Rise: Speeches of Zheng Bijian 1997–2005*. Washington: Brookings Institution Press.

Raimondo Neironi

The US Grand Strategy in the Indo-Pacific and the Quadrilateral Security Dialogue from Trump to Biden

The Quadrilateral Security Dialogue (Quad) was placed more centrally in the formulation of the US Indo-Pacific grand strategy over the past six years. Although President Joe Biden has blunted the idea of an impending clash with China rather than his predecessor, the Quad aims at blocking any Beijing's military adventurism and economic coercion in the Indo-Pacific's diplomatic and security domains. This chapter posits that this minilateral initiative apparently unveils a manifest political fragility. Indeed, while the four maritime democracies has been unanimously emphasized, since its inception, how important it is to make the Indo-Pacific free, open and secure to all countries, the presence of contrasting visions, the lack of a coherent policy response on certain issues – such as climate change – and specific aspects of India's diplomatic posture – its relations with Russia – not only prevent the Quad from turning into a proper military pact, but also indicate that any attempt to deter China's ambitions could be frustrated.

Introduction

The Indo-Pacific region has occupied a critical place in the United States grand strategy since the nineteenth century (Auslin 2020; Green 2017; LaFeber 2013; Perry 1994). Its involvement can be somehow embedded into an historical framework consisting in three specific waves. At the beginning, the US availed of some areas in Asia and the Pacific to hand control of commercial outposts for its Open Door policy at the risk of war and favoured the spread of missionary activities over there (Preston 2016). Then, the second wave started as US military occupied the Philippines and other territories establishing a form of 'administrative colonialism' that lasted until the mid-1940s (Go 2011). Ultimately, the third wave followed the end of World War II, at a time when Washington underwrote the security of a great crescent stretching from Japan to South-East Asia when it realised the region would have been the most consequential and vital for US interests (Ngoei Wen-Qing 2019; Thompson 2019).

In recent decade, US policymakers have regarded the Indo-Pacific as a unified economic and strategic theatre that is owed fundamentally to the relentless ascendancy of China to global power after the early 2000s. As competition between the US and China has built up, a vast array of scholarships has emerged focussing on the reconfiguration of power in the area and the implications of People's Republic of China (PRC) rise for US political and developmental prospects. The rivalry between Washington and Beijing is now persistent and the US claims the Chinese Communist Party (CCP) actively seeks to overturn the established rules-based international order to 're-shape' a world antithetical to the US values and interests (Blinken 2022). As a result, it has so far promoted a series of political initiatives to dispel the perception that it is no longer committed to China's assertiveness in the seas that could jeopardise security of its regional allies and partners. Neither President Biden nor Secretary of State Antony J. Blinken have never referred to China as a revisionist power, however the fact that the CCP is planning on using its economic leverage and diplomatic capabilities to transform both the regional and international system has reached a certain degree of acceptance between some international scholars (Benvenuti et al. 2022).

This chapter analyses the evolution of the Indo-Pacific strategy within the space of six years and explains how the Quadrilateral Security Dialogue (Quad) can be included in a comprehensive American statecraft. It proceeds as follows. The first section examines the fundamental assertions of the US 'grand strategy' in the Indo-Pacific and clarify why since the end of the Pacific War the US has tolerated no power established exclusive hegemonic control over Asia and the Pacific. The second section compares the Indo-Pacific strategies portrayed by the administrations of Donald Trump and Joe Biden. As of today, neither of strategies is mostly declassified, but a close examination of official documents and public speeches reveals enough details to scrutinise. The third section traces the origins of the Quad and explains why it was invigorated by the US and, above all, its security allies. The US stands for the development of a minilateral regional process which is strictly associated with the existing multilateral initiatives in the Indo-Pacific. The fourth and the fifth paragraph finally focus on the relationship between the US and its Quad partners and recognises political limits and strategic discrepancies, chiefly affecting India's diplomatic posture, that make fallacious to brand the strategic dialogue as an authentic pact.

The quest for hegemony in Asia in historical perspective

Understanding what a grand strategy would mean is determinative in analysing foreign policy and national security of the US. Most scholars have long developed influential studies that explained its meaning and the logic behind it. On the whole, this concept constitutes the attempt of a state to establish global hegemony (Layne 2006: 3) employing diplomatic, military, informational and economic tools (Martel 2015: 30; Bacevich 2004: 98) in a comprehensive approach against long-range threats, in times of peace and war. Although there is no consensus in literature about how the term should be defined (Silove 2018: 28; Milevski 2016: 1-11), three distinctive features must be fulfilled when referred to a grand strategy. First, grand strategy assumes the existence of a national interest – that there is a collective entity that strategy seeks to secure and that there are national ends that must be aligned with national means. Second, grand strategy identifies the key threats towards the state and, then, arranges among them to formalise a strategic plan, a view or a behaviour – it depends upon what type of notion scholars expressly subscribe to (Silove 2018: 49). Third, it devises 'affordable ways' (Goddard and Krebs 2015: 8) and means, and mobilise all instruments and resources at its disposal (Biscop 2021: 3) to take on those threats over the long-run. Any strategy worthy of the name aims to protect vital interests, but it also attempts to limit efforts by competitors to increase their power (Bacevich 2004: 87).

For over two centuries, the national interest of the US has corresponded to the assumption that the Pacific Ocean represents a conduit for American goods mostly, but also for people and ideas (Auslin 2020: 175; Green 2017: 5). The US does not tolerate any other power establishing exclusive hegemonic control over the entire area; if anything, it has taken the steps necessary to expand further its economic power there and to cling to its naval and air bases that were scattered around. Primarily, since 1945 America's utmost interest has been to maintain a balance of power in the Pacific and prevent the rise of an aggressive and destabilising hegemon that would threaten its freedom and peace along a critical regional intersection and that also would undermine the security system set by the US after the San Francisco peace treaty, which came into effect in 1952.

After the end of the Pacific War, the 'hub-and-spokes system', otherwise known as the 'San Francisco alliance system', constitutes a comprehensive structure of interrelated political-military and economic commitments between Washington, at the centre of this model, and Japan, the Philippines, Australia and New Zealand, as well as South Korea, Taiwan, and Thailand, at the periphery. By and large, each defence treaty was conceived to ensure a formal military intervention in case of external attack, albeit not an automatic security guarantee. Either way, the rationale behind the creation of the 'hub-and-spokes' system was to establish military and intelligence alliances not just to forestall a 'domino effect' with Asian countries falling to communism, but also to align partners with the US regional interests. In fact, such a system constrained potential erratic allies from engaging in 'adventurist behaviour' that might drag the US into larger military contingencies in the region (Cha 2009/2010: 163). The US took the brunt of Asian security and regional politics underwent 'a huge shift from bloc bipolarity to an American-centred regionalism' (Katzenstein 2005: 43). Harry S. Truman and John Foster Dulles – then, the Special Representative of the US administration in the peace treaty negotiations with Japan (1950-1951) – preferred a NATO-type multilateral alliance to the hub-and-spokes system in East Asia even after the latter emerged (Izumikawa 2020: 20–2; Buckley 2002: 81). Dulles clarified that these security treaties 'involve only islands, where security is strongly influenced by sea and air power' (Ang 2022: 19).

As the Cold War ended, US partners in the region were encouraged to "assume greater responsibility for their own defense." Furthermore, the San Francisco architecture made it difficult to create multilateral security arrangements in Asia since it was no longer required to Asian states to interact with one another (Press-Barnathan 2003: 4). On the basis that the core of San Francisco security system should have remained valid, a specific form of multilateralism developed in the Asia-Pacific above all the 1990s. The main objectives after the Soviet collapse were to reorientate the 'tested' bilateral pacts that reflects the region's diverse security concerns (Baker 1991): they should continue to serve multiple and complex security and economic purposes for both the US and its East Asian partners (Ikenberry 2004: 354); to promote co-operation with certain countries (i.e. Singapore and India) in niche areas where such countries' embedded interests coincided with those of the US (i.e. technology transfer). These all considerations asserted, the US has not only gained primacy, but has managed to establish hegemony in the region directly after China's diplomatic isolation due to the 1989 Tiananmen massacre. This finds reflection in its military preponderance, alliance system, and near-monopolistic role as security public goods provider – but more importantly in the 'disproportionate' American ability to determine regional order (Goh 2019: 617). In fact, while the George H.W. Bush administration was committed to put dialogue with its allies in a good consideration, it discouraged any political initiative coming from them, such as Japanese Foreign Minister Nakayama Taro's proposal of July 1991 for a region-wide security dialogue in Asia.

Yet, Washington concretely anchored its principles of engagement in the region, for the first time, within the *US Security Strategy for the East Asia-Pacific Region*, issued by the Department of Defence (DoD) in 1998. This document was the last formally published US government report on that matter until 2019. Under the Bill Clinton administration, US officials discerned a way to dovetail strategic culture and economic interests (Nye 2001: 95) in a bid to address all unprecedented challenges of that time – such as the 1997-98 Asian financial crisis – by favouring enhancement of existing alliances, arrangement to build 'political, economic and military development within Asia's diverse environment,' and co-operation with allies, partners, and regional great powers such as China and Russia (see United States Government 1998). Economic cooperation serves political purposes and the process of economic liberalisation was seen as an important step towards the larger goals of political security and social well-being (Cossa 2003: 196). A regional intergovernmental framework for security dialogue as the ASEAN Regional Forum was considered as a useful and positive vehicle to express the Pacific identity of the US (Ashizawa: 187). In the last 1990s US officials were committed to shaping national strategy and they were conflated with a string of other tailored strategic documents developing appropriate capabilities and ambitious goals.

Since the China's rise, the Indo-Pacific region is a laboratory of political, diplomatic and economic initiatives. China was not then the issue, but the Obama administration gave considerable attention to multilateralism and global governance, a policy shift from the unilateralist George W. Bush administration. The question of Asia's power balance constitutes just one of the major reasons for the US involvement in the region, which is crucial to success for each of Washington's policy goals in the twenty first century (Campbell 2022: 73, 76-7), as well as in the past.

By the same token, the US fostered a minilateral approach which has been employed to address regional security issues (Tow 2019: 238–39) – traditional and not – generally built on its alliances (Wuthnow 2019: 135): the US-Japan-Australia Trilateral Strategic Dialogue Ministerial (2006) and the US-Japan-India Trilateral Ministerial (2011) find an explanation within this context.

From Trump to Biden: Turning vision into a strategy

The Indo-Pacific social construct is a continuation of previous attempts by US policymakers to fill the void that stems from the failure to adapt the 'hub-and-spokes system' to the changing conditions (Wirth and Jenne 2022: 3). Based on this assertion, the Indo-Pacific initiative would be an Asian one, even though the Trump administration is often credited with its creation. Seven decades after of US global leadership, the Trump administration openly questioned a number of fundamental pillars of American primacy including a belief in the benefits of a free and open global economic system and the web of longstanding bilateral alliances and multilateral fora in Asia. In a sense, the advent of the Trump administration represented a 'watershed moment' for US grand strategy (Clarke 2021: 5).

Nevertheless, while pulling out of the Trans-Pacific Partnership in 2017 and snubbing a range of multilateral initiatives in Asia, the declassified document US Strategic Framework for the Indo-Pacific (2018)[1] has revealed top interests of the US in the region: preserving US economic, diplomatic, and military access to the most populous region of the world; enhancing the credibility and effectiveness of the hub-and-spokes system; maintaining the US primacy in the region. The language of the Trump administration evoked the ideological, 'open-space' rhetoric of the Barack Obama era. But, in its geographical term, the map showing the Indo-Pacific is 'lifted' and moved east (Doyle and Rumley 2019: 78–9). The US Seventh Fleet operate across the Indian and Pacific oceans as a single entwined geostrategic plane.

Trump reiterated its commitment to establishing new alliances and partnerships, while expanding and deepening existing relationships that share principles such as respect for sovereignty, fair and reciprocal trade, and the rule of law. Trump expected Asian states should have accepted larger and more responsible roles for their own defence. He emphasised the importance to reinforce freedom of navigation operations and the peaceful resolution of territorial and maritime disputes in the East and South China seas, in accordance with international law.[2] Furthermore, Trump's 'free' and 'open' vision counted on expanding US's economic engagement in the Indo-Pacific region. On the occasion of the 2017 CEO Summit of the Asia Pacific Economic Co-operation (APEC) in Da Nang, Trump affirmed some Asian countries ignored the rules to gain advantage over those that followed them, causing enormous market-distorting trade practices and policies and threatening the foundations of international trade. Secretary of State Mike Pompeo (2018) said it has never sought domination in the Indo-Pacific, and it has opposed any country that does. Rather, it aspires to a regional order, independent nations that can compete fairly in the international marketplace. The BUILD Act and the Asia Reassurance Initiative Act received strong bipartisan support and were specifically geared toward leveraging the

---

1   United States Government, National Security Council (2018). 'US Strategic Framework for the Indo-Pacific', February <https://trumpwhitehouse.archives.gov/wp-content/uploads/2021/01/IPS-Final-Declass.pdf>, accessed 25 January 2022.

2   The White House (2017). 'National Security Strategy', pp. 46–7 <https://trumpwhitehouse.archives.gov/wp-content/uploads/2017/12/NSS-Final-12-18-2017-0905.pdf>, accessed 25 January 2022.

assets and resources of the private sector and thus emphasise enterprise driven-development finance (Calabrese 2020: 311).

That said, it is necessary to identify the threat and unveil priorities of Trump administration's vision on the Indo-Pacific. It was posed a great deal of attention to China. Until the early 2000s, US policymakers exhaustively debated how to respond to China's rise. As Edward Luce stated (2017) 'Washington settled on a hedging strategy of accommodating China's self-proclaimed peaceful resurgence while' retaining the option of switching to containment if it turned sour.' What has never been in question is the US would do what it takes to preserve its primacy in Asia and the Pacific. China's rapid economic ascent and concomitant strategic importance has been the basis for challenging the still existing order that US helped create and over which it has enjoyed 'unquestioned ascendancy' (Beeson 2019: 251).

The US Indo-Pacific vision acknowledges China as a regional power reluctant to accept the existing order or to talk to the establishment of new shared directives for that order. It expresses an 'an unambiguous commitment to preserve the current order by all

means necessary' (Wesley-Smith and Finin 2021: 439). The US Congress revealed how it is clear that the PRC has chosen to pursue 'an aggressive and assertive foreign policy' involving various levels. This, as well as its rhetoric and actions (Scobell 2021: 79), 'frequently and deliberately undermine US interests and are contrary to core US values and the values of other nations, both in the Indo-Pacific and beyond.' The PRC's objectives are to first establish regional hegemony over the Indo-Pacific and then to use that dominant position to propel the PRC to become the leading world agent, shaping an international system that is conducive to the CCP's interests and consistent with its sovereignty, security, and development ambitions (Strategic Competition Act 2021: 287–89). These assertions received a bipartisan support and are in line with those of the Department of Defence.[3] China would be planning on 'dissolving' US alliances and partners in the region.[4] What ensued is that the US would almost certainly be 'on a collision course' with China in case Beijing should seek to challenge

---

3   United States Government, Office of the Secretary of Defence (2021). 'Military and Security Developments Involving the People's Republic of China', Annual Report to Congress, pp. 1–173 <https://media.defense.gov/2021/Nov/03/2002885874/-1/-1/0/2021-CMPR-FINAL.PDF>, accessed 25 January 2022.
4   The White House (2021). 'United States Strategic Framework for the Indo-Pacific', pp. 1–2 <https://trumpwhitehouse.archives.gov/wp-content/uploads/2021/01/IPS-Final-Declass.pdf>, accessed 25 January 2022.

the current rules-based regional order and reshape a new one in a way that is compatible with its own values and traditions (Cocker 2015: 66).

Trump administration's confrontational approach on China, along with pressing demands for contributing more to the costs of US military presence in Japan and South Korea, undermined the very alliances it needs to fulfil the objectives of Indo-Pacific vision (O'Shea and Maslow 2021: 208). It is a fundamental interest of the US to preserve key liberal principles in the Indo-Pacific, and it cannot do so without 'robust engagement from a strategy that empowers its allies and partners' (Denmark 2020: 227–30). Richard J. Heydarian (2020: 211) suggests Trump's 'America First' policy could lead middle powers in the region to establish a multipolar post-American order. In fact, alliances and partners cannot operate without the US; still less can an indigenous coalition of deterrence succeed in institutionalising an Asian-authentically co-operative mechanism.

Even though it is too premature to assess its engagement in Asia, there are some elements of continuity in the Biden administration's comprehensive commitment. America's long-term ambition in the area remain still the same – the maintenance of free trade, alliances, liberal values and territorial security. Biden is different than Trump to have turned a vision into a strategy. In some ways, this strategy clings to the core of 'Pivot to Asia', due to the presence of its architect in the current administration: embracing and engaging Asian states; preventing hegemony; and creating shared incentives for supporting the 'operating system' and costs for undermining it (Campbell 2017). The general objectives of the Biden administration design for the region, navigating a path through a balancing rivalry with China, restoring confidence with its 'ironclad' allies; and forging constructive ties with partners in the Indo-Pacific. From supply-chain resilience to climate change and infrastructure, the Indo-Pacific region is experiencing a 'governance deficit' that the US should be well placed to address (Crabtree 2021: 63).

The PRC's coercion and aggression are most acute in the Indo-Pacific: from the economic coercion of Australia to the conflict along the Line of Actual Control with India, from the growing pressure on Taiwan to the bullying of neighbours in the East (Japan) and South China Seas (some South-East Asian states). This could undoubtedly hark back to Trump administration's assertions, but difference lies in purpose. The objective is not to 'change' the PRC but to 'shape' the strategic environment in which it operates, building a 'balance of influence' in the world that is 'maximally' favourable to the US and its allies. While the exact meaning of this is unclear, it suggested the wider aim of forging such a regional balance goes beyond the military realm. The Biden administration reckons conflict involving

China over Taiwan, as well as territorial disputes in East and South China seas, would be truly crippling and should be therefore discounted. Just a 'collective effort' over the next decade will determine whether the US plans on developing a 'clear-eyed coexistence' on its interests and values (Campbell and Sullivan 2019).

American strategy will be principled, long-term, and anchored in democratic resilience. 'Integrated deterrence' to dissuade or defeat aggression in any form or domain.[5] Allies and partners will play a heightened role in Biden's Indo-Pacific strategy, modernising treaty alliances with Australia, Japan, South Korea, the Philippines, and Thailand; steadily advancing major defence partnership with India and supporting its role as a net security provider; and building the defence capacity of partners in South and South-East Asia and the Pacific Islands, and investing in regional organisations. Alongside its partners, the US will bring about an Indo-Pacific economic framework – within APEC, in upholding and strengthening the rules-based multilateral trading system, with the World Trade Organisation at its core. This economic framework will help economies to harness rapid technological transformation, including in the digital economy, and adapt to the coming energy and climate transition. Forging unprecedented co-operation, in a democratic way, with those countries who share the free and open vision of the Indo-Pacific. During the East Asia Summit in October 2021, President Biden announced plans for a US-led Indo-Pacific Economic Framework. Secretary Gina M. Raimondo and US Trade Representative (USTR) Katherine Tai held exploratory talks with Japan, Malaysia, Singapore, and South Korea during their overseas visits, but no official negotiations have been launched yet. The US planned Indo-Pacific economic framework will be inclusive and flexible, and will not be structured 'like a typical free trade deal' (Latiff and Lee 2021).

The defence of maritime domain is another important pillar of the US gran strategy. Strengthening maritime domain awareness; promoting the safety and security of sea lines of communication; combating challenges, such as illegal, unreported fishing rely on the UN Convention on the Law of the Sea (UNCLOS) and international law. China's expansive claims to the South China Sea pose the possibility of blocking any efforts to link the Indian Ocean, Asia and the Pacific into an Indo-Pacific construct. If China successfully turns the South China Sea into an inaccessible zone for US, Indian, or South-East Asian naval or maritime

---

5   The White House (2022). 'The Indo-Pacific Strategy of the United States', February, pp. 7–12 <https://www.whitehouse.gov/wp-content/uploads/2022/02/U.S.-Indo-Pacific-Strategy.pdf>, accessed 28 February 2022.

vessels, it could essentially 'put a firebreak' between the Indian and the Pacific oceans (Harold 2014: 90). Any code of conduct on the South China Sea should respect the UNCLOS and the legitimate rights and interests of all stakeholders.

Compared to Trump, Biden elevated the Quad to a leaders' level summit. He has often stressed there are feasible margins to co-operate with China, but similarly it has claimed to take the lead in forcing multi and minilateral initiatives to subdue competing assertive strategy from PRC (Koga 2022). Countering coercion by reinforcing deterrence: the Biden administration has shown diplomatic ability by arranging meetings with allies to apply pressure on China and pushing regional countries to lean on a side between Washington and Beijing (Townshend et al. 2021: 4–5).[6] Biden hopes combination of multi and minilateral initiatives will enable him to accelerate his agenda (Vinjamuri 2021).

The Quad: resumption, common strategy, and anti-China sentiment

The Quad carves a special place in the US grand strategy for the Indo-Pacific. Such unusual strategic and economic co-operation includes the US, its two key defence allies in Asia – Japan and Australia –, and India. The Quad traces its origins to the period post the tsunami in the Indian Ocean in December 2004. Then, the four countries participated in the Tsunami Core Group that was described at the time as a new style of diplomacy. Further, it prompted member countries to establish what would become 'a more robust and durable structure' for co-operation on non-traditional security issues (Envall 2015: 53). This informal initiative served as a template for further interaction on other relevant issues. The desire to construct an innovative security system across the region can be dated back to Japan's Prime Minister Abe Shinzo which spearheaded the original quadrilateral initiative with the support of his Australian and Indian counterparts, John Howard and Manmohan Singh, and the strong backing of US Vice-President Dick Cheney. In that circumstance, US strategic policy in the Indo-Pacific was 'in substantial part' driven by allies and partners, especially Japan (Medcalf 2021). This revival of the quadrilateral meeting was not welcomed in China, that issued formal diplomatic protests to Australia, the US, Japan, Australia and India. However, in July 2007, the then Australia's PM

---

6   The White House (2021). 'Remarks by Vice President Harris on the Indo-Pacific Region', Singapore, 24 August <https://www.whitehouse.gov/briefing-room/speeches-remarks/2021/08/24/remarks-by-vice-president-harris-on-the-indo-pacific-region/>, accessed 25 January 2022.

Kevin Rudd decided to shelve the idea of rejoining blaming the ambiguity of the original proposal and divergent interests of those involved (Flitton 2020). India, in turn, has been cautious about supporting the Japanese initiative. Of the minilateral arrangements that continued to work, there was the Washington-Tokyo-Canberra security triangle which still relies on a sheer geopolitical logic.

Five years on, Abe (2012) authored an opinion piece in *Project Syndicate* advocating the creation of a 'democratic security diamond' in which Japan, the US, Australia and India would 'safeguard the maritime commons stretching from the Indian Ocean region to the Western Pacific to oppose China's get-tough policy. Since then, Australia showed amenable to resurrecting the quadrilateral dialogue and in November 2017, after a decade of dormancy, on the sidelines of the ASEAN Regional Forum (ARF) held in Manila it re-emerged to deepen security cooperation and coordinate alternatives for regional infrastructure financing to the Chinese-led Belt and Road Initiative (BRI). For the first time, ministerial-level officials met in New York in September 2019, thus marking a new milestone for US diplomatic re-engagement with regional allies and partners.

The Quad embraces a framing that initially stressed co-operation on freedom of navigation and overflight in common maritime zones, upheld the UN system and international law, coped with North Korea's nuclear threat and terrorism. Most of ideological structure retains Japan's 'Free and Open Indo-Pacific' (FOIP) strategy (Goh 2022: 35) revealed in August 2016. Japan's FOIP is often confused with the US strategy: while the former considers free and open as a normative construct that is applied to the management of maritime affairs (Yoshimatsu 2019: 447–48), the latter is centred at the more military-oriented Quad (Hosoya 2019: 25). Apart from those principles previously mentioned, the Biden administration has broadened the deeply common enterprise of the quadrilateral dialogue. US National Security Adviser, Jake Sullivan (2021), affirmed the Quad represents 'the kind of new form of partnership' that is going to most fundamentally grapple with a range of issues that they are facing. Primarily, it attempts to deliver regional public goods provision, such as health care and education. Secondly, members are working all among themselves to mutually enhance supply chain resilience, mainly that of semiconductor. Thirdly, the minilateral initiative has begun performing a 'standard-setting function' in critical and emerging technologies (Satoru 2021: 84–5). Until now, tangible outcomes have been achieved in natural disaster risk management and in infrastructure initiative for low- and middle-income countries (Build Back Better World). Since 2015, Quad partners have provided more than $48 billion in official finance for infrastructure in the region.[7] moreover, they pledged to donate at least one billion COVID-19 vaccines by the end of 2022 across the world, manufactured by India's Biological E.[8] Last but not least, in an effort to pre-empt new risky activities in cyberspace, leader-level experts will meet regularly to implement work between government and industry on adopting new standards.

The Quad enjoy the support of four vibrant economies and robust democracies – even as some of these have a damaged reputation (Toohey 2021) – which are able to represent geographically and culturally distinct elements of the Indo-Pacific. However, those countries who advocate this new concept have, tough, distinctive policy agendas and different national interests. Japan and Australia formalised bilateral alliances, respectively in 1960 and 1951 (with New Zealand), that now serve as an 'integrated deterrence' across domains and the spectrum of conflict.[9] Since the dawn of the San Francisco system, Japan and Australia have been viewed the US as a security provider and 'lender of first resort' because these states still trust the US role of benign hegemon in the region. Conversely, India's diplomacy pursued a non-alignment strategy during the Cold War and evolved into a 'multi-alignment' approach (O'Donnell and Papa 2021: 801–22). This has entailed New Delhi to reach out to varied nations. Although national governments have long rejected formal alliance, in reality, India's post-Cold War foreign policy is pervaded by a set of 'complexities' that influence arrangements and partnership Indian government have signed to consolidate national security (Panda 2022: 44).

However, even though different posture on certain diplomatic and security issues might suggest a lack of overarching coordination, they have become temporarily aligned on one shared concern: the recrudescence of China's diplomatic and military activities (Peou 2022: 57). In *The Asian Insider*, Nirmal Ghosh (2021: 6) wondered whether the Quad might be labelled as an anti-China

---

7   The White House (2021). 'Fact Sheet: Quad Leaders' Summit', 24 September <https://www.whitehouse.gov/briefing-room/statements-releases/2021/09/24/fact-sheet-quad-leaders-summit/> accessed 25 January 2022.

8   The White House (2022). 'The Indo-Pacific Strategy of the United States', February, p. 16 <https://www.whitehouse.gov/wp-content/uploads/2022/02/U.S.-Indo-Pacific-Strategy.pdf>, accessed 28 February 2022.

9   The White House (2022). 'Fact Sheet: President's FY23 Budget Restores American Leadership and Confronts Global Threats', 28 March <https://www.whitehouse.gov/omb/briefing-room/2022/03/28/fact-sheet-presidents-fy23-budget-restores-american-leadership-and-confronts-global-threats/>, accessed 30 March 2022.

initiative. There is no denying that the US sees it as a new emerging democratic forum to counter the Chinese leadership's reckless policies in the Indo-Pacific. In some ways, the revival of the dialogue conveys a 'strong deterrent message' to any revisionist attempts of China (Hakata and Cannon 2021: 7). The Biden administration reckons that in recent years China has been acting more aggressively both at home and in the region. US Vice-President Kamala D. Harris[10] and Secretary of State Blinken (The Associated Press 2022) affirmed confrontation with Beijing is 'not inevitable', but the US must stand up with its allies for a rules-based system threatened by any potential aggression from China.

The Quad can be deemed as a formal organisation since no agreements has been signed, no charter approved, no shared budget allocated. Only few tacit obligations are placed on its members and it is based on mutual trust. This grouping pattern is representative of an informal intergovernmental organisation, which is based on regular meetings at the ministerial, senior officials, and working levels but are not gathered by permanent secretariat as happened in the case of ASEAN (Cannon and Rossiter 2022). At this point, it is still debated if the Quad can be considered as a strategic partnership. Based on Wilkins' prominent research (2012: 68), the answer cannot be positive. The minilateral initiative is organised around specific tasks rather than a general security purpose, as a security partnership is expected to be; is primarily 'threat-driven' rather than 'goal-driven'. Officially, no enemy state is identified by the partnership as a threat, though the partnership is very concerned with Chinese assertiveness in territorial disputes (East and South China Sea and Sino-Indian border); ultimately, like a strategic partnership, the Quad tends to be informal in nature and entail lower commitment costs than a formal defence treaty.

Said that, the Quad can be considered as a premier forum opening the chances for a warm-up in bilateral relations that was severely undermined by the Sino-American rivalry. US allies' key policy calculation is to identify, explore and implement other forms of security collaboration with Washington and with each other that are 'less binding but still effective' in fulfilling mutual security aims (Tow 2021: 14). The Quad is complementary to trilateral groupings including the US and new trilateral arrangements which are formed by 'spoke-to-spoke relations' and do not include the US (i.e., Australia-India-Japan). Doubts about

---

10 The White House (2021). Remarks by Vice President Harris on the Indo-Pacific Region, Singapore, 24 August <https://www.whitehouse.gov/briefing-room/speeches-remarks/2021/08/24/remarks-by-vice-president-harris-on-the-indo-pacific-region/>, accessed 25 January 2022.

the reliability of the US as a security guarantor under the Trump administration convinced local actors to develop new forms of co-operation to allay this uncertainty (Nilsson-Wright, 2017: 2).

Political divergence, strategic weakness

While the four maritime democracies identified convergent interests across the two-ocean region, not all consider PRC as illiberal, norm violator or incremental revisionist power. Japan and Australia are in line with the US when viewing China's behaviour in a coercive way. Among policymakers in the Quad's capitals concerns have been mounting about 'unduly provoking or creating a confrontational bulwark' against Beijing (Hakata and Cannon 2021: 9). There is no mention to China's threat in statements. However, Quad can be seen as a 'security platform' in opposition to China's expansionism in East Asia, but it is not a new Manila Pact, signed in 1954. The regional states – Quad members and not – have become wary of the expanding influences of an authoritarian China, while at the same time seeking to develop friendly and co-operative relations with that nation (Jung et al. 2021: 53–4). China converged on strategic interests with Japan and India which has improved their relations and proved China's goodwill towards its historical regional rivals (Shah 2020: 134).

Each US's junior partners is committed to offsetting risks and opportunities derived from relationship with their main economic partner and major provider of security. Nearly every one of American security allies and partners enjoys dominant economic relations with China. Even 2021, China remained the largest two-way trading partner of US, Japan, Australia, and India. Any US strategy cannot ignore this tangible fact (Campbell 2017). Although they depend more on the US than on themselves for their security, Japan and Australia intend to be become less dependent on their main ally and China, and promote alternative security and economic policies with neither each other (Japan-Australia, Japan-India, Australia-India) or other middle powers in the region.

Since the Abe's second term, Japan has planned on reconfiguring its military dependence. Enhancing Japan's defence and technological co-operation with India (April 2020), as well as stepping up reciprocal access agreement with Australia that makes it easier for each nation's troops to operate in each other's country (January 2022), should be defined as the central element of the FOIP to counterbalance China. A 'web of trusted security relations' in every other combination among the Quad members had the effect of preparing to tame Chinese power (Medcalf 2020). Furthermore, it is debated if Japan's FOIP should be regarded as a subtle but indirect swipe at Chinese activities in the South China

Sea (Choong 2019: 416) or a countermeasure against China's BRI. The strategy revolves around idea of 'quality infrastructure' as a principal component of its external infrastructure push (Yoshimatsu 2021). However, Japan has intentionally avoided taking actions that would be perceived by China as containment through its FOIP. Today, Tokyo has maintained its desire, although it has no seat in the Board of Governors of the Asian Infrastructure and Investment Bank, to provide co-operation and financial support for China's BRI, under certain conditions (Sano 2021: 18; Ito 2019: 36). Abe's visit to China in 2018, the two countries exchanged 52 memorandums of cooperation for businesses in third countries, which implied that Japan would not object to the BRI (Ishii 2021: 157). However, Japan is very interested in investing in infrastructure in Asia, especially through the Asian Development Bank, whose is the largest shareholders with the US (each with 15.6 per cent of total shares), the PRC (6.4 per cent), India (6.3 per cent), and Australia (5.8 per cent).[11]

Australia, as well as Japan, certainly sees its bilateral military alliances with the US as the basis of their own security, strengthening their security through the US, not outside it. However, Australians have found it difficult to adopt a self-interested position. The historical basic problem of Australian policymakers, as they look at long-term foreign and defence policies, was how to balance the geographical necessity which arises from being geographically Asian against the attitudes and interests which arise from being ethnically Western predominantly (Bell 1968: 276). Over the past decade, Australia often has pursued foreign policy in the new changing regional order following three reinforcing legs, each of which relies on security from China. One is the ever-tighter alliance with the US, another is engagement with the Quad, and the third has the Indo-Pacific as a strategic concept that seeks to co-opt India into balancing China (Raby 2020). Joining the Quad maintains Australia's less distant from Asia and stops perpetuating its insularity. The 'act of faith' of Australia (Raby 2020) consists in following the US into strategic confrontation with China. Australia has long preferred to balance its core normative and strategic ties with the US against its economic relations with China.

India views Japan and Australia as 'natural partners' in a contested region (ABC News Australia 2022; NDTV 2021). At the same time, New Delhi is convinced of Beijing's unwillingness to endorse India's 'rightful' place in a global

---

11 Asian Development Bank. 'Investors Relations, Credit Fundamentals' <https://www. adb.org/work-with-us/investors/credit-fundamentals#accordion-0-4>, accessed 25 January 2022.

order (Suryanarayana 2021). The US strategy for the Indo-Pacific recognises that India is a like-minded partner and leader in South Asia and the Indian Ocean, active in and connected to South-East Asia, a driving force of the Quad and other regional fora, and an engine for regional growth and development. Between the world's largest democracies there is a 'growing strategic convergence'[12] founded on shared values. This has produced a relationship that is not an alliance but that maintains a certain closeness (Selden 2016: 70). Since 1992, India and US have modest annual naval drills, called *Malabar*. In November 2001, the US and India moved toward military co-operation in the form of defence technology sales agreements and the protection of strategic sea lanes, such as the Bay of Bengal. based on common strategic interests and a convergence of views on many issues, particularly regarding China's threat in the Indian Ocean. Nevertheless, India maintains that it is important to preserve its own strategic autonomy. Decades-old grievances that re-emerge periodically continue to influence the Sino-Indian relationship. In an attempt to counter China's the Twenty-First Century Maritime Silk Road, in 2014 India has launched Project *Mausum* (aimed at re-establishing India's ancient maritime routes with its ancient trade partners within the Indian Ocean) and has sought to enhance its strategic and economic engagements with key regional states with support from Japan and the US (Upadhyaya 2020: 44).

With all said that, among the main risks in minilateral security politics there is its overt political fragility. While there is a 'convergence of strategic interests' among the four parties, there is little evidence of coherent strategic intent among them (Ball et al. 2021: 172–74; O'Neil and West 2021: 2; Choong 2019: 417–23). If Japan and Australia do not intend to contest the systemic preponderance of the US in the region, India is alone among the Quad countries in seeking a multipolar system that could reflect today's realities. Its structural approach is an attempt at constructing an equilibrium that includes 'all nations in this geography as also others beyond who have a stake in it' (Panda 2021: 70).

Climate change exemplifies this situation. The Biden administration has turned up the heat on its allies and partners to reduce carbon emissions. Japan, the world's third-biggest importer of the dirtiest fossil fuel, declined to sign the Glasgow agreement on phasing out coal power because it needed to preserve all its options for power generation. A top US climate official said that Australia's

---

12 The White House (2021). 'US-India Joint Leaders' Statement: A Partnership for Global Good', 24 September <https://www.whitehouse.gov/briefing-room/statements-relea ses/2021/09/24/u-s-india-joint-leaders-statement-a-partnership-for-global-good/> accessed 25 January 2022.

2030 target of reducing emissions by 26-28 % on 2005 levels was 'not sufficient' (Hurst 2021). India has also abstained from signing a global deal made at COP26 to reduce emissions of methane gas. It is one of the most potent greenhouse gases, created by agriculture, fossil fuels and waste, and India is a major emitter. If they do not find a solution, the Quad risks to be considered as unfit and loose grouping such as ARF and ASEAN Plus Three.

Ultimately, another factor that intensifies political fragility can be represented by the official Indian position on Russia. The US remains opposed to India's acquisition of S-400 missile systems from Russia. Recognising the complications that the India-Russia defence partnership creates for US regional strategy, American policymakers still appear to underestimate India's dependence on and commitment to its partnership with Russia, and to overestimate the US ability to reshape Indian preferences (Sameer and Sagerstrom 2021: 151). As in case of the military coup in Myanmar, the Russian invasion of Ukraine has made it clearer divisions between India and the rest of the Quad members which have all hit Russia with sanctions and provided military and financial assistance to Ukraine. In the Indian-Japanese joint statement (19 March 2022) Kishida Fumio and Narendra Modi expressed their 'serious concern' about the ongoing conflict and humanitarian crisis in Ukraine and assessed its broader implications, particularly to the Indo-Pacific region.[13] But India has not criticised Russia's invasion and has abstained from several key UN votes condemning aggression.

Conclusion

Given that its main concern revolves around China, there were worries that the quadrilateral dialogue would securitise the region by becoming a security pact (Kwek 2021). This chapter concluded that there are no margin and perspective to label the Quad as a security pact both for political and strategic reasons. If it is certain that this political initiative, if anything, could pose an effective counterweight to any China's actions in the Indian and Pacific oceans, nothing could look less catchy than the perspective for US allies and partners, at best, to get embroiled and, at worst, to choose a side in the Sino-American rivalry. Within this context, Japan and Australia feel somewhat composed by joining

---

13 Government of India, Ministry of External Affairs (2022). 'India-Japan Summit Joint Statement Partnership for a Peaceful, Stable and Prosperous Post-COVID World', 19 March, <https://www.mea.gov.in/bilateral-documents.htm?dtl/34991/IndiaJapan+Summit+Joint+Statement+Partnership+for+a+Peaceful+Stable+and+Prosperous+PostCOVID+World>, accessed 30 March 2022.

a minilateral forum revolving around the US leadership and adding to formal security alliances. In contrast, India rejects the implicitly hierarchical nature embedded in the Quad. Failing in implementing a coherent policy response, one of two key catalysts for minilateral security along with the application of common values or mutual interests to a specific challenge (Tow 2021: 26), constitutes a serious hurdle to make one step ahead to counter Chinese expansion.

Since it has never referred to a direct adversary, the forum might be branded, if not exclusively, as anti-China. As a matter of fact, it was resurrected at a time when the US-China Comprehensive Economic Dialogue established in April 2017 by President Trump does not make some headway in trade and financial services. At this time, the rationale behind the objective to form a minilateral grouping underpinned by democratic values and spirit of co-operation between authentic partners is to conceive a credible alternative to China's economic development and political authoritarianism, more than constraining any Beijing's attempt to dismantle the existing regional order. Washington has served the Quad as a tool to ensure its control on junior strategic partners and to benefit India's truly collaboration against the backdrop of the important theatre in the Indian Ocean.

The Quad will continue to make sense as long as India, a nuclear power, is part of this initiative. It is a known fact that it constitutes the linchpin of the US grand strategy in the Indo-Pacific for three main reasons. First, New Delhi's recognition of freedom and democratic values, in international relations as well as domestic policy, demonstrates the existence of a credible and lingering alternative to authoritarianism in Asia. Second, engaging Indian Navy means that the US INDOPACOM could conduct a large number of maritime special operations in the Indian Ocean to secure the most important chokepoints of the region. Third, Modi's commitment to manufacturing and donating COVID-19 vaccines across the small- and medium-income countries is due to yield concrete results against the pandemic and China's vaccine diplomacy in Asia. However, while there is some truth in this, there is also little doubt that US might drag India into a proper military pact. Despite dialogue on Kashmir between India and China have been all but thriving this year, it is unlikely that Washington and New Delhi might formalise a stringent arrangement to contain China's military activities along the Line of Actual Control.

Bibliography

ABC News Australia (2022). '"Historic" Trade Agreement with India Signed after Decade of Negotiations', 2 April.

Abe, S. (2012). 'Asia's Democratic Security Diamonds', *Project Syndicate*, 27 December.

Ang, C.G. (2022). *The South-East Asia Treaty Organisation*, Abingdon and New York: Routledge.

Ashizawa, K. (2013). Japan, the US, and Regional Institution-Building in the New Asia. When Identity Matters. New York: Palgrave Macmillan.

Auslin, M. R. (2020). *Asia's New Geopolitics: Essays on Reshaping the Indo-Pacific*. Stanford, CA: Hoover Institution Press.

Bacevich, A. J. (2004). *American Empire: The Realities and Consequences of US Diplomacy*, Cambridge, MA: Harvard University Press, 2004.

Baker III, J.A (1991). 'America in Asia', *Foreign Affairs*, 1st December. <https://www.foreignaffairs.com/articles/asia/1991-12-01/america-asia-emerging-architecture-pacific-community>, accessed 25 January 2022.

Ball, D., et al. (eds) (2021). *Asia's New Geopolitics: Military Power and Regional Order*. Abingdon: Routledge/International Institute for Strategic Studies.

Beeson, M. (2019). 'Asia's Competing Multilateral Initiatives: Quality versus Quantity', *Pacific Review*, 32 (2), 245–55.

–––– (2003). 'Australia's Relationship with the United States: The Case for Greater Independence', *Australian Journal of Political Science*, 38 (3), 387–405.

Bell, C. (1968). 'Australian Defence in the Asian Context', *Journal of the Royal Central Asian Society*, 55 (3), 276–87.

Benvenuti, A. et al. (2022). *China's Foreign Policy. The Emergence of a Great Power*. Abingdon and New York: Routledge.

Biscop, S. (2021). *Grand Strategy in 10 Words: A Guide to Great Power Politics in the 21st Century*. Bristol: Bristol University Press.

Buckley, R. (2002). *The United States in the Asia-Pacific since 1945*. New York, NY: Cambridge University Press.

Calabrese, J. (2020). 'Assuring a Free and Open Indo-Pacific – Rebalancing the US Approach', *Asian Affairs*, 51 (2), 307–27.

Campbell, K.M. (2022). 'America's Rebalancing Towards the Asia-Pacific in Retrospect and Prospect'. In R.G. Patman, P. Köllner, and B. Kiglics (eds), *From Asia-Pacific to Indo-Pacific Diplomacy in a Contested Region*. Singapore: Palgrave Macmillan, 73–89.

–––– (2021). 'In Conversation with Michael Fullilove (Executive Director Lowy Institute), 1st December, <https://www.lowyinstitute.org/publications/conversation-white-house-indo-pacific-coordinator-kurt-campbell>, accessed 25 January 2022.

----- (with Sullivan, J.) (2019), 'Why the Quad Alarms China', *Foreign Affairs*, September/October, <https://www.foreignaffairs.com/articles/china/competition-with-china-without-catastrophe> accessed 25 January 2022.

----- (2017). *The Pivot: The Future of American Statecraft in Asia*. New York, NY: Twelve. [Kindle book]: http://www.amazon.com.

Cannon, B.J., and Rossiter, A. (2022), 'Locating the Quad: Informality, Institutional Flexibility, and Future Alignment in the Indo-Pacific', *International Politics*, <https://link.springer.com/content/pdf/10.1057/s41311-022-00383-y.pdf> accessed 25 January 2022.

Cha, V.D. (2009/2010). 'Powerplay: Origins of the US Alliance System in Asia', *International Security*, 34 (3), 158–96.

Chen, P. (2020). 'The Prospects of the US Alliance System in Asia: Managing from the Hub', *Issues & Studies: A Social Science Quarterly on China, Taiwan, and East Asian Affairs*, 56 (3), 1–34.

Choong, W. (2019). 'The Return of the Indo-Pacific Strategy: An Assessment', *Australian Journal of International Affairs*, 73 (5), 415–30.

Clarke, M. (2021). *American Grand Strategy and National Security. The Dilemmas of Primacy and Decline from the Founding to Trump*. Cham: Palgrave Macmillan.

Cocker, C. (2015). *The Improbable War. China, the United States, and the Logic of Great Power Conflict*. New York, NY: Oxford University Press.

Crabtree, J. (2021). 'America's Architectural Challenge in Southeast Asia', *Survival*, 63 (5), 59–65.

Denmark, A.M. (2020). *US Strategy in the Asian Century: Empowering Allies and Partners*. New York, NY: Columbia University Press.

Dian, M., and Meijer, H. (2020). 'Networking Hegemony: Alliance Dynamics in East Asia', *International Politics*, 57 (2), 131–49.

Doyle, T., and Rumley, D. (2019). *The Rise and Return of the Indo-Pacific*. Oxford: Oxford University Press.

Envall, H.D.P. (2015). 'Community Building in Asia? Trilateral Cooperation in Humanitarian Assistance and Disaster Relief'. In Y. Tatsumi (ed.), *US-Japan-Australia Security Co-operation. Prospects and Challenges*, April. Stimson Center, 51–59.

Flitton, D. (2020). 'Who Really Killed the Quad 1.0?', *The Interpreter*, The Lowy Institute, 2 June.

Ghosh, N. (2021). 'Summit Underscores Biden Administration's Focus on Asia', *The Asian Insider*, April.

Go, J. (2011). *Patterns of Empire: The British and American Empires, 1688 to the Present*. New York, NY: Cambridge University Press.

Goddard, S.E., and Krebs, R.R. (2015). 'Rhetoric, Legitimation, and Grand Strategy', *Security Studies*, 24 (1), 5–36.

Goh, E. (2019). 'Contesting Hegemonic Order: China in East Asia', *Security Studies*, 28 (3), 614–44.

Green, M.J. (2017). *By More than Providence. Grand Strategy and American Power in the Asia Pacific since 1783*. New York, NY: Columbia University Press.

Hakata, K., and Cannon, B.J. (2021). 'The Indo-Pacific as an Emerging Geography of Strategies'. In B.J. Cannon, and K. Hakata (eds), *Indo-Pacific Strategies Navigating Geopolitics at the Dawn of a New Age*. Abingdon and New York, NY: Routledge, 3–21.

Harold, S.W. (2014). 'Extremely Desirable but Exceptionally Difficult. An American Perspective', In M. Malik (ed.), *Maritime Security in the Indo-Pacific Perspectives from China, India, and the United States*. London: Rowman & Littlefield, 85–96.

Heydarian, R.J. (2020). *The Indo-Pacific: Trump, China, and the New Struggle for Global Mastery*. Singapore: Palgrave Macmillan.

Hosoya, Y. (2019). 'FOIP 2.0: The Evolution of Japan's Free and Open Indo-Pacific Strategy', *Asia-Pacific Review*, 26 (1), 18–28.

Hurst, D. (2021). '"Not on the Same Page": Australia Set to Face US Pressure on Climate as Ministers Head to Washington', *The Guardian*, 8 September.

Ikenberry, G.J (2004). 'American Hegemony and East Asian Order', *Australian Journal of International Affairs*, 58 (3), 353–67.

Ishii, J. (2021). 'Indo-Pacific Diplomacy, the Quad and Beyond: Democratic Coalition in the Era of US-China Global Competition'. In E. A. Carr Jr (ed.), *From Trump to Biden and Beyond. Reimagining US-China Relations*. Singapore: Palgrave Macmillan, 151–73.

Ito, A. (2019). 'China's Belt and Road Initiative and Japan's Response: From Non-participation to Conditional Engagement', *East Asia*, 36, 115–28.

Izumikawa, Y. (2020). 'Network Connections and the Emergence of the Hub-and-Spokes Alliance System in East Asia', *International Security*, 45 (2), 7–50.

Jung, S.C., Lee, J., and Lee, J. (2021). 'The Indo-Pacific Strategy and US Alliance Network Expandability: Asian Middle Powers' Positions on Sino-US Geostrategic Competition in Indo-Pacific Region', *Journal of Contemporary China*, 30 (127), 53–68.

Katzenstein, P.J. (2005). *A World of Regions: Asia and Europe in the American Imperium*. Ithaca, NY: Cornell University Press, 2005.

Kitaoka, S. (2019). 'Vision for a Free and Open Indo-Pacific', *Asia-Pacific Review*, 26 (1), 7–17.

Koga, K. (2022). 'A New Strategic Minilateralism in the Indo-Pacific, *Asia Policy*, 17 (4), 27-34.

Kwek, I. (2021). 'The Quad's Uneasy Place in Southeast Asia', *The Interpreter*, The Lowy Institute, 14 April.

LaFeber, W. (2013). *The New Cambridge History of American Foreign Relations.* Cambridge: Cambridge University Press.

Latiff, R., and Lee, L. (2019). 'US Says New Indo-Pacific Economic Framework Not Typical Trade Deal', *Reuters*, 19 November.

Layne, C. (2006). *The Peace of Illusions. American Grad Strategy from 1940 to the Present.* Ithaca, NY and London: Cornell University Press.

Luce, E. (2017). *The Retreat of Western Liberalism.* New York, NY: Atlantic Monthly Press. [Kindle book]: http://www.amazon.com.

Martel, W.C. (2015). *Grand Strategy in Theory and Practice: The Need for an Effective American Foreign Policy.* New York, NY: Cambridge University Press.

Medcalf, R. (2021). 'Declassification of Secret Document Reveals US Strategy in the Indo-Pacific', *The Strategist*, Australian Strategic Policy Institute, 13 January.

–––– (2020). *Contest for the Indo-Pacific. Why China Won't Map the Future.* Carlton: La Trobe University Press. [Kindle book]: http://www.amazon.com.

Milevski, L. (2016). *The Evolution of Modern Grand Strategic Thought.* Oxford: Oxford University Press.

Natalegawa, M. (2018). *Does ASEAN Matter? A View from Within.* Singapore: ISEAS – Yusof Ishak Institute.

NDTV (2021). 'India, Japan "Most Natural" Partners in Region: PM Modi', 15 July.

Ngoei Wen-Qing (2019). *Arc of Containment: Britain, the United States, and Anticommunism in Southeast Asia.* Ithaca, NY: Cornell University Press.

Nilsson-Wright, J. (2017), 'Creative Minilateralism in a Changing Asia: Opportunities for Security Convergence and Co-operation between Australia, India and Japan', *Chatham House*, Research Paper, July <https://www.chathamhouse.org/sites/default/files/images/2017-07-28-Minilateralism.pdf>, accessed 15 January 2022.

Nye, J.S. (2001). 'The "Nye Report": Six Years Later', *International Relations of the Asia-Pacific*, 1 (1), 95-103.

O'Donnell, F., and Papa, M. (2021). 'India's Multi-alignment Management and the Russia-India-China (RIC) Triangle, *International Affairs*, 97 (3), 801–22.

O'Neil, A. and West, L. (2021). 'The Quadrilateral Security Dialogue and Indo-Pacific Minilateralism: Resurrection without Renewal?'. In B. Singh, and S. Teo (eds), *Minilateralism in the Indo-Pacific. The Quadrilateral Security Dialogue, Lancang-Mekong Co-operation Mechanism, and ASEAN*. Abingdon and New York, NY: Routledge, 27–41.

Panda, J. P. (2022). 'The Quad Plus and India's Pointed Alignment Strategy', In J.P. Panda, and Ernest Gunasekara-Rockwell (eds), *Quad Plus and Indo-Pacific: The Changing Profile of International Relations*. Abingdon and New York, NY: Routledge, 44–77.

Peou, S. (2022). *Peace and Security in Indo-Pacific Asia IR Perspectives in Context*. Abingdon and New York, NY: Routledge.

Perry, J. C. (1994). *Facing West: Americans and the Opening of the Pacific*. Westport, CT: Praeger.

Pompeo, M. R. (2018). 'Secretary's Remarks on "America's Indo-Pacific Economic Vision"', 30 July 2018 <https://asean.usmission.gov/sec-pompeo-remarks-on-americas-indo-pacific-economic-vision/>, accessed 25 January 2022.

Press-Barnathan, G. (2003). *Organizing the World: The United States and Regional Co-operation in Asia and Europe*, Abingdon and New York, NY: Routledge.

Preston, A. (2016, 3rd edition), 'The Religious Turn in Diplomatic History'. In F. Costigliola, and M.J. Hogan (eds), *Explaining the History of American Foreign Relations*. New York: Cambridge University Press, 284-303.

Raby, G. (2020). *China's Grand Strategy and Australia's Future in the New Global Order*. Carlton, VIC: Melbourne University Press. [Kindle book]: http://www.amazon.com.

Sameer, L., and Sagerstrom, T. (2021). 'What the India-Russia Defence Partnership Means for US Policy', *Survival*, 63 (4), 149–82.

Sano, S. (2021). 'Japan's Free and Open Indo-Pacific Vision: In Overcoming the Geostrategic Dilemma', In P. Jaiswal, and D. P. Bhatt (eds), *Rebalancing Asia: The Belt and Road Initiative and Indo-Pacific Strategy*. Singapore: Springer, 11–27.

Satoru, M. (2021). 'The Biden Administration's First Year in the Indo-Pacific: Balancing, Order-Building and Managing Competition with China', *Asia-Pacific Review*, 28 (2), 77–106.

Scobell, A. (2021). 'Constructing a US-China Rivalry in the Indo-Pacific and Beyond', *Journal of Contemporary China*, 30 (127), 69–84.

Selden, Z. (2016). *Alignment, Alliance, and American Grand Strategy*. Ann Arbor: Michigan University Press.

Shah, R. (2020). 'Will the Indo-Pacific Strategy Besiege China?', *Australian Journal of Maritime & Ocean Affairs*, 12 (3), 125–37.

Silove, N. (2018). "Beyond the Buzzword: The Three Meanings of 'Grand Strategy'", *Security Studies*, 27 (1), 27-57.

Sullivan, J. (2021). 'In Conversation with Michael Fullilove (Executive Director Lowy Institute), 11 November <https://www.lowyinstitute.org/publications/2021-lowy-lecture-jake-sullivan>, accessed 25 January 2022.

Suryanarayana, P. S. (2021). 'India's Quest for Multipolarity', *RSIS Commentary*, 20 December.

The Associated Press (2022). 'Blinken Says Confrontation with China Not Inevitable', 11 February.

Thompson, S. (2019). *The United States and Southeast Asian Regionalism: Collective Security and Economic Development, 1945-75.* Abingdon and New York: Routledge.

Toohey, T. (2021). 'Quad Queers its Pitch: Champions of Democracy Fail to Walk the Talk', *Pearls and Irritations*, 9 December.

Tow, W. T. (2021). 'Minilateralism and US Security Policy in the Indo-Pacific. The Legacy, Viability and Deficiencies of a New Security Approach'. In B. Singh, and S. Teo (eds), *Minilateralism in the Indo-Pacific. The Quadrilateral Security Dialogue, Lancang-Mekong Co-operation Mechanism, and ASEAN.* Abingdon and New York, NY: Routledge, 13–26.

———— (2019). 'Minilateral Security's Relevance to US Strategy in the Indo-Pacific: Challenges and Prospects', *Pacific Review*, 32 (2), 232–44.

———— (2015). 'The Trilateral Strategic Dialogue, Minilateralism, and Asia-Pacific Order Building'. In Y. Tatsumi (ed.), *US-Japan-Australia Security Co-operation. Prospects and Challenges*, April. Stimson Center, 23–35.

Townshend, A., et al. (2021). 'Correcting the Course: How the Biden Administration Should Compete for Influence in the Indo-Pacific', *United States Studies Centre at the University of Sydney*, August, 1–46.

Upadhyaya, S. (2020). *India's Maritime Strategy Balancing Regional Ambitions and China.* Abingdon and New York, NY: Routledge.

Vinjamuri, L. (2021). 'Biden's Realism Will Drive Competition Among US Allies', *Chatham House*, 23 September.

Wesley-Smith, T., and Finin, G. A. (2021). 'US-Pacific Engagement and the Biden Presidency: The Limits of a China-Centred Approach', *Journal of Pacific History*, 56 (4), 437–58.

Wilkins, T. S. (2012). '"Alignment", not '"Alliance"' – The Shifting Paradigm of International Security Co-operation: Toward a Conceptual Taxonomy of Alignment', *Review of International Studies*, 38, 53–76.

Wirth, C., and Jenne, N. (2022). 'Filling the Void: The Asia-Pacific Problem of Order and Emerging Indo-Pacific Regional Multilateralism', *Contemporary Security Policy*, 1–30.

Wuthnow, J. (2019). 'US 'Minilateralism' in Asia and China's Responses: A New Security Dilemma?', *Journal of Contemporary China*, 28 (115), 133–50.

Yahuda, M. B. (2019, 4th edition). *The International Politics of the Asia-Pacific*. Abingdon and New York, NY: Routledge. [Kindle book]: http://www.ama zon.com.

Yoshimatsu, Y. (2021). 'Japan's Strategic Response to China's Geo-economic Presence: Quality Infrastructure as a Diplomatic Tool, *Pacific Review*, <10.1080/09512748.2021.1947356>, accessed 25 January 2022.

–––––, (2019). 'The Indo-Pacific in Japan's Strategy towards India', *Contemporary Politics*, 25 (4), 438–56.

Francesca Frassineti

Chinese Maritime Coercion in East Asia: Probing the US Alliance System Trigger Points

Over the past several years, the strategic environment in East Asia has faced a complex of security challenges, especially noticeable in the maritime domain. Mounting tensions have risen amid China's growing assertiveness in the context of disputed waters and territories in the East and South China Seas. By skillfully adopting a playbook and toolkit short of direct use of conventional force, the Chinese leadership has sought to advance its objectives and leverage its influence to pressure or punish countries without provoking outright escalation to military confrontation. Amid a destabilised rules-based regional order, the United States and its allies most notably Japan have struggled to devise effective strategies to counter China's maritime challenges in the gray zone due to shortcomings related to existing deterrent strategies, defense planning and diplomacy at the level of individual countries and bilateral security alliance. This chapter examines China's attempts to gain the upper hand through the use of non-state actors, paramilitary and civilian means in the maritime domain. In doing so, the Chinese Communist Party exploits the defining advantages of gray zone activities in terms of deniability and the determination of regional countries to respond. For this reason, it will be stressed the importance of managing gray zone threats with a long-term perspective and a whole-of-government approach aimed to enhance coordination between civilian and military agencies.

Following the Russian Federation (from now on, Russia)'s seizure of the Crimean Peninsula from Ukraine in 2014, the term 'gray zone' has sparked renewed attention and controversy in international affairs. Policy experts and strategists have been engaged in debates regarding the novelty of the gray zone phenomenon and the need for an explicit definition besides outlining its commonly identified characteristics (Brands 2016).[1] Through the use of irregular and local proxy forces ('little green men') operating covertly, along with disinformation tactics, the first-stage of Russia's annexation of Ukraine has become an exemplary case of post-Cold War 'fait accompli' that James J. Wirtz describes as 'the riskiest type

---

1   Recent seminal discussions on gray zone coercion include Carment and Belo (2020); Hicks *et al.* (2019); Morris *et al.* (2019); Hoffman (2016); Mazarr (2015); Kapusta (2015).

of short-of-war strategy animating the gray zone' (2017: 108). Eight years later, Moscow's full-scale invasion and aggression against Ukraine has shown that non-military means coexist with traditional warfare in the attempt to influence and threaten the liberal international order.

Leveraging the advantages typical of the gray zone is not in itself new. Since 1991, the bleak area of limited military competition simmering between the two ends of the war-peace spectrum has been viewed as more significant than ever. This has largely been attributed to the information revolution and technological advancements, which can further enable such aspects of warfare (Knefel 2015; Mazarr 2015). Currently, as the global security environment is being shaped primarily by the United States (U.S.)' strategic competition with Russia and China, low-intensity coercive tactics have become part of the latter's 'repertoire of statecraft' (Goddard et al. 2019) aimed to selectively contest the US-led order.[2] By sidestepping established 'redlines', employing intermediary actors, or presenting fait accompli, both Moscow and Beijing have sought to weaken the US and their partners' determination to respond (Van Jackson 2017).

In East Asia, the People's Republic of China (PRC) has leveraged interoperability across various dimensions following 'a pattern of dialing up and dialing down coercive diplomacy and blending it with diplomacy, trade and investment, and other forms of engagement' (Cronin et al. 2014: 5). Johnston (2013)'s question of 'how new is China's new assertiveness' has fed an animated debate that resembles the controversy mentioned earlier around the novelty of the gray zone term. Many experts date China's assertive shift to 2009 and 2010 (Friedberg 2015; Chan and Li 2015; Johnston 2013; Fravel and Swaine 2011) as efforts to consolidate its maritime and territorial claims have become more noticeable due to the increasing presence of Chinese paramilitary in the South China Sea (SCS) and the submission of a *jiu duan xian* [nine-dash line - 九段线] map to the United Nations (UN).[3] In 2009, the Sino-American confrontation over the USNS

---

2   Since 2017, China and Russia have been described in the US National Security Strategy as challengers to 'American power, influence, and interests, attempting to erode American security and prosperity'. While reaffirming the strategic competition with Beijing and Moscow, the Biden administration's 2022 National Security Strategy has characterized China as the only rivalling nation with 'with both the intent to reshape the international order and, increasingly, the economic, diplomatic, military, and technological power to do it' (p. 23).

3   The nine-dash line is a cartographic representation of China's expansive claims in the SCS formed by a collection of arbitrary dots. The narrative that revolves around it aims to convey the message that the line is part of China's administrative territory. The history of the dashed line pre-dates the 'U-shaped Line' map that China attached

Impeccable incident has reinforced similar arguments put forward by other scholars including Michael Yahuda (2013) and Sarah Raine (2011).[4] Conversely, Richard Q. Turcsányi stresses that the series of events that took place after 2011 (i.e. the cable-cutting, Scarborough Shoal and HYSY 981-oil rig incidents) have shown a qualitative shift in Chinese behavior, unlike the 'policy adjustments' that occurred that same year (2018: 39-54).

In recent years, China's assertiveness especially in the maritime domain has been addressed as one of the leading cases of gray zone challenges by the majority of Western scholars of strategic studies and practitioners. Despite the large consensus on applying the gray zone construct to Chinese coercion at sea, Alessio Patalano contends that when discussing Chinese maritime force, 'the parameters of a hybrid strategy' are more practical to understand 'the functional correlation between Beijing's strategic objectives and maritime claims' (2019: 813). From this perspective, applying the gray zone framework tends to conflate the military and constabulary activities and to confuse efforts aimed to separate the tactics from the overall strategy of the Chinese Communist Party (CCP) in which the use of force is weighed on the context and circumstances rather than on the ambition to avoid armed clashes (Ibid).

A study recently released by the RAND Corporation has found that between 2014 and 2016 the term *huise didai* [gray zone - 灰色地带] has gradually appeared in Chinese media and academic debates and that *feizhanzheng junshi* [non-combat military operations - 非战争军事行动] has been used to refer to 'stability maintenance, rights protection, and security and guarding operations' (Lin *et al.* 2022: 11). As Gui Yongtao notes, the shift might have been accelerated following the publication of the 2010 US Quadrennial Defense Review considered as 'the first significant introduction of the notion of a gray zone into contemporary strategic discussions' (2019: 45-46). In the same year, Japan became the first to explicitly refer to 'a growing number of so-called 'gray zone'

---

to its *note verbale*, which Beijing submitted to the UN on 7 May 2009, in response to Malaysia and Vietnam joint submission that claimed an extended continental shelf in the southern part of the SCS.
    See Permanent Mission of the People's Republic of China, Notes Verbales CML/17/2009 and CML/18/2009, May 7, 2009, <http://www.un.org/Depts/los/clcs_new/submissions_files/mysvnm33_09/chn_2009re_mys_vnm_e.pdf> and <http://www.un.org/Depts/los/clcs_new/submissions_files/vnm37_09/chn_2009re_vnm.pdf>. Accessed 18 April 2022.
4   For an expanded account of the incident including the evidence presented and the arguments made by the governments of the two nations involved, see Odom (2013).

disputes – confrontations over territory, sovereignty and economic interests that are not to escalate into wars' (JMoD 2010: 3). In Tokyo's 2013 National Defense Program Guidelines the gray zone framework has been further elaborated supposedly driven by the need to enhance deterrence vis-à-vis the Chinese behavior in the ECS.

Drawing on extensive literature, this chapter focuses on the Chinese leadership's multi-faceted efforts emerging from the convergence of state and non-state means through non-kinetic capabilities that are arguably aimed to weaken the rule-based international or regional order. By framing Chinese maritime coercion and competition at sea from the perspective of the gray zone conceptualization, this study outlines what material capabilities, legislative developments and tactics have supported the CCP's mounting use of maritime coercion to advance its political and strategic objectives. It is argued that by improving its paramilitary and law enforcement capabilities – and integrating them into the military chain of command – the CCP exploits the defining advantages of gray zone activities in terms of deniability and the determination of regional countries to respond.

Although the focus is on the military and paramilitary spectrum, this chapter acknowledges that Beijing can rely on a diversified toolkit, which includes diplomatic and economic coercion, in the maritime disputes with Southeast Asian claimants and Japan to a lesser degree (Zhang 2019: 139-147). Albeit the obvious caveats inherent in the history-based claims of Beijing's militarized assertions of sovereignty, Chinese maritime coercion holds potential implications for managing other disputes within and beyond this world's region given the risks of a potentially replicable course of actions. Therefore, this chapter aims to contribute to our understanding of the CCP's ongoing attempts to contest the status quo within and beyond the East and South China Seas (ESCS).

Navigating Chinese Maritime Ambitions

Since the early 1990s, the centrality of the maritime domain has regained prominence amid China's broader militarization efforts. In November 2012, the speech of the outgoing Secretary-General Hu Jintao at the 18th Communist Party Congress marked the high point of a decade-long process of growing maritime power ambitions. Hu declared that making China a 'great maritime power' should be one of the CCP's priorities, and thus the power of the PLA Navy (PLAN) ought to be bolstered (Xinhua News Agency 2012). As naval modernisation has been deemed instrumental to China's strategic objectives, the PLAN has received a great bulk of attention underscoring the fundamental role of the maritime space also for the Chinese domestic economic development and protection of Beijing's sovereignty and security interests.[5] Against this backdrop, since 2010, it has been estimated that nine surface combatants are commissioned on average every year, making Beijing's navy 'the largest navy in the world' (DoD 2022, p. 52).

By embracing maritime power as an essential element of the 'China dream' of achieving national rejuvenation by 2049, President Xi Jinping has doubled down on his predecessor's pledge to build a 'great maritime power'. On the one hand, growing amounts of resources are being devoted to enable the PLAN to conduct long-distance operations. On the other, a large share of the official defence budget has been justified by the necessity to deploy new platforms and weapon systems that could potentially allow China to prevent third parties from accessing contested areas and thus deter them from being involved (Erickson 2014). While China's military advantage in its adjoining waters remains unmatched, the capacity of the PLAN to support Beijing's foreign policy objectives and project military power beyond its immediate region still faces some constraints. This includes poor logistic support capabilities and full-sized naval bases for PLAN remote water operations as well as unfavourable maritime geography.

In response to repeated calls and pressures by the central leadership and the military cadres, the Chinese naval forces have been galvanised to show greater resolve to defend the country's rights in the context of maritime and territorial disputes (Jakobson 2014).[6] The CCP remains unwilling to negotiate on these issues given that the islands have been an integral part of the national territory since 'ancient time' (CMFA 1980: 5).[7] Therefore, it is the duty of the PLAN to 'safeguard the motherland's sacred territorial waters' (Liu Huaqing as quoted in BBC News 1993). As a result, over the last decade, China has been engaged in the militarized assertion of power over most of the ESCS seeking to establish compliance with its jurisdictional claims while undermining those of the other claimants (Kuo 2021).

---

5   On the emergence of China's strategy to defend its interests overseas and stabilise the areas where the Chinese human and economic presence is most significant, see Ghiselli (2021).

6   In 1992, the phrase 'maritime rights and interests' first appeared in the Chinese official lexicon with the passage of the Law on the Territorial Sea and Contiguous Zone. Since then, according to Bickford *et al.* (2011), Chinese leaders have regularly reiterated the duty to safeguard them.

7   Chinese Ministry of Foreign Affairs (CMFA) (1980). 'China's Indisputable Sovereignty over the Xisha and Nansha Islands', *Beijing Review*, 7, 15-24, 18 February.

The existence of significant economic interest at stake in the SCS has been well-documented. Aside from one-third of global shipping passing through the Strait of Malacca every year (UNCTAD 2016), the US Energy Information Agency (EIA) estimates that the SCS contains 11 billion barrels of untapped oil and 190 trillion cubic feet of natural gas (2013). Beijing asserts its claim to approximately 90 per cent of this basin, which is not only historically dubious but also without any legal basis from the perspective of international law (Dupuy and Dupuy 2013, Jakobson 2014).

In order to support its claims, the CCP has followed a so-called 'salami-slicing' strategy eventually managing to alter the status quo 'slowly and progressively' by occupying and expanding existing islands, and building new territorial features (Miracola 2018). Although the creation of new islands is not illegal, acting as if this might produce rights challenges maritime law. Some of the already-existing yet enlarged or newly created islands have become *de facto* militarized since they host facilities to support missile batteries and platforms for fighters, bombers and unmanned aerial vehicles. While Beijing has not yet used the artificial outposts in the SCS to interfere with freedom of navigation, these facilities can be strategically significant in terms of enabling China's air power projection onto maritime space, which is the essential objective of the Chinese military conceptualization of layered-defense that the US Department of Defense characterises as 'anti-access' and 'area denial' or A2/AD.

Following the territorial transformation of the SCS according to its strategic objectives, China's posture has been somewhat recalibrated, focusing on consolidating its acquired positions rather than seeking further expansion. In doing so, Beijing has been incentivized to act incrementally via gray zone approaches. This can be attributed also to China's high dependence on global markets to achieve its national rejuvenation goal and thus to the CCP's interest in preventing any inadvertent military escalation that might disrupt regional trade flows (Mazarr 2015). Adding to that, the necessity to keep Southeast Asian countries from enhancing diplomatic and military cooperation with the US, India and Japan (Kraska and Monti 2015).

It is no coincidence that in November 2013, Xi Jinping announced the Belt and Road Initiative (BRI) – then called One Belt, One Road – whose two main maritime corridors pass through the SCS.[8] In this context, the BRI's link with

---

8   Although officially presented as an infrastructural project of economic development, this chapter follows the argument put forward by Zhou Weifeng and Mario Esteban (2018) who frame the BRI as an expression of China's grand strategy.

both the PLA and the Navy has not gone unnoticed. All the more so following the inauguration, in 2016, of the first Chinese overseas naval base in Doraleh (Djibouti), which has given Beijing access to sea routes outside the regional borders and has brought its ships at the gates of the Mediterranean.

During the COVID-19 pandemic, China's determination to assert its jurisdictional claims has sparked withering criticism from the White House leading to an increased US military presence in the SCS aimed to signal Washington's commitment to uphold freedom of navigation and rule of law (Thayer 2021). According to records provided by US Pacific Fleet, the US Navy conducted twenty-two Freedom of Navigation Operations (FONOPs) in the Paracels and Spratlys between 2019 and 2021. Most recently, US Indo-Pacific Commander Admiral John C. Aquilino told reporters that China has 'fully militarized' at least three of the several features that Beijing has built in the hotly contested waters, referring to the completed construction of military facilities on Mischief Reef, Subi Reef and Fiery Cross (Gomez and Favila 2022).

Means and Capabilities: The Second and Third Sea Force

From the Chinese perspective, having a solid navy should be the main pillar of becoming a 'great maritime power'. Nonetheless, the protection and advancement of Beijing's 'maritime rights and interests' (*haiyang quanyi - 海洋权益*) have made it imperative to deploy all of its naval forces for coercive and competitive purposes. To fulfil its nationalist ambitions and most immediate security objectives, Beijing has relied mainly on the China Coast Guard (CCG) and the People's Armed Forces Maritime Militia (PAFMM), the second and third sea forces, respectively, with the first sea force (the PLAN) to supervise coordination and ensure deterrence.

Like the PLAN, both the CCG and the PAFMM have been the targets of organisational changes and capability build-up (Kennedy and Erickson 2017). When the leadership of the Party was handed down to Xi Jinping, China lacked an established coast guard and 'coast-guard like missions were performed by five different agencies' (Martinson 2021: 187-88). Within weeks after taking China's top Party office in November 2012, the new leadership notified the PLAN 'to transfer eleven auxiliary vessels to the nascent Chinese coast guard' and the production of several new classes of ocean patrol vessels was accelerated (Ibid). Having doubled its fleet of large patrol vessels, which now includes more than 140 hulls – in addition to over 120 vessels for limited offshore operations and about 450 coastal patrol boats – the CCG is considered as 'the largest maritime law enforcement fleet in the world' (DoD 2022: 78).

Aside from increasing its material capabilities, the CCG has been bolstered in terms of operational efficiency following a two-step process. At first, in March 2013, the National People's Assembly approved the centralization of bureaucratic control over four of the five existing maritime law enforcement agencies – including the then newly-formed CCG – bringing them under the supervision of a civilian agency, namely the State Oceanic Administration (SoA). However, in 2018, a five-year assessment showed unconvincing results and led to entrust the People's Armed Police (PAP), which directly answers to the Central Military Commission (CMC), with control over the CCG (Zhao 2018). This means that the CCG has been placed within the military chain of command, allowing it to develop as a professional force.

As a corollary to this process, China adopted an *ad hoc* legislation. In 2020, the Supreme People's Court and the Supreme People's Procuratorate issued a notice according to which 'plac(ing) on file for investigation and prosecution over crimes at sea' should fall into the jurisdiction of the CCG (Zou 2021: 187). In January 2021, the first Chinese coast guard law was passed at the XXV Meeting of the Standing Committee of the 13th National People's Congress. While its mandate and role have remained unchanged, in light of what has been described so far, the CCG can arguably operate as the leading Chinese maritime law enforcement agent with larger and more equipped patrol vessels allowing it to be present for extended periods in the disputed areas.[9]

As observed by Lyle J. Morris (2017), the fact that Chinese paramilitary maritime forces are the front-line defenders to assert Beijing's sovereignty claim have induced other regional claimants to do the same, meaning to deploy their coast guards rather than their navies in disputed waters. Accordingly, the more frequent presence of coast guard cutters, which are equipped with advanced military technologies, involved in peacetime patrol missions in areas claimed by multiple states makes it hard to distinguish between actors that are usually involved in 'law enforcement' tasks from those that carry out 'national defence' duties (Ibid).

At the tactical level, China's 'cabbage tactics' imply that its conventional and unconventional forces 'physically encircle contested islands to block all types of access to bring the targeted islands on their knees' (Miracola 2018). While in the

---

9　Officially, the responsibilities of the CCG include 'fighting crime at sea, ensuring maritime safety, supporting the development and exploitation of marine resources, protecting the marine environment, managing fisheries, cracking down on smuggling at sea' (Zhao 2018).

past Chinese ships that detected the presence of foreign vessels within the nine-dash line, used to issue verbal reminders mainly through radio communications, nowadays, the CCG monitoring missions have come to include a more aggressive response. Between 2018 and 2020, the CCG reportedly rammed against Vietnamese fishing boats to reaffirm Chinese sovereignty, escorted Chinese ships along the nine-dash line's western border to conduct seismic surveys in Vietnam's exclusive economic zone, intimidated Malaysia for exploiting seabed resources in its neighboring exclusive economic zone at the southeastern border and joined Chinese fishers when trawling in Indonesia's exclusive economic zone along the southern edge of the nine-dash line (Ku 2020; Fachriansyah and Fadli 2020).

It should be noted that the CCG has refrained from using armed force against foreign vessels so far. However, Ryan D. Martinson (2021) suggests that the Law that came into effect in February 2021 could potentially lead to that outcome due to its very vague language. In particular, he points to the phrasing of articles 21 and 22 related to the circumstances in which the use of naval artillery can be allowed, that is if the CCG suffers an 'attack by weapons and other dangerous methods' or if the purpose is to prevent foreigners from violating 'Chinese sovereignty, sovereign rights and jurisdictional rights'. The lack of clarity is even more troubling in terms of the scope of application since the term 'jurisdictional waters' was left undefined whereas the draft law did specify 'inland waters, territorial sea, contiguous zones, exclusive economic zone and continental shelves'; however, such clarification was then crossed out in response to protests by various regional neighbors (Ibid.).[10]

---

10 As Martinson (2021) notes, based on various Chinese sources, it can be concluded that 'Beijing claims its jurisdiction over the Gulf of Bohai, a large section of the Yellow Sea, the Senkakus in the ECS to the Okinawa Channel and the waterways within the nine-dash line, which demarcates China's claims in the SCS and virtually covers the entire water basin'. See Xi J. (2021). "Comrade Xi Jinping's Remarks to the Eighth Collective Study Session of the CCP Politburo [习近平同志在中共中央政治局第八次集体学习时的讲话]". Interpret: China, Original work published on July 30, 2013, <https://interpret.csis.org/translations/comrade-xi-jinpings-remarks-to-the-eighth-collective-study-session-of-the-ccp-politburo/>. Accessed 18 April 2022; Chu F. (1959) cit. in Cohen and Chiu (197: 484); State Council Information Office of the People's Republic of China (2019). 'Full Text: Diaoyu Dao, an Inherent Territory of China', 26 September, <https://www.fmprc.gov.cn/mfa_eng/topics_665678/diaodao_665718/201209/t20120926_701830.html>. Accessed 18 April 2022.

Alongside the CCG, the PAFMM is the other crucial resource for Beijing's coercion in the maritime gray zone. Records of the presence of Chinese maritime militias can be traced back to the Battle of the Paracel Islands in 1974 (Yoshihara 2016). Since 2015, China has largely relied on irregular forces of full-time and well-paid units – mostly crews of fishermen and civilian vessels without fishing responsibilities – that are trained in the southeastern coastal provinces and respond to a military command and control structure to be deployed on board of fishing vessels for military-like support activities (Kennedy and Erickson 2017: 2-7). The constantly changing identity of the militia has been best captured by the following phrase that can be found in various Chinese sources including the PLA Daily: 'putting on camouflage they become soldiers, taking off their camouflage they become law-abiding fishermen'.[11] For instance, this is the case of the hundreds of ships that arrived, in August 2016, in the contiguous area of the Senkaku Islands (钓鱼岛 Diaoyu dao in Chinese) following a fishing incident.[12] On that occasion, the Japanese Coast Guard spotted 'over 100 maritime militias' on board the vessels 'by uniforms or military uniforms and by the fact that they were giving orders to Chinese fishermen' (Ironna Japan 2016).

According to the literature, gray zone operations confound international legal definitions in terms of the identity of the combatant and what constitutes a war. Uncertainty rises even more when irregular actors are deployed during these operations (Hoffman 2016; Green et al. 2017; Chung 2018; Kaszeta 2018). Therefore, the issue of attribution stands out among the various hurdles when it comes to effectively counteract gray zone coercive acts given that they maximize deniability for actors who implement them. Indeed, the Chinese use of officially non-military resources to expand and reaffirm its administrative control over disputed territories maximizes the potentially for deniability. This creates a destabilizing dynamic for both claimant and non-claimant countries that are faced with the challenge of understanding if the offender's nominally civil resources respond to civil or military command. In the gray zone, the more aggressive provocations are, the easier they can be met since they can be attributed and framed as a severe threat to national interests in a way that makes deterrence

---

11 (穿上迷彩是合格战士, 脱下迷彩是守法渔民). '广西北海军分区加强海上民兵建设 提升装备效能' [Beihai Military Subdistrict of Guangxi Strengthen Maritime Militia Construction, Increases Equipment Performance], *PLA Daily*, 6 January 2014, https://www.chinanews.com.cn/mil/2014/01-06/5700496.shtml> Accessed 18 April 2022.

12 For clarity purposes, hereafter, this chapter will follow Adam P. Liff (2019)'s suggestion to refer to the contested islands as 'the Senkakus' based on the US Board of Geographic Names convention.

credible. However, the fact that in the SCS, the status quo has been gradually changed through incremental actions means that any military operation aimed at blocking or attacking Chinese artificial reefs may backfire and be viewed as excessive and disproportionate. For instance, if a country's warship is forced to change its course because of the aggressive behavior of the PAFMM, it should do that based on a swift assessment of how and whether to respond to a nominally civilian ship. Most importantly, in case of inadvertent escalation, that scenario would likely be presented to the public by the Chinese propaganda as a military attack against an unarmed non-combatant actor.

As shown, the US has increased its presence through maritime patrols, military exercises and assistance to the security of some coastal states. Still, none of these interventions has had the effect of partially reversing or slowing down the pace of Chinese reclamation activities. In December 2020, after thirteen years since its last tri-service maritime strategy, the Pentagon released the strategy *Advantage at Sea: Prevailing with Integrated All-Domain Naval Power* jointly adopted by the US Navy, the Marine Corps and the US Coast Guard. By including explicit reference to the PAFMM as part of China's 'multilayered fleet', the Pentagon has arguably acknowledged that the US naval forces should gain the advantage of operating effectively 'below the threshold of armed conflict' to be able to push back against 'China's and Russia's revisionist approaches in the maritime environment' (2020: 3-9).

China and Japan's Competition in the East China Sea

Compared to Beijing's progress in advancing its sovereign claims in the SCS, Chinese gray zone coercion in the East China Sea (ECS) has been no less destabilising. And all the more so, considering the limited geographical area in which tensions with Japan are cyclically ignited. In a 2013 *Foreign Policy* article, former Australian Prime Minister Kevin Rudd expressed such widely-held concern by referring to a 'Maritime Balkans' and defining the 'fault line' running between China and Japan as 'the most worrying' in contemporary Asia. Here, both Beijing and Tokyo claim rights over an exclusive economic zone (EEZ), which necessarily overlap since the sea separating China and Japan spans only three hundred and sixty nautical miles.

The core of Beijing's gray zone coercion has taken the form of regular deployments of CCG vessels into the Senkakus' contiguous zone (24 nautical miles) and territorial waters (12 nm). Since 1895, Japan has been managing the Senkakus except for the period of the US Civil Administration of the Ryukyu Islands (USCAR), which served as the government of Okinawa from 1950 to 1972. In 1971, China first asserted ownership over the eight uninhabited outcrops that are located about 330 km south-east of China and about 170 km north of the island of Ishigaki in Okinawa prefecture. Aside from the economic benefits of fish stocks and potential hydrocarbon fields, the control of these islets is a matter of national pride for both.[13] Not only Tokyo has remained unwilling to negotiate but Japan has never even officially recognized the existence of a dispute (Chiu 1997).

Japanese sources often indicate that the spiraling of decades-old tensions over the islands started in December 2008, when 'Chinese Government vessels intruded into Japan's territorial waters surrounding the Senkaku Islands for the first time' (JMFA 2013). Nonetheless, it can be argued that the bilateral confrontation entered a new phase following the clash in 2010 between a Chinese fishing trawler and two Japanese Coast Guard vessels. Two years later, underlying frictions erupted as the Japanese government decided to buy three of these islands from private owners to prevent their sale to the nationalist governor of Tokyo Shintaro Ishihara. From the Japanese government's perspective, such a decision was meant to avoid further damage to Tokyo-Beijing relations (Swaine 2013). However, the Japanese move eventually backfired. The Chinese government called the acquisition 'totally illegal and invalid,' making clear that blatant violation of the Chinese territorial sovereignty would have required a strong response (CMFA 2012). As the Chinese Ministry of Foreign Affairs engaged in vitriolic rhetoric, public outcry erupted in China's first and second-tier cities and in Japan underscoring a relevant shift in the sense that public opinion was turning into a salient factor in influencing the pace of progress over this issue (Beukel 2011; Swaine and Fravel 2011; Johnston 2013).[14]

Following the purchase of the islands, China was eager to turn words into deeds. Ships of the China Marine Surveillance crossed the limit of the territorial sea (12 nm) around the Senkakus, making way for intensified intrusions by the Chinese maritime law enforcement vessels. It seemed that China was exercising self-restraint by supporting its claims through the passage of the CCG and PAFMM rather than launching provocative actions that could have led the

---

13 In 2008, Tokyo and Beijing agreed to make the ECS a 'Sea of Peace, Cooperation and Friendship' through jointly developing an area overlapping the median line, and to pursue opportunities for Japanese companies to cooperate in the extraction of oil and gas on the Chinese side of the line. However, due to flaring tensions the agreement has been stalled.

14 On the linkage between the Chinese media coverage and the role of public opinion in the context of the Senkakus dispute, see Chen (2013).

Japanese Coast Guard to respond aggressively (Morris 2017). Yet, in December 2015, Beijing deployed the first armed ship supplied to its coast guard officially on the grounds that the unarmed CCG ships had been facing armed Japanese Coast Guard cutters hence the balance of armaments should be leveled (The South China Morning Post 2015). Then, in August 2016, a swarm of 200-300 Chinese fishing boats and 15 ships of the CCG was deployed in the contiguous area around the Senkakus for four days. On that occasion, the use of cabbage tactics by China severely tested the response capacity of the Japanese Coast Guard. In light of that episode, the quantitative surge in China's activity in the waters surrounding the islands has raised questions about the capability of Japan to handle increased operational pressure and thus coalesce a sufficient number of naval units should China adopt in the future a similar response to an eventual clash at sea (Johnson 2016).

In recent years, the practice of occasional infiltration of Chinese maritime law enforcement vessels in the contiguous zone territorial waters of the Senkakus has been replaced by their near-continuous presence around the features. Through this 'new normal' that China has introduced in the ECS, Beijing seeks to de-legitimize the sovereignty that Tokyo has upheld through the exercise of administrative control (Morris 2017). Between April and August 2020, it has been observed a changing 'modus operandi' of the CCG as its ships have stayed in the Senkakus' territorial waters for 111 days and operated in the contiguous area for 283 days in a row, marking the longest deployment since the Japanese government's purchase of the islands (Tsuruta 2018). Recent shifts in Beijing's constabulary actions have been viewed as part of 'the second phase of the triple Chinese friction strategy' supposedly aimed at taking 'exclusive control of the Senkaku' by challenging the Japanese control instead of being limited to signal the Chinese presence in the area (Patalano 2020).

China has so far refrained from enacting in the ECS the same playbook that we've seen in the SCS – in other words, seeking to take the islands by force – yet the actions of the CCG and the PAFMM pose a significant challenge to the territorial integrity of Japan. From the CCP's perspective, by keeping this competition at the level of law enforcement rights, Beijing 'retains the initiative to challenge the status quo, limit the risk of war, or at least put Japanese authorities in the difficult position of pacing responses that may invite more escalation' (Ibid.).

But Chinese coercive actions targeting Japanese territorial integrity have not been limited to the maritime domain as Beijing has stepped up its activities also in the airspace, especially in the western and southwestern sections of Japan's ADIZ. On 23 November 2013, China brought an additional source of instability by unilaterally declaring an Air Defense Identification Zone (ADIZ) immediately surrounding the Senkakus, which created an overlap with a large portion of Japan's ADIZ; a move designed to strengthen Beijing's maritime and island claims as well to justify aerial activities aimed at defending them.[15] Tokyo lodged 'a serious protest', viewing Beijing's decision as an attempt to force international compliance with Chinese territorial claims (Valencia 2014).

Undoubtedly, China has created a flashpoint that continues to expand in which accidental events could trigger a military confrontation. Following the first violation of the territorial airspace over the Senkakus by a Chinese patrol aircraft, from December 2012 until 2016, the Japanese Self-Defense Air Force scrambled its jets more than 1,000 times up in response to Chinese incursions, outpacing the Cold War-era record of 944 in 1984 (The Japan Times 2017). Washington and its regional allies understand the Chinese ADIZ as a provocation largely due to the fact that it has been declared unilaterally without prior consultation with Japan, in violation of the principle of freedom of overflight on the high seas (UNCLOS). Most of all, they are worried that it might lead Beijing to declare an ADIZ in the SCS.

The practice of announcing designation of the ADIZ has originated in Northeast Asia in the wake of the Second World War and the Korean War but it has never been formally recognised under the international law. The Americans were the first followed by Japan and South Korea and for decades the various areas did not overlap. The extension of the Chinese ADIZ, however, ended up including also a group of submerged maritime feature that Koreans call Ieodo. In response, Seoul has expanded its ADIZ southward to include Ieodo, which has led the Korean ADIZ to overlap with parts of both the Chinese and Japanese ADIZs.

In 2019, the potential for disruption resulting from overlapping claims reached a critical point when Russian and Chinese airplanes intruded into the South Korean ADIZ during a joint air exercise prompting both Japan and South Korea to scramble their jets. The Russian and Chinese pilots continued north, but one of the Russian planes flew within the 12-nm territorial airspace around the Dokdo rocks (called Takeshima by Japan) that are administered by South Korea but claimed by Japan. The South Korean airplanes fired 360 warning shots and protested strongly against the raid. Although Tokyo was furious at Russia's actions, Japan's Foreign Minister Kono rebuked to South Korea for firing warning

---

15 The ADIZ is a designation of the airspace in which countries try to monitor traffic for national security purposes. It typically extends far beyond a state's borders to monitor traffic for national security reasons allowing the identification and interception of an aircraft should it be considered as a threat.

shots in the Japanese airspace because 'Takeshima is Japan's territory' therefore it was 'Japan that should take action against the Russian plane that entered its airspace' (Choe 2019).

Between 2016 and 2018, access without prior notification by Chinese aviation in South Korea's ADIZ increased from 50 to 140 while dropping to 25 in 2019 (Trent 2020: 15). In order to avoid hazardous military incidents, Beijing and Seoul have increased the number of direct hotlines – from the first one established in 2015 to the current five – to connect their navies and air forces (Yonhap 2021). In 2019, a Chinese PLAAF fighter entered Seoul's ADIZ. It was contacted by the South Korean Air Force and asked to provide its flight information. In the midst of the recent spike in the number of Chinese incursions into the Korean ADIZ, information-sharing has partially mitigated South Korean concerns over Beijing's intentions showing how military hotlines might help prevent escalatory outcomes by reducing the risks of miscalculation.

Implications for Japan's Strategic Posture and Coordination with the United States

In 2010, the Japanese government first adopted the term 'gray zones' in official defense documents.[16] Since then, it has been used in reference to 'armed incidents that do not reach the levels of a large-scale attack' and that are mainly the product of China's 'reactive assertiveness' around disputed islands (JMoD 2013). In the 2022 White Paper, the Japanese Ministry of Defense has reiterated 'China's continuous attempt to unilaterally change the status quo by coercion in the East and South China Sea' particularly in reference to the 'expanded and intensified activities of the Chinese Navy and Air Force allegedly based on China's unilateral claims on the Senkakus' (JMoD 2022, p. 45).

From the perspective of force readiness, Tokyo has been building up the southwestern island chain of the Japanese archipelago concentrating ground troops, missiles and structures that follow a multi-stage contingency planning aimed at handling potential escalatory outcomes amid mounting tensions spurred by Chinese incursions around the Senkakus (Ryall 2021). On the other hand, Japanese strategists and policymakers have slowly advanced with regard to conceptualize the gray zone circumstances and related responses mainly due to the gaps in the legal framework. By relying on the CCG vessels

---

16 On a different note, 2010 is very much a symbolic year given that Beijing ousted Tokyo as the second-largest economy in the world.

to assert its claims, China has indeed leveraged the constraints of Japan's legal and constitutional framework regarding the use of force outside unambiguous 'armed attack' scenarios. Although the issue should have been at the core of the bill adopted in September 2015, which largely focused on the limited use of the right to collective self-defense, it was not (Hornung 2018).

This means that no legal context has emerged yet in order to harmonize the mandate of the Japanese Coast Guard – a nonmilitary law-enforcement organization – with that of the Maritime Self-Defense Force – the military component – and to expand the latter's rules of engagement (Pajon 2017). Given the longstanding separation between military and civilian resources typical of the Japanese security system, if a surveillance and security mission that is performed 'in the vicinity of maritime borders and remote islands' exceeds the capabilities of the Japanese Coast Guard, the Japanese Maritime Self-Defense Force can provide support, according to article 82 of the Law on Self-Defense Forces, and that 'would not constitute an orthodox military action but a law enforcement operation' (Furuya 2019: 4). From the perspective of the Japanese government, therefore, this kind of maritime security operation still remains within the boundaries of non-combat activity. On the contrary, as Céline Pajon notes (2017: 123), 'Beijing would consider any intervention by the Japanese Maritime Self-Defense Force in the gray zone as a unilateral decision by the Japanese government in the direction of military escalation'. As a result, Japan is bound to respond to Chinese 'reactive assertiveness' through a suboptimal degree of coordination between its maritime agencies, which constitutes intrinsic shortcomings in any efforts aimed to preserve the Japanese territorial integrity (Ibid.).

Against this backdrop, much of the discussion about Chinese coercion and competition in the ECS has revolve around the constraints facing Japan to effectively devise counterstrategies. In addition to the necessary adjustments in the composition of the Japanese military forces and interoperability between military and civilian bureaucracies, Japanese efforts will have to focus on improving coordination within the framework of the security alliance with the US As stated in Article V of the 1960 US-Japan mutual security treaty, the United States shall intervene in the event of a 'common danger' represented by an 'armed attack against either Party in the territories under the administration of Japan'. Although Japan takes primary responsibility for its defence, in a significant military scenario with China, Tokyo could invoke the treaty provision and seek Washington's assistance.

During numerous Track 1.5 dialogues, South Korean and Japanese officials have reportedly expressed concerns to their US counterparts about the credibility of Washington's security commitments also in terms of gray zone challenges stemming from Chinese coercive and competitive behavior (Schoff and Lee 2019; Glosserman 2015). Back in 2012, as tensions between Beijing and Tokyo flared up, the US Congress reiterated its rhetorical support for Japan by inserting an Authorization Act into the National Defense Plan for 2013 stating among other things that the 'unilateral actions of a third party will not affect the recognition by the United States of the Japanese administration on the Senkaku Islands' (US Congress 2013). During his term, President Obama specified that the United States 'does not believe that [the status of the Senkaku Islands] should be subject to unilateral changes' (BBC News 2014). President Joe Biden called Japanese Prime Minister Yoshihide Suga first among Asian leaders to reaffirm 'the unwavering commitment to the defence of Japan under Article 5 of our security treaty, which includes the Senkaku Islands'. Subsequently, Defense Secretary Lloyd Austin stressed that 'the United States is opposed to unilateral moves to change the status quo'. From the Nixon administration, every US president has made clear that the Treaty should include the island question, yet, the US government's 'neutral stance' with regard to who has sovereignty over the Senkakus has remained unchanged (Johnson 2021).

Following the 2015 Guidelines, the US-Japan security alliance has been reoriented towards a 'seamless' level of cooperation aimed at discouraging Beijing from launching a conventional aggression in the ESCS (Dian 2020). Nevertheless, bilateral tensions and distrust in Northeast Asia are constant matters of concern as confirmed during the US-Japan Security Consultative Committee (2+2) held in January 2023 (DoS 2023). The possibility that an accidental or deliberate collision at sea could rapidly degenerate remains high given the limited success represented by the Maritime and Air Communication Mechanism that went into effect in June 2018 after negotiations had stalled in 2015.[17] Moreover, the changing nature of operations in the gray zone makes it more challenging to reach a consensus between Tokyo and Washington on what constitutes an 'armed attack'. If Japan cannot activate Article 5 of the Treaty, any attempt to formulate a joint response will in fact take place within the logistical, legal, and political constraints of the alliance framework. In particular, strategists will have

---

17 According to the Japanese MFA, this mechanism has been developed 'to promote mutual understanding and confidence between Japan and China and to enhance bilateral defense cooperation, to avoid unexpected collision, and to prevent unforeseen circumstances in the sea and air from developing into military clashes or political or diplomatic issues'. See the Japanese FMA webpage on Japan-China relations.

to navigate between different definitions in the Japanese and US legislations of what constitutes an act of war or an armed attack.

Although highly unlikely that the Japanese ally might be 'peeled away', the pressure of provocations against its sovereignty makes it imperative for Washington to increase cohesion aimed at preventing potential paralysis and further deterioration of the status quo. Moving forward, Japanese and American alliance planners should bolster efforts to update the deterrence capability of the alliance to address these pressing gray zone challenges, even outside the scope of Article 5, especially in light of the potential implications of the recent CCG Law. Within and beyond the maritime domain, sharing early assessments and indicators for detecting and attributing gray zone threats, countering disinformation, and working on public communication will be crucial to managing the uncertainty of the gray zone, thereby, preventing China from presenting them with new escalation dilemmas.

Conclusion

Over more than a decade, China has sought to play an enhanced role in gray zone competition with the US working to gradually increase its upper hand. Unlike Russia's ambition for regime change in Ukraine, Beijing has mostly aimed for strategic advantage in the Indo-Pacific less by confronting the US directly than by leveraging its neighbors to accept Chinese claims and rules. In particular, China has incrementally sought control over strategic waterways in the ESCS. Therefore, this chapter set out to has explored the changes that have been afoot in East Asia's maritime environment, mainly due to the CCP's willingness to step up China's disputed sovereignty claims over large parts of these sea basins, and in doing so contributing to a rapidly deteriorating security context.

Against the backdrop of a changing operational environment, this chapter has examined the drivers, means, and capabilities that have enabled Beijing to pursue its political and strategic objectives while managing to avoid full scale war. The deployment of the CCG and the PAFMM has increased the degree of unpredictability within the overarching framework of the strategic competition with Washington. Besides, by exposing shortcomings in existing deterrent strategies, defense planning, and alliance coordination through its coercive activities in the gray zone, China has tried to drive a wedge between the US and its partners and allies in the region in order to influence the balance of power in East Asia.

The fact that many states in the region are responding to the expansion of the CCG by strengthening their own coast guards has created new dynamics that require a much more efficient command and control architecture between maritime, government, and civilian actors both on land and at sea that can be achieved by strengthening joint exercise programs on a routine basis. Given the growing role of paramilitary actors and resources in the Chinese strategy, joint exercises and simulations should contemplate scenarios in which military escalation stems from actions in the gray zone perpetrated by non-military actors such as militias, seafarers, and fishing boats.

For what concern the dispute between Tokyo and Beijing in the ECS, this is driven in large part by resentment over unresolved historical issues – a cornerstone of the Chinese state-led nationalism in the Xi Jinping's era – amid high levels of mutual distrust. These elements coupled with the fact that the theater in which the respective coast guards and military forces operate is very limited contribute to a persistent high risk of accidental clashes and unintended escalation of tensions. The CCP is expected to proceed with the deployment of ships and planes within the Japanese-administered territory in ways that challenge Japanese jurisdiction but remain below the threshold that would otherwise trigger a military response. Although the mandate of the Japanese Coast Guard has expanded somewhat in recent years, its strictly civilian law enforcement mandate continues to limit its options for responding to its nominal Chinese counterpart, which is best thought of as a paramilitary force rather than a civilian law enforcement agency in light of recent developments in terms of legislative framework and capacity build up.

The case studies that have been examined in this chapter are particularly relevant for a discussion on contemporary gray zone challenges as they shed light on the ambiguity of Chinese coercive maritime behavior. Moreover, they have shown that the deployment of non-state actors and paramilitary and civilian resources further exacerbates political and legislative uncertainty. In light of the above, it can be concluded that the formulation of an effective response to the challenges of the gray zone requires above all a long-term perspective combined with an approach that while mobilizing all the tools available to governments, it focuses on bolstering the collaboration between the civilian and military components.

Bibliography

Beukel, E. (2011). 'Popular nationalism in China and the Sino-Japanese relationship: The conflict in the East China Sea.' *An Introductory Study, DIIS Report*, 1, 1-32.

Bickford, F. et al. (2010). 'China as a Maritime Challenge: The Strategic Dimension', *CNA Research Memorandum*, D0023549.A3/1 Rev, October.

Brands, H. (2016). 'Paradoxes of the gray zone', *Foreign Policy Research Institute*, 5 February, <http://www.fpri.org/article/2016/02/paradoxes-gray-zone/>. Accessed 18 April 2022.

Carment, D. and Belo, D. (2020). 'Non-State Actors and Conflict Management in an Era of Gray-zone Conflict', in Hampson, F., Kent, J. and Ozerdem, A. (eds.) *The Routledge Handbook on Peace, Security, and Development*, 138-148.

Chan, I. and Li, M. (2015). 'New Chinese Leadership, New Policy in the South China Sea Dispute?', *Journal of Chinese Political Science*, 20 (1), 35-50.

Chen, S. (2019). 'When Did Public Opinion on the Senkaku/Diaoyu Island Issue Begin Forming in China?', *Asian Journal of Journalism and Media Studies*, 2, 74-89.

Chinese Ministry of Foreign Affairs (CMFA) (1980). 'China's Indisputable Sovereignty over the Xisha and Nansha Islands', *Beijing Review*, No. 7, 15-24, 18 February.

---- (2012). 'Foreign Ministry Spokesperson Hong Lei's Regular Press Conference', 11 September, <http://np.china-embassy.gov.cn/eng/fyrth/201209/t20120 913_1591456.htm.> Accessed 18 April 2022.

Chiu H. (1997). 'An Analysis of the Sino-Japanese Dispute over the Tiaoyutai Islets', *Chinese Yearbook of International Law & Affairs*, 15, (1996-1997), 9-31.

Congress of the United States of America (2013). *National Defense Authorization Act for Fiscal Year 2013*, 2 January, <https://www.congress.gov/112/plaws/publ239/PLAW-112publ239.pdf.> Accessed 18 April 2022.

Cronin, P.M. et al. (2014). *Tailored Coercion: Competition and Risk in Maritime Asia*, Washington, DC: Center for a New American Century.

Dian, M. (2020). 'Japan, South Korea and the rise of a networked security architecture in East Asia', *International Politics*, 57, 185–207

Dupuy, F. and Dupuy, P.M. (2013). 'A Legal Analysis of China's Historic Rights Claim in the South China Sea', *The American Journal of International Law*, 107 (1), 124-141.

Erickson, A.S. (2014). 'The Budget This Time: Taking the Measure of China's Defense Spending', *Open Forum*, The Asan Forum, <https://theasanforum.org/the-budget-this-time-taking-the-measure-of-chinas-defense-spending/>. Accessed 18 April 2022.

Fachriansyah, R. and Fadli (2020) 'Indonesia talks sovereignty with China following foreign vessel controversy', *The Jakarta Post*, 14 September, <https://www.thejakartapost.com/news/2020/09/14/indonesia-talks-sovereignty-with-china-following-foreign-vessel-controversy.html>. Accessed 18 April 2022.

Friedberg, A. (2015). 'The Sources of Chines Conduct: Explaining Beijing's Assertiveness', *The Washington Quarterly*, 37 (4), 133-150.

'Full text of Hu Jintao's report at 18th Party Congress' (2012). *Xinhua News Agency*, 17 November, <http://us.china-embassy.gov.cn/eng/zt_120777/18cpc ncl/201211/t20121127_4917578.html>. Accessed 18 April 2022.

'Full text of Xi Jinping's report at 19th CCP National Congress' (2017). *China Daily*, 18 October, https://www.chinadaily.com.cn/china/19thcpcnationalc ongress/2017-11/04/content_34115212.htm>. Accessed 18 April 2022.

Furuya, K. (2019). 'Maritime Security: The Architecture of Japan's Maritime-Security System in the East China Sea,' *Naval War College Review*, 72 (4), 27-51.

Glosserman, B. (2015). 'Struggling with the Gray Zone: Trilateral Cooperation to Strengthen Deterrence in Northeast Asia,' *Pacific Forum CSIS*, 15 (13), 1-44, <https://www.files.ethz.ch/isn/194801/issuesinsights_vol15no13.pdf>. Accessed 18 April 2022.

Goddard, S.E. et al. (2019). 'Repertoires of statecraft: instruments and logics of power politics', *International Relations*, 33 (2), 304-321.

Gomez, J. and Favila, A. (2022). 'AP Exclusive: US admiral say China fully militarized isles', *The Associated Press*, March 22, <https://apnews.com/arti cle/business-china-beijing-xi-jinping-south-china-sea-d229070bc2373be1c a515390960a6e6c>. Accessed 18 April 2022.

Gui Y. (2019). '灰色地带' 之争: 美日对华博弈的新态势'[Competing in the Gray-Zone': A New Situation in U.S.-China Engagement with China], *Japanese Studies*, 1, 45-70.

Harold, S.W. et al. (2017). 'The U.S.-Japan Alliance and Deterring Gray Zone Coercion in the Maritime, Cyber, and Space Domains', *RAND Corporation*, <https://www.rand.org/content/dam/rand/pubs/conf_proceedings/CF300/ CF379/RAND_CF379.pdf>. Accessed 18 April 2022.

Hicks, K. et.al. (2019). 'By Other Means, Part II: U.S. Priorities in the Gray Zone', *Center for Strategic and International Studies*, <https://www.csis.org/analysis/ other-means-part-ii-us-priorities-gray-zone>. Accessed 18 April 2022.

Hoffman, F. G. (2016). 'The contemporary spectrum of conflict: Protracted, gray zone, ambiguous, and hybrid modes of war', *The Heritage Foundation*, <https://www.heritage.org/sites/default/files/2019-10/2016_IndexOfUSMilit aryStrength_The%20Contemporary%20Spectrum%20of%20Conflict_Pro tracted%20Gray%20Zone%20Ambiguous%20and%20Hybrid%20Modes%20 of%20War.pdf>. Accessed 18 April 2022.

Hornung, J.W. (2018). 'Japan's 2015 Security Legislation: Change Rooted Firmly in Continuity', in McCarthy, M. (*ed.*), *Routledge Handbook of Japanese Foreign Policy*, London: Routledge.

Jackson, V. (2017). 'Tactics of Strategic Competition', *Naval War College Review*, 70 (3), 39-61.

Jakobson, L. (2014). 'China's Unpredictable Maritime Security Actors', *Lowy Institute*, <https://www.lowyinstitute.org/sites/default/files/chinas-unpred ictable-maritime-security-actors_3.pdf>. Accessed 18 April 2022.

'Japan Coast Guard says armed Chinese ships enter disputed waters for the first time' (2015). *The South China Morning Post*, 26 December, <https://www. scmp.com/news/asia/east-asia/article/1894919/japan-coast-guard-says-armed-chinese-ships-enter-disputed-waters>. Accessed 18 April 2022.

'Japan scrambled jets against approaching aircraft a record 883 times over nine months; most incidents involved China' (2017). *The Japan Times*, 21 January, <https://www.japantimes.co.jp/news/2017/01/21/national/japan-scrambled-jets-approaching-aircraft-record-883-times-nine-months-incidents-invol ved-china/>. Accessed 18 April 2022.

Johnson, J. (2016). 'Chinese Senkaku swarm tactic spells trouble for Japan', *The Japan Times*, 7 August, <https://www.japantimes.co.jp/news/2016/08/07/ national/politics diplomacy/senkaku-swarm-tactic-spells-trouble-tokyo/>. Accessed 18 April 2022.

---- (2021). 'New U.S. defense chief confirms Senkaku fall under security treaty', *The Japan Times*, 24 January, <https://www.japantimes.co.jp/news/2021/01/ 24/national/politics-diplomacy/us-japan-defense-senkakus/>. Accessed 18 April 2022.

Jonhston A.I. (2013). 'How new and assertive is China's new assertiveness?', *International Security*, 37 (4), 7-48.

Kapusta, P. (2015). 'The gray zone', *Special Warfare*, 8 (4), 18–25.

Kaszeta, D. (2018). 'The Forensic Challenge', *The Journal of Complex Operations*, 7(3), 85-89.

Kennedy, C.M. and Erickson, A.S. (2017). 'China's Third Sea Force, The People's Armed Forces Maritime Militia: Tethered to the PLA', *China Maritime Report No. 1*, Naval War College China Maritime Studies Institute, <https://digital-commons.usnwc.edu/cgi/viewcontent.cgi?article=1000&context=cmsi-marit ime-reports>. Accessed 18 April 2022.

Knefel, J. (2015). 'The Gray Zones is the Future of War: Ongoing, Low-Level, and Undeclared', *Inverse Culture*, 12 July, <https://www.inverse.com/article/ 8838-the-gray-zone-is-the-future-of-war-ongoing-low-level-and-undecla red>. Accessed 18 April 2022.

Kraska, J. and Monti, M. (2015). 'The Law of Naval Warfare and China's Maritime Militia', *International Law Studies*, 91 (1), 450–467.

Kubo, N., Sieg, L. and Stewart, P. (2014). 'Japan, U.S. Differ on China in Talks on 'Grey Zone' Military Threats', *Reuters*, 10 March, <https://www.reuters.com/ article/us-japan-china-defence-idUSBREA280RD20140309>. Accessed 18 April 2022.

Lin, B. et al. (2022). 'Competition in the Gray Zone: Countering China's Coercion Against U.S. Allies and Partners in the Indo-Pacific', *RAND Corporation*, <https://www.rand.org/content/dam/rand/pubs/research_reports/RRA500/RRA594-1/RAND_RRA594-1.pdf>. Accessed 18 April 2022.

Martinson R.D. (2021). 'Gauging the real risks of China's new coastguard law', *Australian Strategic Policy Institute*, 23 February, <https://www.aspistrategist.org.au/gauging-the-real-risks-of-chinas-new-coastguard-law/>. Accessed 18 April 2022.

---- (2020). 'Appendix I—The China Coast Guard: A Uniformed Armed Service', in M. A. McDevitt, *China as a Twenty-First-Century Naval Power: Theory, Practice, and Implications*, Annapolis, MD: Naval Institute Press, 187–206.

Ministry of Defense of Japan (JMoD) (2010). *National Defense Program Guidelines for FY 2011 and Beyond*, Tokyo, 17 December 2010.

---- (2013). *National Defense Program Guidelines for FY 2014 and Beyond*, Tokyo, 17 December 2013.

---- (2022). *Defense of Japan 2022*, Tokyo, 21 July 2022.

Ministry of Foreign Affairs of Japan (JMFA) (2013). *Position Paper: Japan-China Relations Surrounding the Situation of the Senkaku Islands*, Tokyo, 7 February, 2013.

Miracola, S. (2018). 'Chinese Hybrid Warfare', *Istituto per gli Studi di Politica Internazionale (ISPI)*, 21 December, <https://www.ispionline.it/en/publication/chinese-hybrid-warfare-21853>. Accessed 18 April 2022.

Morris, L.J. (2017). 'Blunt Defenders of Sovereignty: The Rise of Coast Guards in East and Southeast Asia', *Naval War College Review*, 70 (2), 75-112.

Morris, L.J. et al. (2019). 'Gaining Competitive Advantage in the Gray Zone: Response Options for Coercive Aggression Below the Threshold of Major War', *RAND Corporation*, <https://www.rand.org/content/dam/rand/pubs/research_reports/RR2900/RR2942/RAND_RR2942.pdf>. Accessed 18 April 2022.

'Obama Asia tour: US-Japan treaty 'covers disputed islands'' (2014). *BBC News*, 24 April, <https://www.bbc.co.uk/news/world-asia-27137272>. Accessed 18 April 2022.

Odom, J.G. (2013). 'The 'Case' of USNS Impeccable Versus 5 Chinese Ships: A Close Examination of the Facts, the Evidence, and the Law', in Van Dyke, J. et al. (eds.) *Governing Ocean Resources: New Challenges and Emerging Regimes*, 307-341.

Pajon, C. (2017). 'Japan's Coast Guard and Maritime Self-Defense Force in the East China Sea: Can a Black-and-White System Adapt to a Gray-Zone Reality?', *Asia Policy*, n. 23.

Patalano, A. (2019). 'When strategy is 'hybrid' and not 'grey': reviewing Chinese military and constabulary coercion at sea', *The Pacific Review*, 31 (6), 811-832.

---- (2020). 'What is China's Strategy in the Senkaku Islands?', *War on the Rocks*, <https://warontherocks.com/2020/09/what-is-chinas-strategy-in-the-senk aku-islands/>. Accessed 18 April 2022.

Raine, S. (2011). 'Beijing's South China Sea Debate', *Global Politics and Strategy*, 53 (5), 69-88.

Ryall, J. (2021). 'Japan's ground troops to get transport ships amid concerns over China's military build-up in Indo-Pacific', *The South China Morning Post*, 15 February, <https://www.scmp.com/week-asia/politics/article/3121781/jap ans-ground-troops-get-transport-ships-amid-concerns-over>. Accessed 18 April 2022.

'S. Korea, China agree to establish two more military hotlines' (2021). *Yonhap*, 2 March, <https://en.yna.co.kr/view/AEN20210302009600325>. Accessed 18 April 2022.

Schoff, J.L. and Lee, P.K. (2019). 'Sustaining Strong Partnerships: The First Trilateral Dialogue Initiative (TDI) Workshop', *Carnegie Endowment for International Peace*, <https://carnegieendowment.org/2019/04/25/sustain ing-strong-partnerships-first-trilateral-dialogue-initiative-tdi-workshop-pub-78971>. Accessed 18 April 2022.

Choe, S.H. (2019). 'South Korean fighter jets fire hundreds of warning shots after Russian warplanes' incursions', *The New York Times*, 23 July, <https://www.nytimes.com/2019/07/23/world/asia/south-korean-warning-shots-russia-pla nes.html>. Accessed 18 April 2022.

'Summary of World Broadcasts: Far East' (1993). *BBC News*, 8 February, <https://catalogue.nla.gov.au/Record/1818020>. Accessed 18 April 2022.

Swaine, M. and Fravel, T.M. (2011). 'China's Assertive Behavior – Part two: The Maritime Periphery', *Carnegie Endowment for International Peace*, <https://carnegieendowment.org/2011/06/24/china-s-assertive-behavior-part-two-maritime-periphery-pub-44829>. Accessed 18 April 2022.

'尖閣諸島を襲う中国漁船に乗船する「海上民兵」の正体 [The True Colours of the Maritime Militia Embarked on the Chinese Fishing Vessels Attacking the Senkaku]' (2016). *SAPIO*, November, <http://ironna.jp/article/4598>. Accessed 25 March 2022.

Thayer, C. (2021). 'COVID-19 masks mischief in the South China Sea', *East Asia Forum*, 13 January, <https://www.eastasiaforum.org/2021/01/13/covid-19-masks-mischief-in-the-south-china-sea/>. Accessed 18 April 2022.

Trent, M. (2020). 'Over the Line: The Implications of China's ADIZ Intrusions in Northeast Asia', *Federation of American Scientists*, <https://fas.org/publicat ion/adiz-report/>. Accessed 18 April 2022.

Tsuruta, J. (2020). 'The Chinese Coast Guard and the Senkaku: Activities of the last year suggest what the future might hold', *The Diplomat*, 30 December, <https://thediplomat.com/2020/12/the-chinese-coast-guard-and-the-senk aku/>. Accessed 18 April 2022.

Turcsányi, R.Q. (2018). *Chinese Assertiveness in the South China Sea: Power Sources, Domestic Politics, and Reactive Foreign Policy*, Berlin: Springer International Publishing.

United Nations Conference on Trade and Development (UNCTAD) (2016). *Review of Maritime Transport*, <https://unctad.org/system/files/official-document/rmt2016_en.pdf>. Accessed 18 April 2022.

United States Department of Defense (2022). *Annual Report to Congress: Military and Security Developments Involving the People's Republic of China*, 29 November, <https://www.defense.gov/News/Releases/Release/Article/3230 516/2022-report-on-military-and-security-developments-involving-the-peoples-republi/>. Accessed 2 February 2023.

United States Department of State (2023). *Joint Statement of the 2023 U.S.–Japan Security Consultative Committee ("2+2")*, 11 January, <https://www.state.gov/2023-u-s-japan-security-consultative-committee/>. Accessed 2 February 203.

Valencia, M.J. (2014). 'The East China Sea Disputes: History, Status, and Ways Forward', *Asian Perspective*, 38 (2), 183-218.

Vu, K. (2020). 'Vietnam protests Beijing's sinking of South China Sea boat', *Reuters*, 4 April, <https://www.reuters.com/article/vietnam-china-southchina sea-idAFL4N2BS031>. Accessed 18 April 2022.

Yahuda, M. (2013). 'China's New Assertiveness in the South China Sea', *Journal of Contemporary China*, 22 (81), 446-459.

Yoshihara, T. (2016). 'The 1974 Paracels Sea Battle: A Campaign Appraisal', *Naval War College Review*, 69 (2), 41-65.

Zhang, K. (2019). 'Cautious Bully: Reputation, Resolve, and Beijing's Use of Coercion in the South China Sea', *International Security*, 44 (1), 117-159.

Zhao, L. (2018). 'Enforcement powers of China Coast Guard expanded', *China Daily*, 23 June, <https://www.chinadaily.com.cn/cndy/2018-06/23/content_3 6439266.htm>. Accessed 18 April 2022.

Zou, K. (2021). *International Law of the Sea in the Twenty-first Century: State Practice in East Asia*, Singapore: World Scientific Publishing.

Simone Zuccarelli

The Anglosphere's Role in an Increasingly Chaotic Eurasia and Beyond

The Anglosphere is well connected thanks to cultural, security and economic ties. With the progressive regionalisation of the international system, the relative decline of the United States, the return of competition between the great powers and the consequences of Brexit, this subsystem could play an increasingly important global role. The specificity of the Anglosphere and its relevant and growing role in international politics were recently highlighted on the occasion of the Hong Kong protests and the Russian invasion of Ukraine. A detailed analysis of the history of the Anglosphere, its importance, the existing relations between English-speaking countries, the role of the Special Relationship and, above all, the potential transformation of the Anglosphere in the next decade could provide a number of relevant insights to better understand how the US alliance system will evolve, what shape the international system will take, what role the Special Relationship will play and what future awaits English-speaking countries in an increasingly chaotic world.

Thirty years after *the end of history*, history has returned with a vengeance. Old and new threats are shaping the international order and Europe, after the hard years of the Covid pandemic, is witnessing a war unlike any in more than seventy years. The rest of the world is becoming increasingly unstable, as the United States is progressively losing its ability to shape and guide the international order, which is also being undermined by the rise of China as the United States' peer competitor. Essentially, great power competition is back and the world is evolving into a multipolar (dis)order.

The new reality is fostering the resumption of the debate on the possibility of strengthening ties between English-speaking countries, leading to the creation of a more integrated Anglosphere. This subsystem is already well-connected thanks to cultural, security, and economic ties, but advocates of the Anglosphere do not consider this sufficient, especially in light of the growing challenges emanating from the world stage.

Over the past three decades, such thinking has been supported mainly by Conservative politicians and pundits and has gained traction in the aftermath of Brexit, partly because the United Kingdom needs to find a new equilibrium after the withdrawal from the European Union. At the same time, the progressive deterioration of the security scenario has forced the United States to strengthen its commitment to the *Special Relationship* with London, and globally an axis between English-speaking nations is becoming increasingly attractive.

Anglosphere: a brief history of an idea

In order to better understand what an Anglo-Saxon alignment would look like and what impact it would have on US foreign policy, the post-Brexit UK and the international system as a whole, it is firstly essential to examine the origins of the idea of the Anglosphere and its recent development. Although the term only emerged in 1995, and has not been clearly defined since, the debate around the idea of an alliance of Anglo-Saxon nations is much older and has been conducted on both shores of the Atlantic since the nineteenth century. The concept of the Anglosphere emerged as a British one in the late Victorian era, when important figures such as Prime Minister Robert Peel, Richard Cobden and John Stuart Mill supported the 'vision of a global order based on free trade, peace, and progress' (Howe 2007: 27). In the beginning, the main concern was how to strengthen and improve the Empire. The Victorian intellectuals and politicians concerned with the future of the Empire sought to propose new ideas to better integrate the Anglo-world and create a 'Greater Britain' (Kenny and Pearce 2018). One of the products of this thinking was the Imperial Federation League, founded in 1884, whose aim was to 'secure by federation the permanent unity of the Empire' (Kenny and Pearce 2018: 17).

The United States, however, has always occupied a privileged place in the reflections on the Anglosphere. Although the relationship between the British Empire and the United States remained strained after the War of 1812, a relevant number of British decision-makers and intellectuals at the beginning of the twentieth century advocated the idea of increased cooperation, even a union, between London and Washington. In the late nineteenth century, the idea of Anglo-American hegemony in the 'civilised world' gained strength (Ovendale 1998: 4). By the end of the nineteenth century, 'Britain became more popular in America than it had ever been, and enthusiasm for a common Anglo-Saxon heritage was evidenced. There was talk of an alliance, and even a reunion between the two countries' (Ovendale 1998: 6).

Indeed, it was already clear that Britain and the United States 'besides having a large number of cultural similarities [...] looked at the world in a different way than have most of the European countries. The British Empire was, and the United States is, concerned not just with the balance of power in one particular corner of the world, but with the evolution of what we today call "world order"' (Mead 2002: xvi). Furthermore, the Darwinian era brought with it the struggle between races. The idea of a *Saxondom*, namely the uniqueness and superiority of the Anglo-Saxon race, became widespread and contributed to the rapprochement between London and Washington and the emergence of the idea of the Anglosphere (Vucetic 2011). President Theodore Roosevelt, for example, considered the Anglo-Saxons to be the most advanced race and believed that they were in a struggle with barbarian civilisations (Hunt 2009). The same conception of the world resonates with another US President: Woodrow Wilson. The twenty-eighth President 'long celebrated liberty as the flower of the Anglo-American tradition' (Hunt 2009: 130). He also held British tradition and culture in high esteem and considered Anglo-Saxons at the top of the racial hierarchy. The First World War reinforced the belief in the uniqueness of the English-speaking world, which was dedicated to leading humanity towards progress and freedom.

However, it was only after the Second World War that this liberal-internationalist vision was translated into a comprehensive network of institutions. And because the United States and the United Kingdom held such a similar worldview, a peaceful transition of hegemonic power was possible for the first time in history (Schake 2017). Even before the war, London was well aware that its relationship with Washington was becoming increasingly unbalanced, with the latter that was slowly but steadily taking the lead. Therefore, Britain gradually adopted a more subtle strategy to remain relevant in the new environment. Harold Macmillan summed up this approach in the *darkest hour*: 'These Americans represent the new Roman Empire and we Britons, like the Greeks of old, must teach them how to make it go' (Nicholls 1974: 70). The British, therefore, could at most aspire to occasionally influence the Americans. Indeed, after the Second World War London helped convince the Americans that their active leadership was necessary for the survival of the West. Moreover, it was Churchill, also a Briton, who was instrumental in redefining the concept of the Anglosphere. In his opinion, the common history and culture of the English-speaking peoples should form the basis for the idea of the Anglosphere. In particular, he emphasised the profound links between the English-speaking people, envisioned an Anglo-American hegemony and paved the way for the creation of the *Special Relationship* (Kenny and Pearce 2018), a term coined by Churchill himself and used in its current meaning during his speech at Fulton, on 5 March 1946. On the same occasion Churchill announced the descent of the *Iron Curtain* across Europe. Basically, the original Cold Warrior was Britain, not the United States.[1]

---

1   'To an extent American historians have persisted in writing about the Cold War as if,

Despite differing views on how the post-World War II scenario should be handled, Washington increased its support for London, for example by recognising its role in the Middle East and relieving it of the burden of fighting communism in Greece. At the same time, the two allies maintained their strong wartime relationship. Most notably, in 1946, the UKUSA Agreement on cooperation in signals intelligence was signed. In the following years, Canada (1948), Australia and New Zealand (1956) joined the pact, which then became known as *Five Eyes*, the strongest and longest-running multilateral intelligence agreement in the world.

Moreover, after the Second World War, all British *Dominions* began to look to the United States for leadership in the English-speaking world. In particular, due to the progressive withdrawal of the United Kingdom from the Pacific region and its severe weakening after the war, Australia and New Zealand needed a stronger relationship with the United States, which was now the paramount Pacific power. Initially, Washington was much more cautious about concluding a formal treaty, but the developing dynamics in the Pacific region – Korean War above all – made the Americans change their minds. In 1951, Australia, New Zealand and the United States signed the ANZUS Treaty, which stipulated that an attack on one of the three parties would trigger a response from the other signatories. The United Kingdom was not invited to join the treaty, but the former *Dominions* saw ANZUS as complementary to their relationship with London (McIntyre 1995). As the UK was part of the Commonwealth and had the same Head of State, its intervention in the event of war was a foregone conclusion.

Furthermore, the British Empire was badly affected by the war and suffered a fatal blow in 1947. First, the signing of the GATT agreement effectively ended the Imperial Preference System introduced in 1932. Second, India, the *Jewel of the Crown*, gained independence and this dramatically weakened the Empire (Borsani 2017). Third, London announced the termination of its mandate in Palestine, as it was unable to preserve the stability in the region, further weakening its position in the Middle East. Finally, New Zealand adopted the Westminster Statute of 1931, becoming fully independent. It thus became clear that the United Kingdom's only foreign policy option was to rely on the United

---

on the Western side, only the United States had a role to play. As the British documents became available in the Public Record Office in London a group of historians has increasingly challenged this 'Americocentric' view of the origins of the Cold War, and has seen Britain as the original Cold Warrior, one determined to educate the United States to the realities of what it perceived as the Soviet threat' (Ovendale 1998: 40).

States. London was gradually becoming too weak and had to align its positions with Washington's one, trying to influence it whenever possible. The conclusions of the Strand Committee in 1949 are straightforward: 'The interests of the United Kingdom therefore demand that her present policy of close Anglo-American cooperation in world affairs should continue. Such cooperation will involve our sustained political, military and economic effort' (Ovendale 1998: 83).

A few years later it became clear that London's best policy was to accept Washington's leadership. In 1956, the UK joined France and Israel in trying to resolve the Suez Crisis militarily, but American pressure forced London to change its mind. The lesson for the United Kingdom was harsh but clear: the only way forward was to be Washington's junior partner. But it was a lesson for the United States too[2]: in order to maintain good relations with the Arab states and in the name of anti-colonialism, Washington created a rift with its allies. Nevertheless, it soon became clear that the main threat to US interests even in the Middle East was the Soviet Union and that the strong position *vis-à-vis* Paris and London was not too wise strategically. Egyptian President Gamal Abdel Nasser continued his opposition to the West, the United States was not improving its standing among the non-aligned countries and 'America's attempt to dissociate from Europe had landed it in the position of having to assume by itself the burden of protecting every free (that is, noncommunist) nation in every region of the globe' (Kissinger 1994: 549). The task was confirmed on 5 January 1957, a few weeks after the end of the Suez Crisis, when the American President Dwight Eisenhower was forced to proclaim the *Eisenhower Doctrine* to protect the Middle East from communist aggression. Moreover, the US President immediately sought to recover the *Special Relationship* by meeting with the new British Prime Minister Macmillan in Bermuda and then in Washington, strengthening cooperation between the two countries. The fracture was thus repaired, and ten years after the demise of its great power status, London fully recognized its position as a junior partner of the US (Sayle 2019).

In the years that followed, the relationship between the two allies remained essentially unchanged: The US supported the United Kingdom in various meaningful ways – starting with nuclear and economic cooperation – and the two parts maintained an 'everyday close working relationship' (Ovendale 1998: 134). American officials in London stressed that 'we need the support and

---

2   And Eisenhower quickly regretted his management of the Suez Crisis. Later, he confided to Nixon that he considered Suez as 'his major foreign policy mistake' (Doran 2016: 241).

the sympathy of the British. If they are unable to go it alone, in their relative weakness, neither can we everywhere. […] We consult together more frequently and more extensively than with any third countries. On many matters and in widely different circumstances our policies are made to fit agreed lines of action' (Ovendale 1998: 134). Under Prime Minister Edward Heath, however, it seemed that the United Kingdom was slowly retreating from its global role and instead opting for a European dimension. In 1973, London finally joined the European Community. While the relationship with the US cooled but remained more or less the same, this was not the case with relations with the former *Dominions*. Those relations did not dissolve, but since 'the Commonwealth could not provide a viable alternative to Europe in the mid-1970s' (Dunin-Wasowicz 2015) London preferred the European sphere. The United States was encountering similar difficulties in its relationship with English-speaking allies too. While the ANZUS worked well for many years, to such an extent that Australia and New Zealand actively supported the US effort in Vietnam, it changed during the Eighties because of New Zealand's decision to declare the country a nuclear-free zone in 1984; US nuclear submarines were thus prohibited from visit New Zealand ports. In response, in 1986, Washington suspended its treaty obligations towards Wellington.

At the same time, however, with Margaret Thatcher at Downing Street and Ronald Reagan in the White House, the *Special Relationship* regained vigour. On 20 February 1985, to celebrate the 200th anniversary of diplomatic relations between the two countries, the British Prime Minister affirmed:

> Mr. President, over the 200 years that our countries have dealt with each other, it has not always been plain sailing, but one thing has not changed: the joint common sense which is an essential part of our common heritage has always led the two governments to resolve their differences and to work constructively together for our common purpose. Our joint interest prevails and I know they will continue to prevail. There is a union of mind and purpose between our peoples which is remarkable and which makes our relationship truly a special one. I am often asked if it is special, and why, and I say: "It is special. It just is and that is that!"

Ronald Reagan added: 'There has been something very special about the friendships between the leaders of our two countries and may I say to my friend the Prime Minister, I would like to add two more names to this list of affection—Thatcher and Reagan'. Moreover, in her speech to the College of Europe in 1988 Thatcher manifested her opposition to the further centralization of powers in

Brussels.[3] Her preference for strengthening both the *Special Relationship* and the Anglosphere as a whole was obvious. In the end, however, the faction within the Conservative Party which wanted more integration in the European Union prevailed and John Major replaced Margaret Thatcher. With the end of the Cold War and the signing of the Maastricht Treaty by the United Kingdom in 1992, the time for the idea of the Anglosphere and even of the *Special Relationship* seemed to be over (Dickie 1994).

The transatlantic dilemma: European Integration or Atlantic Option?

In the late 1990s and early 2000s, the idea of the Anglosphere was 'incubated, nurtured [...] reconfigured [...] and powerfully reinvented' (Kenny and Pearce 2018). What emerged from this debate not only shaped the way in which the Anglosphere was perceived, but also provided a strong basis for the Brexit campaign. Moreover, the foreign policies of the largest English-speaking countries, and the United Kingdom in particular, are increasingly moving in the direction elaborated by Anglosphere theorists over the last two decades. To better understand today's choices, it is therefore crucial to have an insight into their thinking.

After some misunderstandings, the UK-US relationship quickly regained momentum. In 1995, Bill Clinton travelled to the United Kingdom and gave a powerful speech at Westminster about the special bond between the two countries. Specifically, the US President recalled that:

> Other times in other places are littered with the vows of friendship sworn during battle and then abandoned in peacetime. This one stands alone, unbroken, above all the rest, a model for the ties that should bind all democracies.
> To honor that alliance and the Prime Minister who worked so mightily to create it, I am pleased to announce here, in the home of British freedom, that the United States will name one of the newest and most powerful of its surface ships, a guided missile destroyer, the United States Ship Winston Churchill. [...]
> My friends, we have stood together in the darkest moments of our century. Let us now resolve to stand together for the bright and shining prospect of the next century.

---

3   'But working more closely together does not require power to be centralised in Brussels or decisions to be taken by an appointed bureaucracy. Certainly we want to see Europe more united and with a greater sense of common purpose. But it must be in a way which preserves the different traditions, parliamentary powers and sense of national pride in one's own country' (Thatcher 1988).

The election of Tony Blair in 1997 further strengthened the *Special Relationship*. Not only did he harmonise much better with Clinton than Major, but he was also able to establish a great relationship with Bush Jr.[4] As a result, the bond between London and Washington further solidified in the 2000s. But while the UK's approach to foreign policy seemed settled – with an abandonment of the Imperial past, a solid European collocation, and a special relationship with the US – some positions that were thought to be out of fashion slowly but steadily re-emerged. Along with a growing Euroscepticism, the idea of the Anglosphere, which had been sidelined throughout the Cold War, also returned to the fore.

Indeed, the progressive recovery of the British economy, the centralist tendencies of the European project and the demise of the Soviet Union opened a political space for the proponents of a global dimension for London based on privileged relations with the other English-speaking nations. This tendency gradually gained strength, especially in the Conservative Party. As early as 1992 and 1993, during the debate on the implementation of the Maastricht Treaty, a deeply Eurosceptic component loudly criticised John Major for his support of the Treaty. The *Maastricht Rebels* wanted a different course for the United Kingdom: *our home is where our language is* (Baxendale and Wellings 1992: 129). In the following years, Eurosceptic sentiment increased, and the UK Independence Party (UKIP) was able to secure 6.5 % of the vote in the 1999 European Parliament elections. At the dawn of the 2000s, the ground was prepared for the return of the Anglosphere debate.

The effort was almost exclusively on the Conservative side of the political spectrum. In 1999, Margaret Thatcher gave a speech to the English-Speaking Union[5] in which she affirmed that 'the security of the world would largely depend

---

4   As Bush recalls in his memoirs: 'I went to the Oval Office on September 12 at my usual time […] my first call was with Prime Minister Tony Blair of Great Britain. Tony began by saying he was "in a state of shock" and that he would stand with America "one hundred percent" in fighting terror. There was no equivocation in his voice. The conversation helped cement the closest friendship I would form with any foreign leader. As the year passed and the wartime decision grew tougher, some of our allies wavered. Tony Blair never did' (Bush 2010: 140).

5   The US branch of the ESU 'arose [in 1920] from the conviction of its founder Sir Evelyn Wrench and a group of like-minded American and British friends, that maintenance of the close personal and national ties forged during World War I was necessary for the preservation of peace. Sir Evelyn firmly believed that given the opportunity to know one another personally, people who shared a common language would soon discover that they also shared similar values, whatever their differences in nationality or background'. – English-Speaking Union Website, <https://www.esuus.org/esu/about/mission/> accessed 31 march 2022.

on the close co-operation of the English speaking people'. She highlighted the unique values of the English-speaking people and the English language, 'the language of liberty'. She criticized the 'attempt to create a new, autonomous European defence structure [and] the utopian venture of creating a single European super-state'. Above all, she stated that a 'new political alliance of the English-speaking people would allow us to foster those values that have been so important in our peace and prosperity and thus encourage the same peace and prosperity around the world' (Thatcher 1999).

The great British historian Robert Conquest agreed with Margaret Thatcher. In the same year that she made her speech, he advocated the creation of an English-Speaking Union (Conquest 2001). He also criticised the European Union, considering it 'artificial and unconvincing', and invited to 'turn to a grouping that would be natural rather than artificial [...] it hardly needs saying that what comes to mind is some form of unity between countries of the same legal and political – and linguistic and cultural – traditions: which is to say an Association of the United States, the United Kingdom, Canada, Australia and New Zealand' (Conquest 1999). He added that technological developments had made the idea of an English-Speaking Union possible as the physical distance was not very significant in the modern world. A similar position was taken by Conrad Black, who criticised the European Union and advocated for an Atlantic Option for the United Kingdom (Black 1999).

While the debate on the union of the English-speaking countries was mainly conducted in Britain, it slowly spread to the US and other Commonwealth countries. The Hudson Institute, in particular, began to organise various conferences on the Anglosphere, attended by important transatlantic politicians and intellectuals (Kenny and Pearce 2018). In 2005[6], the Hudson Institute organised a book forum to discuss *The Anglosphere Challenge: Why the English-Speaking Nations Will Lead the Way in the Twenty-First Century*, written by businessman James Bennett. At this event, it became clear that a growing number of Americans and Brits perceived 'the European Union as a very serious long-term threat to American interests'. Since the United Kingdom had too much

---

6   In the same year, Robert Conquest resumed the idea of the Anglosphere in *Dragons of Expectation* and *Our Island Story* was republished. The second one, in particular 'helped Eurosceptics reimagine Britain outside the EU' (Wellings 2016: 370) and signaled the progressive affirmation of a nostalgic view of Britain and the will to restore its past glory.

to lose in this scenario, the only conceivable alternative was to leave the EU in favour of the union of English-speaking Nations.

In the following years, the idea of the Anglosphere gained ground also in the former *Dominions*, that since 2000 have become increasingly embedded in regional and global dynamics. In 2006, London and Canberra established the Australia-UK Ministerial Dialogue (AUKMIN), strengthening their partnership (Baxendale and Wellings 2015). Furthermore, John Howard, Australia's Prime Minister from 1996 to 2007, said in 2011 that the 'values that bind the United States, Great Britain, Canada, Australia, New Zealand [...] the bonds that keep us together are deeper and more abiding, in my experience, than the bonds between any other countries with which my country has been associated over my time in politics' (Howard 2011). At the same time, the Brexit front was emerging in the United Kingdom, and relations with the former *Dominions* were a major issue. In 2013, Boris Johnson – the man who, along with Nigel Farage, has probably been the most prominent actor in the United Kingdom's exit from the European Union – wrote that in 1973 '[W]e betrayed our relationships with Commonwealth countries such as Australia and New Zealand, and entered into preferential trading arrangements with what was then the European Economic Community'. He invited London to 'undo the damage of 1973' and laid the foundations for the future Brexit debate: 'When Britain joined the Common Market, it was at a time when the establishment was defeatist, declinist and obsessed with the idea that we were being left out of the most powerful economic club in the world. In those days [...] it was assumed that in order to be "internationalist" it was enough to be European. Well, it is perfectly obvious, in 2013, that that is no longer enough - and that we need to seek a wider destiny for our country' (Johnson 2013).

The aspiration for a Global Britain capable of restoring ties especially with its former kith and kin colonies, and the debate about the Anglosphere that has emerged since the end of the Cold War have strongly influenced the Brexit campaign. The Eurosceptic leaders invoked both the cultural and the 'economic potential of the Anglosphere as an alternative to the membership of the EU' (Mycook and Wellings 2017). Moreover, the United Kingdom's membership in the European Union was 'presented [by Brexiteers] as an interregnum in England's imperial past and its global future' (Wellings 2016: 369). The idea of Global Britain[7] was based, above all, on the aspiration to restore a strong

---

7   Theresa May: 'June the 23rd was not the moment Britain chose to step back from the world. It was the moment we chose to build a truly Global Britain [...] the great prize for this country – the opportunity ahead – is to use this moment to build a truly Global Britain. A country that reaches out to old friends and new allies. A great, global,

relationship with the other English-speaking countries (Kenny and Pearce 2018)[8]; basically, with Brexit the UK chose the Anglosphere over the Eurosphere and 'created space for "core" Anglosphere nations to consider how they might deepen some of their ties in ways that reinforce existing linkages' (Gregg 2020).

The future of the Anglosphere in the coming multipolar world

Brexit has changed the course of British foreign policy, completing a historical phase that began with the pro-European turn in 1973 (Borsani 2017) and paved the way for the establishment of a more coordinated and solid Anglospherical system. Indeed, the regained autonomy and the new position outside the European Union – but not outside Europe – forced London to partially reorient its foreign policy. The Anglospheric strategy that had been outlined in previous years and supported by the Conservatives in all the major English-speaking countries was ready to be implemented. Moreover, it is significant that the British are once again pushing the other Anglosphere countries in a particular direction.

First, great efforts were made to strengthen the *Special Relationship* with the United States. While the Democrats repeatedly expressed their concern and opposition to a possible United Kingdom exit from the EU, the Republicans, on the other hand, took a very different view[9]. In particular, the election of Donald Trump, a Brexit supporter[10], a few months after the referendum, secured a powerful ally in Washington. Indeed, the first foreign leader invited to the White House shortly after Trump's inauguration was British Prime Minister Theresa May, a clear sign of the new US Administration's strategic goals. The importance

---

trading nation'. – Time (2017). 'Read Theresa May's Speech Laying Out the U.K's Plan for Brexit', *Time*, 17 January, <https://time.com/4636141/theresa-may-brexit-speech-transcript/> accessed 31 March 2022.

8   For instance, David Davis made it clear in 2016: 'We must see Brexit as a great opportunity to refocus our economy on global, rather the regional, trade. This is an opportunity to renew our strong relationships with Commonwealth and Anglosphere countries. […] We share history, culture and language. We have family ties. We even share similar legal systems. […] it is time we unshackled ourselves, and began to focus policy on trading with the wider world, rather than just within Europe'.

9   President Obama advised UK citizens against withdrawing from the EU. On the contrary, many US Republicans suggested otherwise (Wellings 2017). For instance, after Brexit House Speaker Paul Ryan said: 'We need to emphasize that they are our indispensable ally […] We have a special relationship' (Cassella 2016).

10   BBC Website (2016). 'EU referendum: Donald Trump backs Brexit', 6 May, <https://www.bbc.com/news/uk-politics-eu-referendum-36219612> accessed 31 March 2022.

of the *Special Relationship* was at the heart of the talks and the US President reaffirmed his support for Brexit: 'I think Brexit is going to be a wonderful thing for your country' (Sparrow 2017).

Secondly, London immediately worked to improve its relations with Canberra. It is no coincidence that the first free trade agreement to be negotiated from scratch since the UK left the EU was concluded with Australia in June 2021 (Taylor 2021). And it is also no coincidence[11] that it was a Conservative Prime Minister, Scott Morrison, who signed the agreement on behalf of Australia.

However, the progressive strengthening of the relations between the English-speaking countries can only be partly explained by the ideological dimension and London's activism. Indeed, the return of great power competition and the rise of China have forced the other pole of the *Special Relationship*, the United States, to strengthen its network of alliances. To cope with the harsh reality that is emerging, Washington needs a solid core made up of countries that not only share similar strategic goals, but also the same culture, values, history, language and institutional traditions. The AUKUS trilateral security pact, announced in September 2021, goes exactly in this direction. Under the pact, Australia, the United Kingdom and the United States 'resolve to deepen diplomatic, security, and defence cooperation in the Indo-Pacific region, including by working with partners, to meet the challenges of the twenty-first century'.[12] With AUKUS, Canberra will gain crucial strategic support to counter China's assertiveness; London will retrieve its global projection and aspirations[13]; Washington will be able to rely on a robust security system capable of effectively supporting its containment policy towards China.

Two crises have already provided a glimpse into the evolving global dynamics and the future of the international system. The first concerns the protests in Hong Kong in 2019 and 2020. While the European Union remained more on the sidelines, the three AUKUS countries, joined by Canada and New Zealand[14],

---

11   Indeed, John Howard, the conservative former Australian Prime Minister, backed the Brexit campaign: 'The European project is fundamentally flawed [...] If I were British [...] I'd vote to leave. You have lost your sovereignty' (Smyth 2016).

12   *Joint Leaders Statement on Aukus* (2021, 16 September). <https://www.pm.gov.au/media/joint-leaders-statement-aukus> accessed 1 April 2022.

13   See: *Global Britain in a competitive age: The Integrated Review of Security, Defence, Development and Foreign Policy* (2021, March).

14   However, New Zealand keeps a more independent attitude. Wellington remained outside the AUKUS and maintains its historical position as a nuclear-free zone. Moreover, it is cautious in criticizing China, its main economic partner. Hence, while Australia is increasingly integrating in the US-UK system of alliances, New Zealand

immediately took a strong common position and condemned Chinese repression. The US Congress passed the *Hong Kong Human Rights and Democracy Act* in November 2019, and Australia suspended the extradition arrangements with Hong Kong. In addition, the UK offered a pathway to British citizenship for up to three million people living in Hong Kong. London also decided to restore its historic presence in the Indo-Pacific; in September 2021, the Royal Navy decided to deploy there two patrol vessels for five years. Furthermore, a British *Carrier Strike Group* was briefly deployed in the Indo-Pacific as 'a demonstration of Prime Minister Boris Johnson's vision of a "Global Britain"'.[15]

The same alignment was confirmed during the Russian invasion of Ukraine, which started on 24 February 2022. As expected, the United States led the way in responding to Russian aggression and pushed for a common Western position, especially on sanctions. Moreover, despite its geographical distance from the crisis, Australia has sanctioned Russia – including President Putin – and provided support for the supply of weapons to the Ukrainians. However, as in the Hong Kong crisis, the United Kingdom was the most active country in countering Russia. In particular, London led the group of European countries that opposed the Russian Federation the most. Even before the Russian invasion, the United Kingdom announced a trilateral security pact with Poland and Ukraine. Later, it was the country that called more vociferously for additional support for Kyiv, sent a relevant stock of weapons to Ukraine and imposed one of the strictest sanctions packages against Russia. Moreover, the British are more willing to support Ukraine than the French, the Germans and even the Americans (Kendrick 2022). The Kremlin spokesman acknowledged London's assertiveness and declared British Prime Minister Boris Johnson 'the most active participant in the race to be anti-Russian'.[16]

---

remains at the sidelines. As it was said recently, 'Despite Australia and New Zealand are culturally quite similar and geographically in similar positions, but they are poles apart in terms of the way they see the world [AUKUS] underlines that they're going in very different directions' (McClure 2021).

15 *UK Carrier Strike Group in the Indo-Pacific* (2021, 23 July). <https://www.gov.uk/gov ernment/news/uk-carrier-strike-group-in-the-indo-pacific> accessed 31 March 2022.

16 Reuters (2022). *Kremlin says UK's Johnson is most active anti-Russian leader – RIA*, 24 March <https://www.reuters.com/world/europe/kremlin-says-uks-johnson-is-most-active-anti-russian-leader-ria-2022-03-24/> accessed 1 April 2022.

Conclusions

In recent years, China has grown stronger, Russia has returned, and the Anglosphere has solidified. Many experts[17] and politicians[18] feared that the United Kingdom's role outside the European Union would be diminished and that the country would lose its value *vis-à-vis* the United States. On the contrary, London is in the process of partially regaining its historic role: It is increasingly playing a balancing role in Europe, confronting Russia in a 21st-century great game, projecting its power around the globe once again, and reaffirming its invaluable status for the United States, which needs solid and loyal allies more than ever. For its part, Washington, despite the return of an Administration sceptical regarding Brexit[19], is insisting on the *Special Relationship*: Boris Johnson was the first European leader to be called by US President Joe Biden and, as mentioned above, the United States signed a relevant trilateral agreement with the United Kingdom and Australia.

The relative decline of the United States and the rise of China as a peer competitor will force Washington to bolster its partnerships, especially with close allies. It is therefore likely that *the Special Relationship* will be further strengthened in the coming years. And for the first time in history, maintaining this relationship will be as important to Washington as it already is for London.[20]

---

17 'Many of us on this side of the Atlantic worried that Brexit was going to damage Britain's readiness and its ability to be a major player. I think that the jury is still out but the UK has been heading in the right direction and the Biden administration has taken notice' (Smith 2021).

18 Reuters (2016). 'Ex-UK PM Major says relations with U.S. would "wither" after Brexit', 29 April <https://www.reuters.com/article/us-britain-eu-major-idUSKCN0XQ0S6> accessed 1 April 2022.

19 Like Barak Obama, President Biden also opposed Brexit. After the referendum he condemned 'reactionary politicians and demagogues [...] We'd have preferred a different outcome' (Dettmer 2021).

20 Careful observers of the Anglosphere had already predicted this outcome several years ago: 'Ora, l'eventualità di un declino americano comporterebbe l'aumento dell'importanza strategica della Gran Bretagna per gli Stati Uniti, sorta di rovesciamento epocale nel rapporto della speciale relazione: per Washington il mantenimento di un rapporto speciale con Londra diventerebbe decisivo, rendendo finalmente bilaterale la specialità della relazione angloamericana' [Now, the eventuality of an American decline would entail an increase in Britain's strategic importance to the United States, a sort of epochal reversal in the special relationship: for Washington, maintaining a special relationship with London would become crucial, finally making bilateral the speciality of the Anglo-American relationship] (Bellocchio 2006: 98).

Consequently, the Anglosphere will gradually evolve into a more structured system of alliance. Moreover, 'cooperation rooted in collective identity [is] more enduring than the same processes locked in by international institutions alone' (Vucetic 2011: 151). Therefore, increased integration between countries that share the same language and similar values, culture, history and strategic interests may be the best way for the English-speaking nations to cope with the security risks of the emerging multipolar world.

Furthermore, the war in Ukraine has once again shown that Anglo-American national interests do not necessarily coincide with European ones. France and Germany, in particular, have tried vigorously to reach a diplomatic understanding with Russia for both strategic and economic reasons. Once the war began, behind a solid common front, differences emerged on how to proceed, especially on the scale of the sanctions package. Moreover, since his election, President Emmanuel Macron has stated the need for a rapprochement with Russia several times. For example, in 2019 he clearly set out his vision: 'I believe we must build a new architecture based on trust and security in Europe, because the European continent will never be stable, will never be secure, if we do not ease and clarify our relations with Russia. That is not in the interest of some of our allies, let's be clear about that. Some of them will urge us to impose more sanctions on Russia because it is in their interest'. Although the Russian invasion of Ukraine has forced Macron to temporarily back down, France's position is unlikely to change much in the future. Likewise, other European countries, like Germany[21] and Italy, partly share France's position on Russia, which will make it difficult to maintain a solid common Euro-Atlantic approach in the future. On the contrary, the Anglosphere, especially the United Kingdom and the United States, will probably continue to aggressively contain and confront Russia.

In addition, at least two other relevant issues will push the core Anglosphere countries to work closely together. First, some Western allies and partner countries such as Turkey, India and Israel are taking a generally neutral stance towards Russian actions. For example, Ankara refused to impose sanctions on Russia despite its NATO membership. Moreover, many allies and partners of the United States are taking an ambiguous stance toward China. For example, the European Union tried to reach an investment agreement with China in 2020

---

21 Shortly after the war started, German Chancellor Scholz told Ukrainian President Zelensky that 'Ukraine should renounce its NATO aspirations and declare neutrality as part of a wider European security deal between the West and Russia' (Gordon et. al. 2022).

despite Washington's opposition: 'While the investment deal will not progress in the near future, this does not mean the EU will decouple and diversify away from Beijing overnight […] "there is a lot at stake economically" in Europe's trade relations with China' (Yuen Yee 2022). It seems clear that only the solid Anglosphere core is willing to fully follow the United States closely on these and other relevant issues.

Second, even if Washington would like to have a more Pacific-oriented NATO, and even if the Alliance has started to focus more on China, NATO is likely to remain Eurocentric, especially with the strong return of Russia. Moreover, European countries have neither the capabilities nor the will to assist the United States in the Indo-Pacific. Only the United Kingdom is adapting its grand strategy to a global and ambitious one and is willing to act to maintain an open and stable Indo-Pacific. And it is significant that despite Russia's invasion of Ukraine, Washington's focus remains mainly on China. On 28 March 2022, US Deputy Secretary of Defense Kathleen Hicks stated: 'The people of Ukraine are foremost on our minds. Russia poses an acute threat to the world order, as illustrated by its unprovoked invasion and vicious tactics. Even as we confront Russia's malign activities, the defense strategy describes how the department will act urgently to sustain and strengthen deterrence, with the PRC as our most consequential strategic competitor and pacing challenge. The PRC has the military, economic and technological potential to challenge the international system and our interests within it'.[22]

Therefore, the best strategic solution for the United States is to strengthen its *Special Relationship* with the United Kingdom and its ties with other English-speaking countries that are more eager to side with Washington. In particular, Australia, the United Kingdom and the United States can together control many strategic positions around the globe and effectively exercise the dominion of the seas. Moreover, the Anglosphere may turn out to be one of the most prominent aggregations in an international system that also seems to be developing along civilisational lines. If China will continue to gain strength as a peer-competitor of the United States, if Russia will remain an acute threat, and if power flow from the West to the Rest will not stop, the Anglosphere, structured around an

---

22 *Deputy Secretary of Defense Dr. Kathleen Hicks Remarks on President Biden's Fiscal 2023 Defense Budget* (2022, March 28). <https://www.defense.gov/News/Transcripts/Transcript/Article/2980638/deputy-secretary-of-defense-dr-kathleen-hicks-remarks-on-president-bidens-fisca/> accessed 1 April 2022.

AUKUS core, could institutionalise itself in the coming decades and become one of the poles of the international system.

In 1999, Robert Conquest wrote that 'if the United States and the rest of the English-speaking world would combine their strengths, they would once again provide a strong centre around which a new world community could develop'. When he wrote that, it was probably too early, but today the union of the Anglosphere world may be the best way for the English-speaking countries, and especially for the United Kingdom and the United States, to preserve their security, defend their national interests and succeed in the chaotic world we have entered.

Bibliography

Baxendale, H., Wellings, B. (2014). 'Euroscepticism and the Anglosphere: Traditions and Dilemmas in Contemporary English Nationalism', *JCMS Journal of Common Market Studies*, 53 (1), 1–17.

Bellocchio, L. (2006). *Anglosfera. Forma e forza del nuovo Pan*-Anglismo. Genova: il melangolo.

Black, C. (1999). 'Britain's Atlantic Option. And America's Stake', *The National Interest*, 55, Spring, 15–24.

Borsani, D. (2017). 'Ritorno all'Anglosfera? Una prospettiva storica sui rapporti tra Gran Bretagna e Stati Uniti al tempo di Trump'. In M. De Leonardis (ed.), *Effetto Trump? Gli Stati Uniti nel sistema internazionale fra continuità e mutamento*, pp. 59–82. Milano: EDUCatt.

Bush, G. W. (2010). *Decision* Points. London: Virgin Books.

Cassella, M. (2016). *Ryan calls for post-Brexit trade deal with U.K.* Politico, 28 June <https://www.politico.com/story/2016/06/paul-ryan-brexit-trade-224 878> accessed 31 March 2022.

Clinton, W. J. (1995). *Remarks to the Parliament of the United Kingdom in London*, 29 November.

Conquest, R. (1999). 'Toward an English-Speaking Union', *The National Interest*, 57, Fall, 64–70.

—— (2001). *Reflections on a Ravaged Century*. New York – London: W. W. Norton & Company.

—— (2005). *Dragons of Expectations: Reality And Delusion In The Course Of History*. London: Gerald Duckworth.

Davis, D. (2016). *Britain would be better off out of the EU – and here's why*, 4 February <http://www.conservativehome.com/platform/2016/02/david-davis-britain-would-be-better-off-out-of-the-eu-and-heres-why.html> accessed 31 March 2022.

Dettmer, J. (2021). 'Role Reversal for US and Post-Brexit Britain', *Voa News*, 22 January, <https://www.voanews.com/a/europe_role-reversal-us-and-post-brexit-britain/6201110.html> accessed 31 March 2022.

Dickie, J. (1994). *'Special' No More. Anglo-American Relations: Rhetoric and Reality*. London: Weidenfeld & Nicholson.

Doran, M. (2016). *Ike's Gamble. America's Rise to Dominance in the Middle* East. New York: Free Press.

Dunin-Wasowicz, R. (2015). 'The power of the Anglosphere in Eurosceptical thought', 10 December <https://blogs.lse.ac.uk/brexit/2015/12/10/anglosph ere-is-the-other-side-of-the-eurosceptic-coin-a-conception-of-britains-ident ity-and-place-in-the-world/> accessed 1 April 2022.

Gordon, M. R., Pancevski, B., Bisserbe, N., and Walker, M. (2022). 'Vladimir Putin's 20-Year March to War in Ukraine – and How the West Mishandled It', *The Wall Street Journal*, 1 April <https://www.wsj.com/articles/vladimir-put ins-20-year-march-to-war-in-ukraineand-how-the-west-mishandled-it-1164 8826461> accessed 2 April 2022.

Gregg, S. (2020). 'Getting Real About the Anglosphere', *Law & Liberty*, 17 February <https://lawliberty.org/getting-real-about-the-anglosphere/> accessed 31 March 2022.

Howard, J. (2011). 'The Anglosphere and the Advance of Freedom'. *The Heritage Foundation*, 3 January <https://www.heritage.org/report/the-anglosphere-and-the-advance-freedom> accessed 31 March 2022.

Howe, A. (2007). 'Free trade and global order: the rise and fall of a Victorian vision'. In B. Duncan (ed.), *Victorian Visions of Global Order. Empire and International Relations in Nineteenth-Century Political Thought*, pp. 26–46. Cambridge: Cambridge University Press.

Hunt, M. H. (2009). *Ideology and U.S. Foreign Policy*. New Haven and London: Yale University Press.

Johnson, B. (2013). 'The Aussies are just like us, so let's stop kicking them out'. *The Telegraph*, 25 August <https://www.telegraph.co.uk/news/politics/10265 619/The-Aussies-are-just-like-us-so-lets-stop-kicking-them-out.html> accessed 31 March 2022.

Kampmark, B. (2008). 'The Greeks of Old. Modelling the British Empire for a twenty-first century America'. In K. Christie (ed.) *United States Foreign Policy and National Identity in the 21st Century*. London: Routhledge, pp. 101–114.

Kendrick, M. (2022). 'British Are Most Eager to Support Ukraine Out of NATO's Four Biggest Economies', *Morning Consult*, 25 February <https://morningcons ult.com/2022/02/25/ukraine-invasion-polling-european-views/> accessed 31 March 2022.

Kenny, M., and Pearce, N. (2018). *Shadows of Empire. The Anglosphere in British Politics*. Medford: Polity Press.

Kissinger, H. (1994). *Diplomacy*. New York: Simon & Schuster.

Macron, E. (2019). *Ambassadors' conference – Speech by M. Emmanuel Macron, President of the* Republic, 27 August <https://lv.ambafrance.org/Ambassad ors-conference-Speech-by-M-Emmanuel-Macron-President-of-the-Repub lic> accessed 31 March 2022.

McClure, T. (2021). 'Aukus submarines banned from New Zealand as pact exposes divide with western allies', *The Guardian*, 16 September <https:// www.theguardian.com/world/2021/sep/16/aukus-submarines-banned-as- pact-exposes-divide-between-new-zealand-and-western-allies> accessed 31 March 2022.

McIntyre, D. W. (1995). *Background to the Anzus Pact: Policy-Making, Strategy and Diplomacy, 1945–55*. London: Palgrave Macmillan.

Mead, W. R. (2002). *Special Providence: American foreign policy and how it changed the* world. New York: Routledge.

Mycook, A., and Wellings, B. (2017). 'The Anglosphere: Past, present and future', *The British Academy Review*, 31, 12 November <https://www.thebritishacad emy.ac.uk/publishing/review/31/anglosphere-past-present-and-future/> accessed 31 March 2022.

Nicholls, A. J. (1974). *Semblance of Peace*. London. Palgrave Macmillan

Ovendale, R. (1998). *Anglo-American Relations in the Twentieth Century*. London: Macmillan.

Sayle, T. A. (2019). *Enduring Alliance. A History of NATO and the Postwar Global Order*. Ithaca: Cornell University Press.

Schake, K. (2017). *Safe Passage: The Transition from British to American Hegemony*. Cambridge: Harvard University Press.

Smith, D. (2021). 'US-UK 'special relationship' faces new challenges despite signs of healing'. *The Guardian*, 22 September <https://www.theguardian.com/ world/2021/sep/22/us-uk-special-relationship-faces-new-challenges-desp ite-signs-of-healing> accessed 1 April 2022.

Smyth, J. (2016). 'Former Australian premier John Howard backs Britain to leave EU', *Financial Times*, 6 April <https://www.ft.com/content/0abe0092-fbee- 11e5-8f41-df5bda8beb40> accessed 1 April 2022.

Sparrow, A. (2017). ' "Trump '100% behind Nato", says May at joint White House press conference – as it happened', *The Guardian*, 27 January <https://www. theguardian.com/politics/blog/live/2017/jan/27/donald-trump-and-ther esa-may-hold-joint-white-house-press-conference-politics-live> accessed 1 April 2022.

Taylor, H. (2021). 'UK-Australia post-Brexit trade deal agreed in broad terms', *The Guardian*, 15 June <https://www.theguardian.com/politics/2021/jun/15/uk-australia-trade-deal-agreed-and-set-to-be-announced-on-tuesday> accessed 1 April 2022.

Thatcher, M. (1988). *Speech to the College of Europe ("The Bruges Speech")*, 20 September <https://www.margaretthatcher.org/document/107332> accessed 31 March 2022.

–––– (1999). *The Language of Liberty: The Inauguration of The Thatcher Lecture Series*. English-Speaking Union, New York, 7 December.

Vucetic, S. (2011). *The Anglosphere: A Genealogy of a Racialized Identity in International Relations*. Stanford: Stanford University Press.

Wellings, B. (2017). 'The Anglosphere in the Brexit Referendum'. *Revue Francaise de Civilisation Britannique*, XXII – 2.

Yuen Yee, W. (2022). 'Is the EU-China Investment Agreement Dead?', *The Diplomat*, 26 March <https://thediplomat.com/2022/03/is-the-eu-china-investment-agreement-dead/> accessed 31 March 2022.

Lorenzo Medici – Valentina Sommella[1]

The Roles of China and the WHO in the Fight Against COVID-19 under the Trump Presidency and its Global Consequences

With an enormous loss of life and half of the world's population in isolation at home, the COVID-19 pandemic has become a global impact event. Even if the geopolitical implications may appear less significant when compared to health and safety, they will prove important in the medium to long term, especially if placed in the context of Chinese peaceful development and amidst growing concerns that the rise of China has aroused – and still arouses – in the US and globally. The Chinese political and academic world rejects such concerns, particularly those regarding Chinese foreign policy and allegations of hegemonic purposes, as the People's Republic of China (PRC) has been engaged for years in a significant effort to show itself to the world as a 'Responsible great power', actively contributing to the international community. This essay intends to discuss if the current COVID-19 pandemic - from an adverse event and initially likely to result in a loss of image for the PRC - could ultimately offer the PRC an additional international opportunity.

Introduction

With the enormous loss of life, the COVID-19 pandemic has become a global impact event. Even though the geopolitical implications may appear less significant when compared to health and safety, they will prove important in the medium to long term, especially if seen in the context of Chinese *heping fazhan* (和平发展) [peaceful development] and amid the growing concerns that the rise of China has aroused – and still arouses – in the US and globally.[2]

---

1 Although the entire work was thought through and planned by both the authors, it is possible to ascribe sections 1, 2 and 3 mainly to Valentina Sommella and section 4 mainly to Lorenzo Medici. The introduction and the conclusions were written in collaboration by both the authors. The article was submitted in March 2022.

2 In continuity with Deng Xiaoping's theory, from 2003 the Chinese leadership much insisted on the concept of *heping jueqi* (和平崛起) [peaceful rise], underlining that Chinese growth did not pose a threat to international peace and stability. On the contrary, other nations could obtain significant benefits and opportunities from that growth. The expression 'peaceful rise' was then replaced with 'peaceful development' to mitigate the concept of 'rise', which could be perceived to mean 'elevating above' and therefore imply 'overcoming' another power. The Chinese leadership instead wishes to

During Donald Trump's Presidency, Graham Allison's volume *Destined for War. Can America and China Escape Thucydides's Trap?* (2017) rekindled the academic debate on *Zhongguo weixie lun* (中国威胁论) [China threat theory], which was elaborated in the second half of the 1990s by American scholars, according to which China's economic and military rise poses a threat to global security (Roy 1996; Yee and Storey 2002). Allison takes up the issue of the traditional Sino-American rivalry focusing on the concept of the 'Thucydides Trap', i.e., that war is likely when an emerging power threatens a hegemonic one. This happened between Athens and Sparta in the Peloponnesian war of 431–404 BC and also at other similar times in history, such as in the case of the challenge at sea by Wilhelminian Germany to Great Britain, the hegemonic power before the Great War. According to Allison, in the last 500 years in twelve cases out of sixteen in which a hegemonic power was facing a rising power war became inevitable (Allison 2017; Sommella 2019).

According to the American scholar, both Xi Jinping and Donald Trump represented the national aspirations of their countries, and the aim of both presidents was to 'make their nations great again', each of them considering the other nation's interests to be an obstacle to achieving their own aim. Referring also to the 'clash of civilizations' foreshadowed by Huntington, Allison states that the concept of *Zhongguo meng* (中国梦) [Chinese dream], which is a *leitmotiv* in Xi's political discourse and is understood in the perspective of the great *zhenxing Zhonghua* (振兴中华) [rejuvenation of the Chinese nation], makes it difficult for China to become a 'responsible stakeholder' (Huntington 1996; Allison 2017).

The Chinese political and academic world rejects such concerns, particularly those regarding Chinese foreign policy and allegations of hegemonic aims, as the People's Republic of China (PRC) has for years been engaged in a significant effort to show itself to the world as *fuzeren daguo* (负责人大国) [responsible great power] actively contributing to the international community (Onnis 2013). The current COVID-19 pandemic, an adverse event initially likely to result in a loss of image for the PRC, could ultimately offer China an additional international opportunity (Onnis 2021).

---

focus on the concept of 'development', which does not imply potential contrasts, and so to reassure international observers who are worried about Chinese growth. See Zheng, B. (2005). *China's Peaceful Rise. Speeches of Zheng Bijian: 1997–2005*. Washington, DC.: Brookings Institution Press; Zheng, B. (2005), 'China's "Peaceful Rise" to Great-Power Status', *Foreign Affairs*, 84/5, 18–24.

The analysis in this paper of the role China played on the occasion of the COVID-19 pandemic, which will have repercussions that are still difficult to define, is limited to the years of the Trump presidency, during which Chinese action was internationally approved but also heavily criticized.

The 'Chinese Virus'

According to the Chinese authorities, the pandemic originated at the end of 2019 in Wuhan in Hubei province and was contained by the Beijing government with very stringent measures, which, starting on 23 January 2020, involved a complete lockdown of the entire city. These measures, which were harsher than those then implemented in other countries and more easily applicable in a state where decisions are made by the Politburo of the Chinese Communist Party (CCP), made it possible to effectively control the epidemic curve and resulted in a relatively limited number of infections and victims. At the time of writing these data are significantly lower than those of other nations,[3] particularly considering the relation between the population size and the number of infections, which for China should have been much higher. Therefore, the data are likely to have been underestimated, also considering reports from Chinese civil society and health personnel, who were warned and censored by local authorities (Romaniuk and Burgers 2020).

With the spread of the pandemic in other countries – including the United States – China very quickly went from being the only state affected by the virus to the first to manage to contain it and, according to the Chinese Communist Party narrative, to defeat it. Political discourse in Beijing therefore highlighted the sacrifice made by China, which first fought against the new virus to prevent it spreading internally and then also globally, underlining that the efficient and decisive Chinese response could set an example to and help countries around the world that were still facing the most critical phases in what became a global pandemic (Niquet 2020).

China has identified the virus as *renlei de gongdi* (人类的公敌) [a common enemy of all mankind], *mogui* (魔鬼) [a demon] to be fought against together globally within *mingyun gongtongti* (命运共同体) [the Community of Shared Destiny]. President Xi Jinping included promotion of this international community among the main points in his *Xi Jinping xin shidai Zhongguo tese*

---

3 'COVID Live - Coronavirus Statistics', *Worldometer*, <https://www.worldometers.info/coronavirus/> accessed 7 February 2022.

shehui zhuyi sixiang (习近平新时代中国特色社会主义思想) [Thoughts on Socialism with Chinese Characteristics for a New Era], which was inserted in the statute of the CCP at the nineteenth congress in October 2017 and then in the preamble to the Constitution of the People's Republic with the latest revision in March 2018. From the beginning, the 'Community of Shared Destiny' appeared to be connected to the *yi dai yi lu* (一带一路) [Belt and Road Initiative], which was launched in 2013 and was also included in the party statute, thus recognizing how extraordinary this foreign policy initiative is and how important it is in Xi's diplomatic strategy.

Although China was the first nation in which the virus spread, for the Beijing government it did not necessarily originate in the country. The appointment in January 2020 of epidemiologist and pulmonologist Zhong Nanshan as head of the Senior Expert Group in the Chinese Commission for Public Health (NHC) had strategic value. Zhong is a scientist internationally renowned for his role in the discovery of Sars in 2003 and for having criticized the government approach that minimized the impact of the epidemic. In the following years he has dealt with issues relating to food security and pollution, giving public health priority over economic needs.

A figure outside the government establishment, in the initial phase of the COVID-19 pandemic 'the Sars hero' played an important role in reassuring Chinese citizens about its duration and proper management by the Chinese government (Perry 2020). However, Zhong's eleven-day delay in reporting the first death in Wuhan – together with the recklessness of Hubei Province experts and officials in downplaying the true extent of the infection in the early stages of the pandemic – not only had negative consequences for China but also for other countries that have had extreme difficulty in managing the new coronavirus.[4]

In March 2020, Zhong Nanshan questioned the Chinese origin of the virus, corroborating Beijing's official statements (Shikun 2020). The Chinese media then started to talk about the 'Japanese virus' or the 'Italian virus', referring to countries in which it initially spread, in an evident attempt to define its origin, to the point of exploiting in December 2020 declarations by the German virologist Alexander Kekulé, director of the Institute for Biosecurity Research in Halle,

---

4   According to a study by British, American and Chinese researchers on the effectiveness of 'non-pharmaceutical interventions' in containing COVID-19, if the restrictive measures had been introduced one, two or three weeks earlier in China the number of cases could have been reduced by 66, 86 and 95 per cent respectively, also favouring a significant reduction in the number of areas affected (Lai Shengjie et al. 2020).

on the virus originating in northern Italy (Hernández 2020). Chinese Foreign Ministry spokesman and Deputy Director of the Information Department Zhao Lijian even tweeted in March 2020 that the coronavirus may have been brought to Wuhan by the US military, urging the United States to show greater transparency.[5]

Tension with the US, which was already very strong following recent trade disputes – which added to traditional reasons for Sino-American contrast – were therefore also evident regarding the debate on the virus. On several occasions, Trump publicly denounced the Chinese origin of the virus, underlining evidence that the Chinese leadership did not intend to take it for granted but instead tended to highlight the role that China could play in the common fight against the virus (Rogers et al. 2020).

In fact, according to Xi Jinping the PRC needed to intensify its international communication skills so as 'jiang hao Zhongguo gushi' (讲好中国故事) [to tell China's stories well] (Xi 2017). In this sense, the narrative of the COVID-19 pandemic offered the country where the pandemic originated, and which was identified as responsible for its diffusion, an important opportunity for redemption. This is the reason why this redemption was not only pursued *ex post* by supporting countries in distress but also *ex ante* by questioning the Chinese origin of the virus.

The New 'Health Silk Road' as a Soft Power Tool

For several years, Xi's China has been aiming to strengthen its image as a 'responsible great power'. Starting in the early 2000s, the PRC has implemented a series of (mainly economic, financial and communication) strategies that aim to strengthen its *ruan shili* (软实力) [soft power] and improve its image in the eyes of international public opinion, constituting a real 'charm offensive' (Kurlantzick 2007). The PRC has invested a great deal overseas to promote study of the Chinese language and culture, opening numerous Confucius Institutes, increasingly using 'cultural diplomacy' as an important tool to make its image more attractive and working hard to spread knowledge of Chinese civilization not only on the Asian continent but all over the world (Shambough 2013; Zappone 2017).

However, China's economic growth is still associated with environmental pollution, food safety problems, relatively low wages, pockets of unemployment and poverty still present in large areas of the internal regions and a lack of

---

5   <https://twitter.com/zlj517/status/1238111898828066823> accessed 7 February 2022.

transparency, for example in the timely communication of information of public interest and international significance or regarding the *Zhongguo touzi youxian zeren gongsi* (中国投资有限责任公司) [China Investment Corporation, CIC] sovereign fund. This was established in Beijing in September 2007 and aroused strong interest among the international community, but also fears and criticisms due to concern that it may be driven by political-strategic interests (Arduino 2009).

The lack of protection of some fundamental freedoms in the Chinese political system and China's poor human rights record are factors that in the West do not play in favour of Chinese soft power and they seem to contradict the aim of achieving a 'hexie shehui' (和谐社会) [harmonious society], which is repeatedly proposed by the Chinese leadership (Cheng 2012). In one of the rankings that measure soft power, the People's Republic came twenty-seventh, confirming the gap that separates it from many European countries and the United States (*The Soft Power 30* 2019). However, according to some Chinese academics, the aim is not only to bridge this gap with Western countries but to provide a better model of society than that proposed above all by the United States (Yan 2011).[6]

Announced in September 2013 at the Nazarbayev University of Astana, the capital of Kazakhstan, the Belt and Road Initiative has grown over the years to become an ambitious plan that can be declined in multiple directions: from the classic geopolitical strategic land and sea routes to the Arctic and the new space frontier, and up to the most sophisticated articulations of a *shuzi sichou zhilu* (数字丝绸之路) [Digital Silk Road], a Green Silk Road and a *jiankang sichou zhilu* (健康丝绸之路) [Health Silk Road] the latter being inaugurated precisely on the occasion of the current pandemic.

Through the Health Silk Road, China has provided medical equipment, services, and expert advice to more than 120 countries, also thanks to financial

6   For an in-depth analysis of the Chinese point of view, see Leonard, M. (2008). *What Does China Think?* London: Fourth Estate; Zhang, W. (2008). *Zhongguo chudong quanqiu* (中国触动全球) [The China Ripple]. Beijing: Xinhua Chubanshe; Zhang, W. (2011). *Zhongguo zhenhan: yige wenmingxing guojia de jueqi* (中国震撼:一个文明型国家的崛起) (Shangai: Shiji Chuban Jituan) [The China Wave. Rise of a Civilizational State] (New Jersey, Shangai, Singapore: World Century, 2012); Zhang, W. (2014). *Zhongguo chaoyue: yige wenmingxing guojia de guangrong yu mengxiang* (中国超越:一个文明型国家的光荣与梦想) (Shanghai: Shiji Chuban Jituan) [The China Horizon: Glory and Dream of a Civilizational State] (New Jersey, Shanghai, Singapore: World Century, 2016).

support from the Asian Infrastructure Investment Bank (AIIB),[7] helping them to strengthen their public health facilities. In South Asia, as BRI partners Bangladesh, Nepal, Pakistan, and Sri Lanka benefited immediately from the Chinese experience, with provision of medical equipment and infrastructure assistance, such as the building of a makeshift hospital in Pakistan. Over time, this collaboration could extend to common long-term policies in biomedical technology, synthetic biology and telemedicine (Pal and Vir Singh 2020).

In the same month of March 2020 in which Trump declared a travel ban on Europe,[8] China made every effort to show itself to be a reliable partner and a generous friend. According to the authorities in Beijing, in the common fight against the virus the experience and the contribution of China – which, in the words of Xi Jinping, had already fought and won its 'renmin zhanzheng' (人民战争) [people's war] – could be decisive (Gallelli 2020). As a country hit by the pandemic and forced to take measures of exceptional gravity, China proposed itself as a leading country in the war against COVID-19 and a 'global donor' to nations in distress, donating 20 million dollars to the World Health Organization (WHO) to combat the coronavirus and sending test kits to Cambodia and other neighbouring Asian states (such as Pakistan, Bangladesh, Nepal and Myanmar), and doctors and masks to the most affected European countries and to Central Asia and Africa. By sending health supplies and medical products, China was investing in so-called 'mask diplomacy'. The health crisis thus turned into a geopolitical opportunity and the BRI into a Health Silk Road. Health aid therefore became a tool in the vast soft power operation which Beijing's attention had long been directed to increasing.

At a meeting of the World Health Assembly in May 2020, Xi Jinping announced that China considered its vaccines against COVID-19 a 'global public good' and pledged to offer them globally, whether through donations, sales, or

---

7   The AIIB was proposed by the People's Republic of China, founded in Beijing in October 2014 and is an international financial institution. There were fifty-seven AIIB founding countries and the main objective of the bank – which currently has 104 members – is to provide and develop infrastructure projects in the Asia-Pacific region, thus promoting economic-social development of the region. From the beginning projects were financed in various Asian countries and the 2017 programme extended loans to countries not strictly belonging to the Asian area to contribute to global growth.

8   'Coronavirus: Trump suspends travel from Europe to US' (2020), BBC News, 12 March, <https://www.bbc.com/news/world-us-canada-51846923> accessed 7 February 2022.

loans to purchase them, with the latter option open to some Latin American and Caribbean countries. This *yimiao waijiao* (疫苗外交) ['vaccine diplomacy'] followed in the wake of previous Chinese 'win-win diplomacy' initiatives such as the BRI, in which infrastructure and connecting lines brought development to many countries, but in exchange for recognition and respect for Chinese *hexin liyi* (核心利益) [core interests] such as the question of Taiwan and claims over the South China Sea (Beeson and Li 2016).

Furthermore, China's 'vaccine diplomacy' can be considered a natural continuation of its 'mask diplomacy', even though policies relating to vaccines and their approval process are longer and more rigorous than those relating to masks and personal protective equipment. Therefore, while Western countries have with few exceptions mainly used Pfizer and Moderna vaccines, the vaccines produced in China based on an 'inactivated virus' were initially offered to its neighbours and developing countries, and then also penetrated some countries in Eastern Europe and the Balkans which, as in the case of Serbia, already had preferential relationships with Beijing (Karásková and Blablová 2021). A case of particular interest is that of Taiwan, which the PRC offered to provide with the vaccines made necessary by an increase in cases which occurred in May 2021. This collided with a refusal and an accusation by the Taiwanese authorities that China was exercising 'political pressure' to thwart Taipei's efforts to acquire vaccines elsewhere (Hickey 2021). Neither did South Korea, a traditional ally of the United States on the Asian chessboard, buy Chinese vaccines in order to avoid sending negative signals to Washington, yet another sign that vaccination policies have strong geopolitical connotations (Jin 2021).

Xi Jinping referred to shared management of the pandemic on several occasions, highlighting five priority points promoted by China: the value and dignity of human life; the importance of a scientific approach to the issue and a coordinated and systemic response; international solidarity and cooperation; fairness and equity in the production and distribution of vaccines (with particular attention to the difficulties of developing countries); and the role of the United Nations (UN) and the WHO in improving the public health governance system. These points summarize a white paper published on 7 June 2020 by China's State Council Information Office entitled Fighting COVID-19: China in Action. The white paper is divided in four sections and documents the rapid Chinese response to the emergency from the end of December 2019 and underlines that China regularly transmitted information relating to the COVID crisis in a transparent manner with the priority objective, mentioned several times in the text, of 'saving as many lives as possible, by every possible means'.[9]

At a Global Health Summit in Rome, Xi also recalled PRC initiatives in the aftermath of the start of the pandemic: supplying free vaccines to more than eighty developing countries and exporting them to forty-three countries; investing $2 billion in assistance in responding to COVID-19; and dispatching medical supplies to more than 150 countries and thirteen international organizations (280 billion masks, 3.4 billion protective suits and 4 billion test kits). Xi mentioned a joint China-UN project to create a global humanitarian response hub in the PRC and the G20 debt suspension initiative for poorer countries and announced that China would provide an additional $3 billion in international aid over the following three years to support the response to COVID-19 and economic and social recovery in developing countries. Xi recalled that China had already provided 300 million doses of vaccines globally, and confirmed its future commitment and willingness to transfer Chinese technologies to other developing countries and a renunciation of intellectual property rights on vaccines (Xi 2021).

In fact, China has been very attentive to the COVID-19 Vaccines Global Access (COVAX) initiative, which was launched in April 2020 and supported by the UN, and which also includes developing countries, to accelerate production and fair access to COVID-19 diagnostic tests, therapies, and vaccines. Promoting a new *guoji guanxi minzhuhua* (国际关系民主化) [democratization of international relations] at the cultural level, China increasingly tends to present itself as a leading country in the framework of 'South-South cooperation' requesting 'a fairer international political and economic order'. Although only two, Sinopharm and Sinovac, of the five vaccines produced in China have been validated by the WHO, the others have also been distributed abroad and, although not very widespread in Western countries, they have been widely used in countries in the Global South (Mallapaty 2021).

---

9   China's State Council Information Office (2020). 'Fighting COVID-19: China in Action', 7 June, <http://english.www.gov.cn/news/topnews/202006/07/content_WS5 edc559ac6d066592a449030.html?fbclid=IwAR1KLXuojJDpiRXgDqCFHU1m9Ne vq6-2ORxYWgTy8jUYtUBGmblG5kuG4Pk> accessed 7 February 2022. On the role and importance of the Chinese white papers, see Samarani, G. (2018). 'Informare il mondo. Il ruolo dei "libri bianchi" del governo cinese'. In Graziani, S. (2018), 'Cina globale: soft power e proiezione internazionale', *Sulla Via del Catai. Rivista semestrale sulle relazioni culturali tra Europa e Cina*, 11(18), 109–117.

The Global Consequences of the Pandemic

There are many questions about the possible medium-long-term consequences of the pandemic and the US's ability to safeguard the 'liberal international order' even in the post-COVID world and maintain leadership that during the twentieth century was characterized by globally decisive initiatives, to the point of defining the last century as the 'American century' (Kissinger 2020). The ongoing debates on the rise of China, on the 'Thucydides trap' and on the possibility that the 21ˢᵗ century is the 'Chinese century' therefore remain more relevant than ever, and the alleged lack of solidarity of the Trump presidency does not seem to have questioned the model of globalization led by the West and based on values shared by Western democracies (Campbell and Doshi 2020).

In the 2017 United States National Security Strategy (NSS) China is defined as a 'revisionist power' which wants 'to shape a world antithetical to U.S. values and interests', trying 'to displace the United States in the Indo-Pacific region' and to reshape the international order in its favour. The NSS underlined that 'China's infrastructure investments and trade strategies reinforce its geopolitical aspirations', threatening the sovereignty and stability of other nations.[10]

Likewise, in the 2018 United States National Defense Strategy (NDS) China is defined as 'a strategic competitor using predatory economics to intimidate its neighbours while militarizing features in the South China Sea'. Consequently, the US should give priority in the coming years to the Indo-Pacific as a key region to counter China, which is seeking 'Indo-Pacific regional hegemony in the near-term'.[11] In fact, in June 2019 the US Department of Defense published its first Indo-Pacific Strategy Report, specifying policies to adopt and measures to take in the Indo-Pacific region.

The pandemic had – and still has – a strong impact on the economies of many countries, with domino effects that could also slow down and reshape the BRI projects, despite Xi's repeated guarantees to maintain the commitments made and the objectives identified by the Chinese government. Due to the consequences of the pandemic on the Chinese gross domestic product, many resources have

---

10 The White House (2017). *National Security Strategy of the United States of America.* Washington, DC. <https://trumpwhitehouse.archives.gov/wp-content/uploads/2017/12/NSS-Final-12-18-2017-0905.pdf> accessed 7 February 2022.

11 Department of Defense (2018). 'Summary of the 2018 National Defense Strategy of the United States of America. Sharpening the American Military's Competitive Edge', 19 January, <https://dod.defense.gov/Portals/1/Documents/pubs/2018-National-Defense-Strategy-Summary.pdf> accessed 7 February 2022.

in fact been redirected to domestic recovery rather than abroad, confirming an economic trend decided by the Chinese leadership for some time aimed at developing domestic consumption to support GDP growth and avoiding putting emphasis on exports (Woetzel et al. 2019; Weizhen and Tan 2019; Kemp 2020).

At the same time, China has begun to limit its dependence on Western supply chains in some sectors, for example by reducing its purchases of technological components from other states and favouring their production domestically to strengthen the Digital Silk Road (Baker McKenzie 2020). The People's Republic of China had already invested in big data and artificial intelligence (AI), and the need to monitor the virus using digital technologies allowed it to connect the Digital Silk Road to the Health Silk Road and develop further new applications to use in different areas, from online commercial platforms to telecommunications, from cloud computing to mobile payment systems and smart cities.

The pandemic, which has led many governments to monitor their populations, has increased developing country demand for Chinese telecommunications and surveillance tools, with all the implications and consequences, including negative ones, that this entails in terms of limiting personal freedoms, controlling oppositions and suppression of possible dissent by authoritarian governments. Conversely, the American and European response in the digital sector was less rapid, partly in compliance with privacy regulations, which are less stringent in China (Kurlantzick 2020).

There is therefore a risk of accelerating political effects of the rise of Asia and of the 'Easternization' process – shifting the barycentre of international relations towards the East – favouring 'globalization with Chinese characteristics', a path the Beijing government is already following. If the stability of its economy allows it, it is likely that the Chinese government will take a decisive step in this direction in the post-covid world too (Rachman 2017; Sommella 2019). Since the early 2000s, following an article by Joshua Cooper Ramo, who first spoke of a *Beijing gongshi* (北京共识) [Beijing Consensus], there has been much discussion, first in the West and then in China, on the possibility of providing developing countries with a possible *Zhongguo moshi* (中国模式) [China Model], an alternative model to the 'Washington Consensus' (Ramo 2004).

After China's responsible management of the 2008 financial crisis – with the Chinese economic stimulus playing an important role in reviving global demand (Samarani and Scarpari 2009; Congiu 2010) – some scholars have gone so far as to extend 'the Chinese model' from the economic sphere to the political and cultural ones (Jacques 2009; Subramanian 2011). According to Stefan Halper, for example, the Chinese 'authoritarian' model guarantees not only rapid economic progress but also socio-political stability, which contrasts with many countries in which democratization processes have been accompanied by significant political and social unrest (Halper 2010). For many non-Western countries involved in the BRI, the Chinese authoritarian model is quite attractive, both because of its intrinsic promise of greater and faster well-being and because it is not forcibly exported, as the United States and even the European Union have sometimes tried to do with their democratic models in some Middle Eastern and African countries.

In the current pandemic, the Chinese state media have emphasized how the PRC system has been able to guarantee effective application of lockdowns and procedures to control violations of government prescriptions compared to democratic systems, thus implying a more effective model worth imitating in many countries of the world (Fumian 2020). However, at the same time this has sparked criticism in Western liberal societies and helped rekindle the debate on China's lack of democracy and its authoritarian methods (Onnis 2021), and arguments that only a democratic China would be more attractive in terms of soft power and would acquire the legitimacy to apply for world leadership (Sommella 2019).

China, the WHO, and the Management of the COVID-19 Pandemic

Created in 1948, the World Health Organization, a specialized agency of the United Nations, aims to realize the right of every person to enjoy the best physical and mental health. In the decades of its activity, the agency has achieved important aims such as reducing infant mortality, increasing life expectancy, eliminating smallpox, and decreasing the incidence of infectious diseases such as polio (Beigbeder 1995). However, in recent years the WHO has been in the headlines due to a series of criticisms that have directly or indirectly involved China. Some criticism, advanced above all by Western countries, has been directed at its operating costs. It has been emphasized that the WHO has spent about 200 million dollars a year on travel (7–8 per cent of the budget), a figure higher than the costs incurred for mental health campaigns, HIV/AIDS, tuberculosis and malaria added together. In particular, Margaret Chan, a Hong Kong citizen and head of the organization from 2007 to 2017 representing the People's Republic of China, was criticized for staying in $1,000 a night hotels while visiting West Africa in 2016 (Cheng 2017).

Chan's leadership also received negative reviews of its management of swine flu in 2009, when the WHO was accused of exaggerating the danger.[12] In contrast, during the Ebola epidemic in West Africa between 2014 and 2016

---

12 'WHO admits errors in handling flu pandemic' (2010). *NBC news*, 12 April, <https://www.nbcnews.com/id/wbna36421914> accessed 7 February 2022.

the organization was stigmatized for its lack of responsiveness, communication deficit and poor coordination with national governments in dealing with the health emergency (Hoffman and Røttingen 2014; The World Health Organization 2016). Furthermore, it was thought that Chan, who was considered very close to the Beijing government, would make the organization a springboard for traditional Chinese medicine, the treatments of which are considered by the scientific community to be largely ineffective or even dangerous, not to mention disastrous for many animal species that have become at risk of extinction as they are killed, despite being protected, because they are at the basis of many traditional remedies (Rencken and Dorlo 2019; Hunt 2019).[13]

Ethiopian Tedros Adhanom Ghebreyesus, WHO director since 1 July 2017, has also been a target of attacks. Immediately after his election, Tedros favoured the appointment of former Zimbabwean president Robert Mugabe as WHO goodwill ambassador, an appointment immediately revoked after consistent criticism regarding Mugabe's poor record of human rights violations and the deterioration of public health in Zimbabwe.[14] Above all, Tedros, whose election was backed by China, which in recent years has increased its contribution to the organization by 50 per cent (Mazumdaru 2020), was accused of not opposing Beijing's request to prevent Taiwan's participation (excluded by the WHO in 1972 in favour of the PRC) in meetings of the organization. Taiwan's presence as an observer was in fact allowed between 2009 and 2016, but since 2017 the WHO has no longer permitted Taiwanese delegates to attend the Annual Assembly. International pressure for Taiwan's participation has increased following the COVID-19 pandemic. The effective response of the Taipei government, despite its exclusion from emergency meetings, has reinforced both its request for

---

13 'The World Health Organization's decision about traditional Chinese medicine could backfire' (2019). *Nature*, 570, 5.

14 'Robert Mugabe's WHO appointment condemned as "an insult"' (2017). *BBC*, 21 October, <https://www.bbc.com/news/world-africa-41702662> accessed 7 February 2022; 'WHO chief "rethinking" appointment of Zimbabwe's Mugabe as "goodwill ambassador" after widespread condemnation' (2017). *The Globe and Mail*, 21 October, <https://www.theglobeandmail.com/news/world/shock-as-zimbabwes-mugabe-named-who-goodwill-ambassador/article36681266/> accessed 7 February 2022; 'WHO cancels Robert Mugabe goodwill ambassador role' (2017). *BBC*, 22 October, <https://www.bbc.com/news/world-africa-41713919> accessed 7 February 2022.

membership of the WHO and accusations of China having excessive political influence on the organization (Timsit and Hui 2020).

The WHO's initial action to combat COVID-19 generated further tensions that risked weakening the agency's future action. The management of the pandemic by the WHO has in fact been questioned due to alleged subjection to the People's Republic of China, unlike what happened with the Sars epidemic of 2002–2004 when the organization accused China of not having provided reliable information. In particular, the WHO was accused of aligning itself with the positions of Beijing, congratulating it for the measures adopted and for transparency in its initial communications, despite accusations made in many quarters that the Chinese government had initially hidden the presence of the virus on its territory and once it made it public that it concealed the real scale of the epidemic by providing unreliable statistics on the numbers of infections and deaths (Borger 2020).

Criticisms were also advanced regarding the lack of clarity in the first measures suggested to deal with the pandemic (initial advice against the widespread use of masks, for example) (The World Health Organization 2020a), and of the WHO declaring itself opposed to measures taken by many countries to limit border entry, which were deemed ineffective or even counterproductive by the organization (The World Health Organization 2020b). In particular, the agency negatively judged the decisions taken between January and March 2020 by US President Donald Trump to close the borders, first to travellers from China and then from Europe (Beaubien 2020).

For his part, in April 2020 Trump announced suspension of American funding of the WHO and that he intended to withdraw from the organization, accusing it of slowness in warning of the risk of human transmission of the virus and in sounding the alarm of a global threat, and of having covered up the Chinese omissions in line with what the Beijing authorities declared (Knutson 2020; Lasserre 2020; Samuels 2020).[15] Trump's decision – which was later revoked by new President Joe Biden – risked greatly weakening the agency's work, as the United States was the WHO's main financier, with 893 million dollars of (fixed and voluntary) contributions to the 2018–2019 budget, equal to 20 per cent of the total, and instead strengthening China's position (Perper 2020).

In fact, the criticisms levelled at the World Health Organization regarding its management of COVID-19 do not appear fully founded. The uncertainty

---

15 'Coronavirus: US to halt funding to WHO, says Trump' (2020). *BBC*, 15 April, <https://www.bbc.com/news/world-us-canada-52289056> accessed 7 February 2022.

about its health recommendations was also due to the not always unambiguous positions of scientists on the nature of the virus and how it spread. The WHO has denied the allegations that it endorsed the alleged omissions by the Beijing government, recalling that it had raised the alarm on human-to-human transmission of COVID-19 as early as mid-January 2020, before Chinese studies communicated clear evidence of this type of transmission (Watts and Stracqualursi 2020). Then, affirming that the organization's action is conditioned by Beijing's funding is not supported by the fact that the Chinese contribution to the budget, despite increases in recent years, is equal to a tenth of that of the United States (Huang 2020).

However, between April and May 2020, China and the WHO again ended up in the dock because of suspicions launched by US intelligence agencies about a virus leak from a Wuhan-based laboratory. The accusation was supported by the Trump administration, while the government of Australia called for an independent international investigation (Rincon 2020; Corera 2020; Probyn 2020).[16] China denied the lab-leak theory of COVID's origin and opposed the investigation.[17] The irritation was such as to give rise to a trade war with Australia, with related customs sanctions, and to the arrest on a charge of spying on an Australian citizen of Chinese origin (Kassam 2020; Mao 2021).[18]

Conclusions

This article aimed to reconstruct the roles of the People's Republic of China and the World Health Organization in the fight against COVID-19 under the Trump administration, highlighting the importance of the production and dissemination of vaccines to China, the image of which was initially badly damaged by the outbreak of the pandemic. Its internal and external narrative was precisely aimed at limiting the damage to its reputation, which was revealed by several international polls.

What emerges is strong Sino-American rivalry, which has also appeared in the public debate and in the WHO relating to the genesis and spread of the

16 'Coronavirus: Trump stands by China lab origin theory for virus' (2020). *BBC*, 1 May, <https://www.bbc.com/news/world-us-canada-52496098> accessed 7 February 2022.
17 'Coronavirus: China rejects call for probe into origins of disease' (2020). *BBC*, 24 April, <https://www.bbc.com/news/world-asia-china-52420536> accessed 7 February 2022.
18 'Australia says it is "seriously concerned" about journalist's year-long detention in China', (2021). *CNBC*, 13 August, <https://www.cnbc.com/2021/08/13/australia-concerned-about-journalists-yearlong-detention-in-china.html> accessed 7 February 2022.

virus, increasing traditional tensions between the two countries, which were particularly strong under the Trump administration also in consideration of the trade war. On the contrary, not only the current pandemic but also other global priority issues such as nuclear proliferation, energy security and climate change require serious and constant efforts at joint US-China cooperation to build a 'Pacific Community'. Washington and Beijing should work on developing this to complement – and not replace – the Atlantic one (Kissinger 2011).

However, beyond declarations of intent, such cooperation in this delicate moment still appears distant as the relations between the two powers seem to have reached their lowest point since the period following the events in Tian'anmen in 1989, while a new 'Chinese exceptionalism' seems to be opposed with increasing vigour to the traditional 'American exceptionalism' (Berrettini 2017).

President Xi, a decision-making leader inside China and an assertive one outside the country, has in fact definitively abandoned the *taoguang yanghui* (韬光养晦) [low profile] approach which since Deng Xiaoping had characterized the previous Chinese administrations (Yan 2014) to play a significant role in post-covid global governance, as is also demonstrated by initiatives undertaken during the health emergency such as the Health Silk Road, the contributions made by the Asian Infrastructure Investment Bank and 'vaccine diplomacy'.

Bibliography

Allison, G. (2017). *Destined for War. Can America and China Escape Thucydides's Trap?* Melbourne–London: Scribe.

Arduino, A. (2009). *Il fondo sovrano cinese*. Pavia: O barra O edizioni.

'Australia says it is "seriously concerned" about journalist's year-long detention in China', (2021). *CNBC*, 13 August, <https://www.cnbc.com/2021/08/13/australia-concerned-about-journalists-yearlong-detention-in-china.html> accessed 7 February 2022.

Baker McKenzie, and Silk Road Associates (SRA) (2020). 'Understanding How COVID-19 Alters BRI', <https://www.bakermckenzie.com/-/media/files/insight/publications/2020/03/covid19-bri-short-report.pdf> accessed 7 February 2022.

Beaubien, J. (2020). 'Public Health Experts Question Trump's Ban On Most Travelers From Europe', *NPR*, 12 March, <https://www.npr.org/sections/health-shots/2020/03/12/815146007/public-health-experts-question-trumps-ban-on-most-travelers-from-europe?t=1630487303142> accessed 7 February 2022.

Beeson, M., and Li, F. (2016). 'China's Place in Regional and Global Governance: A New World Comes Into View', *Global Policy*, 7(4), 491–499.

Beigbeder, Y. (1995). *L'Organisation mondiale de la santé*. Genève: Graduate Institute Publications.

Berrettini, M. (2017). *Verso un nuovo equilibrio globale. Le relazioni internazionali in prospettiva storica*. Roma: Carocci.

Borger, J. (2020). 'Caught in a superpower struggle: the inside story of the WHO's response to coronavirus', *The Guardian*, 18 April.

Campbell, K. M., and Doshi, R. (2020). 'The Coronavirus Could Reshape Global Order', *Foreign Affairs*, 18 March.

Cheng, M. (2017). 'AP Exclusive: Health agency spends more on travel than AIDS', *AP News*, 22 May.

Cheng, Q. (2012). 'Challenges for China's harmonious diplomacy'. In H., Lai, and Y., Lu (eds), *China's Soft Power and International Relations*. New York: Routledge.

China's State Council Information Office (2020). 'Fighting COVID-19: China in Action', 7 June, <http://english.www.gov.cn/news/topnews/202006/07/content_WS5edc559ac6d066592a449030.html?fbclid=IwAR1KLXuojJDpiRXgDqCFHU1m9Nevq6-2ORxYWgTy8jUYtUBGmblG5kuG4Pk> accessed 7 February 2022.

Congiu, F. (2010). 'Il processo di modernizzazione cinese tra "multipolarismo e polarizzazione"'. In M., Torri, and N., Mocci (eds), *L'Asia di Obama e della crisi economica globale. Asia Maior*, Milano: Guerini.

Corera, G. (2020). 'Coronavirus: US allies tread lightly around Trump lab claims', *BBC News*, 5 May.

'Coronavirus: Trump suspends travel from Europe to US' (2020). *BBC News*, 12 March, <https://www.bbc.com/news/world-us-canada-51846923> accessed 7 February 2022.

'Coronavirus: US to halt funding to WHO, says Trump' (2020). *BBC*, 15 April, <https://www.bbc.com/news/world-us-canada-52289056> accessed 7 February 2022.

'Coronavirus: China rejects call for probe into origins of disease' (2020). *BBC*, 24 April, <https://www.bbc.com/news/world-asia-china-52420536> accessed 7 February 2022.

'Coronavirus: Trump stands by China lab origin theory for virus' (2020). *BBC*, 1 May, <https://www.bbc.com/news/world-us-canada-52496098> accessed 7 February 2022.

'COVID Live - Coronavirus Statistics' (2022). *Worldometer*, <https://www.world ometers.info/coronavirus/> accessed 7 February 2022.

Department of Defense (2018). 'Summary of the 2018 National Defense Strategy of the United States of America. Sharpening the American Military's Competitive Edge', 19 January, <https://dod.defense.gov/Portals/1/Docume nts/pubs/2018-National-Defense-Strategy-Summary.pdf>   accessed   7 February 2022.

Fumian, M. (2020). 'Stati di quarantena', *Sinosfere*, 9, 116–128.

Gallelli, B. (2020). 'Una nuova "guerra di popolo" per raccontare la "storia della Cina"', *Sinosfere*, 10, 3–15.

Halper, S. (2010). *The Beijing Consensus*. New York: Basic Books.

Hernández, J.C. (2020). 'China Peddles Falsehoods to Obscure Origin of Covid Pandemic', *The New York Times*, 6 December.

Hickey, D. V. (2021). 'The US Must Defend Taiwan – From COVID-19', *The Diplomat*, 29 May.

Hoffman, S. J., and Røttingen, J. - A. (2014). 'Split WHO in two: strengthening political decision-making and securing independent scientific advice', *Public Health Journal*, 128 (2), 188–194.

Hunt, K. (2019). 'Chinese medicine gains WHO acceptance but it has many critics', *CNN*, 26 May.

Huntington, S. (1996). *The Clash of Civilizations and the Remaking of World Order*. New York: Simon & Schuster.

Jacques, M. (2009). *When China Rules the World*. London: Allen Lane.

Jin, K. (2021). 'Why Isn't South Korea Buying Chinese Vaccines?', *The Diplomat*, 28 April.

Karásková, I. and Blablová, V. (2021). 'The Logic of China's Vaccine Diplomacy', *The Diplomat*, 24 March.

Kassam, N. (2020). 'Great expectations: The unraveling of the Australia-China relationship', *Brookings*, 20 July.

Kemp, J. (2020). 'COLUMN-China's internal not export market matters more for world economy', *Reuters*, 3 March.

Kissinger, H. (2011). *On China*. New York: Penguin Press.

–––– (2020). 'The Coronavirus Pandemic Will Forever Alter the World Order', *The Wall Street Journal*, 3 April.

Knutson, J. (2020). 'Trump administration notifies UN of intent to withdraw from WHO', *Axios*, 7 July.

Kurlantzick, J. (2007). *Charm Offensive. How China's Soft Power Is Transforming the World*. New Haven and London: Yale University Press.

–––– (2020). 'China's Digital Silk Road Initiative: A Boon for Developing Countries or a Danger to Freedom?', *The Diplomat*, 17 December.

Lai, S., et al. (2020). 'Effect of non-pharmaceutical interventions to contain COVID-19 in China', *Nature*, 585, 410–413.

Lasserre, I. (2020). 'Comment la Chine tire les ficelles de l'Organisation mondiale de la santé', *Le Figaro*, 9 April.

Leonard, M. (2008). *What Does China Think?* London: Fourth Estate.

Mallapaty, S. (2021). 'China's COVID vaccines are going global – but questions remain', *Nature*, 593, 178–179.

Mao, F. (2021). 'Cheng Lei: Why has an Australian TV anchor been detained by China?', *BBC News*, 9 February.

Mazumdaru, S., 'What influence does China have over the WHO?' (2020). *DW*, 17 April, <https://www.dw.com/en/what-influence-does-china-have-over-the-who/a-53161220> accessed 7 February 2022.

Niquet, V. (2020). 'China's Coronavirus Information Warfare', *The Diplomat*, 24 March.

Onnis, B. (2013). 'Has China Plans for World Domination?', *Comparative Civilizations Review*, 68 (68), 55–73.

–––– (2021). 'COVID-19 and China's global image', *Policy Briefs*, 57.

Pal, D., and Vir Singh, S. (2020). 'Multilateralism With Chinese Characteristics: Bringing in the Hub-and-Spoke', *The Diplomat*, 10 July.

Perper, R. (2020). 'China is injecting millions into WHO as the US cuts funds. Experts say Beijing is trying to boost its influence over the agency and its "deeply compromised" chief', *Business Insider*, 24 April.

Perry, M. (2020). 'COVID-19: Dr. Zhong Nanshan Is In', *The Diplomat*, 21 February.

Pien Huang (2020). 'Trump And WHO: How Much Does The U.S. Give? What's The Impact Of A Halt In Funding?', *NPR*, 15 April, <https://www.npr.org/sections/goatsandsoda/2020/04/15/834666123/trump-and-who-how-much-does-the-u-s-give-whats-the-impact-of-a-halt-in-funding accessed> 7 February 2022.

Probyn, A. (2020). 'Coronavirus investigation call has made Australia a target, but we're not alone in feeling China's wrath', *ABC*, 29 April, <https://www.abc.net.au/news/2020-04-30/coronavirus-china-diplomatic-backlash/12198674> accessed 7 February 2022.

Rachman, G. (2017). *Easternisation. War and Peace in the Asian Century*. London: Vintage.

Ramo, J. C. (2004). *The Beijing Consensus*. London: The Foreign Policy Center.

Rencken, C. N. M., and Dorlo, Th. P. C. (2019). 'Quackery at WHO: A Chinese Affair', *Skeptical Inquirer*, 43 (5), 39–43.

Rincon, P. (2020). 'Coronavirus: Is there any evidence for lab release theory?', *BBC News*, 1 May.

'Robert Mugabe's WHO appointment condemned as "an insult"' (2017). *BBC*, 21 October, <https://www.bbc.com/news/world-africa-41702662> accessed 7 February 2022.

Rogers, K., et al. (2020). 'Trump Defends Using 'Chinese Virus' Label, Ignoring Growing Criticism', *The New York Times*, 18 March.

Romaniuk, S. N., and Burgers, T. (2020). 'Can China's COVID-19 Statistics Be Trusted?', *The Diplomat*, 26 March.

Roy, D. (1996). 'The "China Threat" Issue: Major Arguments', *Asian Survey*, 36 (8), 758–751.

Samarani, G., and Scarpari, M. (eds) (2009). *La Cina. Verso la modernità*, vol. III. Torino: Einaudi.

Samarani, G. (2018). 'Informare il mondo. Il ruolo dei "libri bianchi" del governo cinese'. In S. Graziani, 'Cina globale: soft power e proiezione internazionale', *Sulla Via del Catai. Rivista semestrale sulle relazioni culturali tra Europa e Cina* 11/18 (2018), 109–117.

Samuels, B. (2020). 'Trump administration moves to formally withdraw US from WHO', *The Hill*, 7 July.

Shambough, D. (2013). *China Goes Global. The Partial Power*. Oxford: Oxford University Press.

Shikun, M. (2020). 'Where Did COVID-19 Originate?', *China-US Focus*, 10 March.

Sommella, V. (2019). 'New American Perspectives on the "China Threat" Issue. Peter Navarro and the "Thucydides's Trap"', *Nuova Rivista Storica*, 103 (2), 377–416.

Subramanian, A. (2011). *Eclipse: Living in the Shadow of China's Economic Dominance*. Washington DC: Peterson Institute for International Economics.

'The Soft Power 30. A Global Ranking of Soft Power' (2019). Portland: USC Center on Public Diplomacy, <https://softpower30.com> accessed 7 February 2022.

'The World Health Organization's decision about traditional Chinese medicine could backfire' (2019). *Nature*, 570, 5.

Timsit, A. and Hui, M. (2020). 'Taiwan's status could disrupt the most important global health meeting of this pandemic', *Quartz*, 16 May, <https://qz.com/1857449/taiwan-china-relations-take-center-stage-at-who-meeting/> accessed 7 February 2022.

Watts, A., and Stracqualursi, V. (2020). 'WHO defends coronavirus response after Trump criticism', *CNN Business*, 8 April.

Weizhen, T. (2019). 'China will likely wait out the trade war as it bets on its own economy', *CNBC*, 29 August.

Woetzel, J., et al. (2019). 'China and the world: Inside the dynamics of a changing relationship', *McKinsey Global Institute*, 1 July.

White House, The (2017). *National Security Strategy of the United States of America*. Washington, DC. <https://trumpwhitehouse.archives.gov/wp-content/uploads/2017/12/NSS-Final-12-18-2017-0905.pdf> accessed 7 February 2022.

'WHO admits errors in handling flu pandemic' (2010). *NBC news*, 12 April, <https://www.nbcnews.com/id/wbna36421914> accessed 7 February 2022.

'WHO chief "rethinking" appointment of Zimbabwe's Mugabe as "goodwill ambassador" after widespread condemnation' (2017). *The Globe and Mail*, 21 October, <https://www.theglobeandmail.com/news/world/shock-as-zimbabwes-mugabe-named-who-goodwill-ambassador/article36681266/> accessed 7 February 2022.

'WHO cancels Robert Mugabe goodwill ambassador role' (2017). *BBC*, 22 October, <https://www.bbc.com/news/world-africa-41713919> accessed 7 February 2022.

World Health Organization, The (2016). 'Implementation of the International Health Regulations (2005). Report of the Review Committee on the Role of the International Health Regulations (2005) in the Ebola Outbreak and Response', 13 May, <https://apps.who.int/gb/ebwha/pdf_files/WHA69/A69_21-en.pdf> accessed 7 February 2022.

———— (2020a). 'Rational use of personal protective equipment for coronavirus disease 2019 (COVID-19)', 27 February, <https://apps.who.int/iris/bitstream/handle/10665/331215/WHO-2019-nCov-IPCPPE_use-2020.1-eng.pdf> accessed 7 February 2022.

———— (2020b). 'Updated WHO recommendations for international traffic in relation to COVID-19 outbreak', 29 February, <https://www.who.int/news-room/articles-detail/updated-who-recommendations-for-international-traffic-in-relation-to-covid-19-outbreak accessed> 7 February 2022.

Xi, J. (2017). 'Secure a Decisive Victory in Building a Moderately Prosperous Society in All Respects and Strive for the Great Success of Socialism with

Chinese Characteristics for a New Era', 18 October, <https://www.chinada ily.com.cn/china/19thcpcnationalcongress/2017-11/04/content_34115212. htm> accessed 7 February 2022.

–––– (2021). 'Working Together to Build a Global Community of Health for All', 21 May, <http://www.xinhuanet.com/english/2021-05/21/c_139961512.htm> accessed 7 February 2022.

Yan, X. (2011). *Ancient Chinese Thought, Modern Chinese Power*. Princeton and Oxford: Princeton University Press.

–––– (2014). 'From Keeping a Low Profile to Striving for Achievement', *The Chinese Journal of International Politics*, 7 (2), 153–184.

Yee, H., and Storey, I. (2002). *The China Threat: Perceptions, Myths and Reality*. London-New York: RoutledgeCurzon.

Zappone, T. (2017). *La comunicazione politica cinese rivolta all'estero*. Milano: Ledizioni.

Zhang, W. (2008). *Zhongguo chudong quanqiu* (中国触动全球) [The China Ripple]. Beijing: Xinhua Chubanshe.

–––– (2011). *Zhongguo zhenhan: yige wenmingxing guojia de jueqi* (中国震撼:一个文明型国家的崛起) [*The China Wave. Rise of a Civilizational State*]. Shangai: Shiji Chuban Jituan.

–––– (2014). *Zhongguo chaoyue: yige wenmingxing guojia de guangrong yu mengxiang* (中国超越:一个文明型国家的光荣与梦想) [*The China Horizon: Glory and Dream of a Civilizational State*]. Shanghai: Shiji Chuban Jituan.

Zheng, B. (2005). *China's Peaceful Rise. Speeches of Zheng Bijian: 1997-2005*. Washington, DC.: Brookings Institution Press.

–––– (2005). 'China's "Peaceful Rise" to Great-Power Status', *Foreign Affairs*, 84 (5), 18–24.

Gianluca Pastori

The Belt and Road Initiative and Beijing's Evolving Role in Middle Asia

Since it was first announced in 2013, the Belt and Road Initiative (BRI) has undergone several transformations, retaining its economic and commercial value while strengthening its political dimension and becoming the primary tool for expanding Beijing's influence in the international arena. Initially a limited (albeit ambitious) effort to streamline land and sea routes between Asia and Europe and "break the bottleneck of Asian connectivity", its scope and geographical reach have expanded over time. Now a global initiative spanning several continents, the BRI continues to pay special attention to Middle Asia, a critical geographic pivot, and a key prize in Beijing's quest for regional hegemony. Middle Asia has always been a sensitive spot. Situated at the crossroads of different spheres of influence, it has traditionally been the most effective link between Europe and Asia. At the same time, the fragmentation of the local power system has often made it difficult to control. In recent years, the interplay of Russian, Western and, increasingly, Chinese interests has overlapped with these traditional dynamics, creating new tensions and alignments. Against this backdrop, countries such as Pakistan, Iran, Afghanistan, and the former Soviet republics of Central Asia have been able to reshape their geopolitical roles and strengthen their positions vis-à-vis their potential partners. This growing activism has forced Beijing to adapt its approach to the region and develop more flexible strategies to extend its influence. As far as Middle Asia is concerned, the idea is that many endogenous and exogenous elements are working together to contain China's rise. The interplay of these elements determines how Beijing could promote its vision and support its interests in this highly integrated geopolitical environment and the limits of its actions in dealing with its regional and global partners.

Introduction

Launched with much fanfare in 2013, the Belt and Road Initiative (BRI) is arguably the most ambitious and successful international programme the People's Republic of China (PRC) promoted. By 2018, the PRC had signed up seventy-two countries in Asia, the Middle East, Africa, and Europe to participate in various aspects of the BRI. Together, these countries represent more than one-third of the world's gross domestic product (GDP) and more than half of the world's population. Overall, 125 countries have signed some form of BRI-related agreement with China. In 2017, the BRI was formally incorporated into the Chinese constitution 'as a sign of the initiative's centrality to Beijing's sense of its global destiny' (Dunne 2021). Since its announcement, the initiative has undergone several transformations that have strengthened its political dimension and made it a primary tool for spreading Beijing's influence abroad. At the same time, it has retained its original economic and commercial value. Initially a limited (albeit ambitious) effort to streamline land and sea routes between Asia and Europe and 'break the bottleneck in Asia's connectivity'[1] by reviving the appeal of the ancient Silk Road, its scope and geographical reach have expanded over time. At present, the BRI is a global initiative, with its multiple ramifications extending to Africa, the Indo-Pacific and Latin America, as well as to Europe, Inner Asia, and the Middle East. From this perspective, the BRI is now a central element of Xi Jinping's 'major country diplomacy' strategy, which calls for the PRC to enhance its standing in global affairs in parallel with the rise of its power and status.

With the launch of the BRI, Middle Asia[2] has become increasingly important to the PRC's global strategy. The region has always been a sensitive one. Situated at the crossroads of different spheres of influence, it forms the core of the Eurasian landmass and has traditionally provided the most effective link between Europe and Asia. Bordering the Gulf and the northern shore of the western Indian Ocean, Middle Asia was also the theatre of the Anglo-Russian Great Game in the nineteenth century. In these years, the Tsarist Empire extended its territorial control southwards to the Amu Darya River, which today marks the Afghan Uzbek border. However, the Russian grip on the region consolidated only during the Soviet period, when its territory was formally incorporated into the Union as those of the newly formed republics of Kazakhstan, Kyrgyzstan,

---

1   Connectivity Spearheads Development and Partnership Enables Cooperation. Address by H.E. Xi Jinping President of the People's Republic of China at Dialogue on Strengthening Connectivity Partnership, Beijing, 8 November 2014, <https://www.fmprc.gov.cn/ce/ceindo/eng/jrzg/t1211795.htm> accessed 20 April 2023.

2   This chapter refers to 'Middle Asia' as the part of continental Asia stretching from the Caspian Sea in the west to central China in the east, and from southern Russia in the north to northern India in the south. Roughly speaking, it includes the former Soviet republics of Kazakhstan, Kyrgyzstan, Tajikistan, Turkmenistan, and Uzbekistan, along with the autonomous regions of Inner Mongolia, Tibet, and Xinjiang Uygur, as well as Afghanistan and the adjoining regions of other Asian countries, like Iran and Pakistan.

Tajikistan, Turkmenistan, and Uzbekistan. After the dissolution of the Soviet Union, the interplay of Russian and Western interests and the region's relative isolation allowed the local elites to consolidate their power. At the same time, the global competition overlapped with local power dynamics to produce new tensions and alignments. Against this backdrop, countries like Pakistan, Iran, Afghanistan, and the former Soviet Central Asian republics were able to reshape their geopolitical roles and strengthen their positions vis-à-vis their potential partners. These developments influenced the PRC's posture and helped shape Beijing's vision of the region's potential. Chinese activism, in turn, triggered a general adjustment process whose impacts went far beyond the expected outcomes of the BRI and affected the region's power system in multiple and sometimes unpredictable ways.

Perhaps the most notable of these outcomes has been Beijing's increasing involvement in the political and security dynamics of the Gulf. Iran's active participation in the BRI and the role of Arab oil and gas producers in meeting China's growing energy needs give Beijing a vested interest in regional stability. On the other hand, the BRI provided Beijing with leverage to influence local actors and take a more active stance in their interactions. China's critical role in promoting diplomatic rapprochement between Iran and Saudi Arabia is the most striking example of Beijing's new regional influence. China's 'friendship' allows the increasingly ambitious Arab monarchies to loosen their traditional ties with the US and 'swing' between Washington and alternative allegiances according to their contingent needs. At the same time, China's role as Iran's most important economic and trade partner[3] also gives it relevant bargaining power in the political sphere. Coupled with the strategic reorientation underway and the declining US regional footprint, these elements make the Gulf scenario increasingly multipolar and increasingly interconnected with other regional theatres, mainly Central Asia. From this perspective, the global reach of the BRI somewhat mirrors the global dimension of the current US-China competition. In the same way, Beijing's decision to rely on economic integration, infrastructure,

---

3   According to the figures of the London-based Bourse & Bazaar Foundation, in 2022, the total value of Chinese exports to Iran reached $9.47 billion, while imports from Iran totalled $6.36 billion. Compared to 2021, the value of the China-Iran bilateral trade rose by approximately $1 billion, entirely reflecting the growth in Chinese exports to Iran. <https://www.bourseandbazaar.com/china-iran-trade-reports/december-2022> accessed 20 April 2023.

and soft power to support its new international role somewhat forced its US counterpart to do the same, highlighting the weakness of a political system that is often reluctant to make long-term commitments due to its volatile domestic situation.

From this perspective, the BRI has promoted Middle Asia dynamism, both politically and economically. Over the past decade, it has spurred Middle Asian countries to build a new network of relationships and allowed them to develop different and more sophisticated postures. Its effects have been manifold. On the one hand, China's initiative raised Beijing's regional profile, broke Central Asia's traditional dependence on Russia and provided it with new opportunities to open its economies to the external world. On the other hand, it offered Central Asia and the Gulf a valuable alternative to US alignment at a time when the US – for a variety of reasons – was revising its international priorities and reducing its commitment to the region. Moreover, this new dynamic drew other players into the game, creating new possible poles of attraction and allowing for further changes in the existing balance of power. While investment and trade remained at the forefront of the various programmes, establishing networks of influence became increasingly important. The COVID-19 pandemic significantly impacted this scenario, both quantitatively and qualitatively. However, it did not affect its basic characteristics. Despite the economic and social consequences of the pandemic and Beijing's difficulties in dealing with it (Davidson and Yu 2023; Hawkins 2023; Oyen 2023), the BRI remains a cornerstone of China's regional strategy. At the same time, new and more ambitious initiatives have been launched to integrate and complement it and extend its scope to new areas and actors. The process is still in its early stages, but some elements are already emerging, most notably in terms of Middle Asia's gradual shift towards an increasingly multipolar power system.

Central Asia's shifting sands

China's attention to Central Asia dates to the early 1990s, when the dissolution of the Soviet Union, the weakening of Moscow's control over the region and the emergence of independent Kazakhstan, Kyrgyzstan, Tajikistan, Turkmenistan, and Uzbekistan presented Beijing with a complex and volatile mix of opportunities and challenges. From a Chinese perspective, Central Asia's fragile economies and newly established political systems could check the return of Russian influence. At the same time, their delicate ethnic balance, mutual rivalries, separatist tensions, and the potentially destabilising effects of this state of affairs heightened its concerns, already fuelled by ongoing nationalist tensions in Tibet and Xinjiang.

China coveted Central Asia's (then largely untapped) energy resources to fuel its economic rise. But here, too, Beijing could not compete with the lure of the Western majors, which flocked to the region in the first half of the decade before taking a more cautious approach in the following years. On the diplomatic front, China was still rebuilding its international image after the Tiananmen events (15 April-4 June 1989) and could offer little more than scanty interest to the fledgling Central Asian republics. The focus was on regional security. On 26 April 1996, the PRC, Kazakhstan, Kyrgyzstan, Russia, and Tajikistan (the 'Shanghai Five') signed the Treaty on Deepening Military Trust in Border Regions in Shanghai, the forerunner of the Shanghai Cooperation Organisation (SCO). The following year, they went one step further by signing the Treaty on Reduction of Military Forces in Border Regions (Moscow 24 April 1997).

Beyond the Joint Declaration on a Multipolar World and the Establishment of a New International Order agreed on the eve of the 1997 Treaty[4], the signing of the Shanghai Cooperation Organisation Declaration (15 June 2001) gave impetus to the process. The SCO included Uzbekistan in the 'Shanghai Five' group and deepened cooperation in the fight against terrorism, separatism, and extremism. Unsurprisingly, in the aftermath of the 9/11 attacks, counterterrorism was a good umbrella to cover all members' security concerns. The following years saw further initiatives: the Tashkent Summit of 16-17 June 2004 established the Regional Anti-Terrorist Structure (RATS). On 21 April 2006, the SCO announced new plans to combat transnational drug crime, and in October 2007, it signed an agreement with the Russian-led Collective Security Treaty Organisation (CSTO) to expand bilateral cooperation on security, counter-crime, and the struggle against drug trafficking[5]. But while security remained one of the SCO's pillars, its goals were more ambitious. According to its Charter, its goals and tasks include

---

4   Russian-Chinese Joint Declaration on a Multipolar World and the Establishment of a New International Order, adopted in Moscow on 23 April 1997, *United Nations Digital Library*, <https://digitallibrary.un.org/record/234074> accessed 20 April 2023.

5   The CSTO legal foundations lie in the Collective Security Treaty that Armenia, Kazakhstan, Kyrgyzstan, Russia, Tajikistan, and Uzbekistan signed in Tashkent in May 1992. The following year, Azerbaijan, Belarus, and Georgia joined the founding counties, raising the number of member states to nine. The CST aimed to give birth to a collective security system. In this sense, Article 4 established that aggression against one member state (defined as an 'armed attack menacing to safety, stability, territorial integrity and sovereignty') will be considered as aggression against all members and that, upon the request, the allies will send all necessary help, including military force. Despite ups and downs, in April 1999, Armenia, Belarus, Kazakhstan, Kyrgyzstan, Russia, and Tajikistan agreed on the treaty renewal, and in 2002 gave birth to the

to encourage the efficient regional cooperation in such spheres as politics, trade and economic, defense, law enforcement, environment protection, culture, science and technology, education, energy, transport, credit and finance, and also other spheres of common interest; to facilitate the comprehensive and balanced economic growth, social and cultural development in the region through joint action on the basis of equal partnership for the purpose of a steady increase of living standards and improvement of living conditions of the people of member States; to coordinate approaches to integration into the global economy[6].

These 'soft' dimensions became increasingly important after the PRC joined the World Trade Organisation (WTO) in December 2001. Building on the positive relationship established within the SCO, since the mid-2000s, China has been able to break Russia's de facto monopoly over the transit of natural resources from the former Soviet Central Asian countries. Beijing also became the largest trading partner for Uzbekistan, Turkmenistan and Kyrgyzstan and the largest investor in Kyrgyzstan and Tajikistan. To enhance its regional role, in 2010, Beijing also proposed the establishment of an SCO development bank and an SCO free trade area. In addition, participation in the SCO facilitated the strengthening of bilateral ties, positively impacting the economic and trade sectors. According to the Chinese Ministry of Commerce, trade between China and the former Soviet Central Asian countries has increased more than a hundredfold since their independence. According to the same source, outbound direct investment from China to Kazakhstan, Kyrgyzstan, Tajikistan,

---

CSTO, adopting the CSTO Charter (Chisinau, 7 October). CSTO mission gradually expanded beyond CST's original scope and now includes – besides preventing the threat and repelling armed attacks against member states – countering the challenges and threats to the member states' security, including combating international terrorism, the traffic of narcotic drugs, psychotropic substances and their precursors, weapons and ammunition, and any other types of transnational organized crime; implementing measures to protect civilians from the dangers arising from the conduct of hostilities or as its result; tackling emergencies and providing emergency humanitarian assistance; strengthening the protection of borders and state and military facilities of the member states and carrying out peacekeeping operations and other tasks determined by the CSTO Collective Security Council. To perform these tasks, the CSTO also developed its own military structure, including Peacekeeping Forces of about 3,600 troops, Rapid Deployment Collective Forces of the Central Asian Region of about 5,000 troops, Collective Rapid Reaction Forces of about 18,000 troops, and a Collective Air Force.

6   Charter of the Shanghai Cooperation Organization. Saint Petersburg, 7 June 2002, in *Treaty Series. Treaties and international agreements registered or filed and recorded with the Secretariat of the United Nations*, 2896 (2018), New York: United Nations, p.246.

Turkmenistan, and Uzbekistan exceeded $14 billion in 2021, and the value of trade between China and the five countries exceeded $44.6 billion. However, the situation remains structurally unbalanced. For Beijing, the Central Asian countries account for only a tiny fraction of its total trade; conversely, the PRC is a strategic trading partner for the five former Soviet republics. For instance, in 2018, former Soviet Central Asia accounted for a mere 0.8 per cent of China's imports and 0.9 per cent of its exports. In the same year, China received about 22 per cent of all Central Asian exports and was the source of 37 per cent of the region's imports (Umarov 2020).

More recently, fears of China's 'soft hegemony' have emerged as a growing concern. Unfulfilled promises, the debt trap, the weight of Chinese capital and labour in projects, and a widespread belief that Beijing puts its interests ahead of its partners' have fuelled widespread resentment. In countries such as Kazakhstan and Kyrgyzstan, Sinophobia is rising, drawing on well-established cultural patterns (Peyrouse 2016; Owen 2017; Kumakura 2020). The main political consequence has been a tactical rapprochement with Russia, especially in the military sphere. Currently, Kazakhstan, Kyrgyzstan and Tajikistan host Russian military personnel and infrastructure; the 6,000-7,000-man Russian 201st Military Base in Dushanbe (formerly the 201st Motor Rifle Division) is the largest Russian military facility abroad in terms of personnel. Russia also maintains other major strategic facilities, including the Kant Airbase in Kyrgyzstan, the Baikonur Cosmodrome in Kazakhstan, and several radar stations and test sites all over the region. Russia plays a crucial role in the region's arms market, accounting for more than 60 per cent of trade in 2015-20 (Jardine and Lemon 2020). Since 2014, the US and NATO withdrawal from Afghanistan has renewed Russia's regional activism. The CSTO was another framework that allowed Russia to expand its military presence in Central Asia. For their part, the five former-Soviet Central Asian leaders seem to regard Moscow as a guarantee of their political stability, even if the initial mistrust and the Russian invasion of Ukraine seem to have weakened the bond. Kazakh President Kassym-Jomart Tokayev's request for CSTO assistance in restoring public order after the January 2022 riots is a telling sign of this relationship[7].

This approach to regional dynamics fits well with the needs of the five former Soviet republics and their willingness to reduce their dependence on a single patron. However, Russia and China seem to regard the existing functional

---

7   TASS (2022). 'Kazakhstan's president requests CSTO assistance in overcoming terrorist threat', 5 January <https://tass.com/world/1384229> accessed 20 April 2023.

division of labour (with Moscow dealing with 'hard' security and Beijing with trade and development) as temporary. Cracks are already appearing in its fabric. On the one hand, Russia is raising its profile in the economic sphere, with energy being the backbone of Moscow's relations with Turkmenistan and providing a valuable tool for untangling the traditionally complex relationship with Uzbekistan, especially after the election of President Shavkat Mirziyoyev in September 2016. Russia is also active in the infrastructure sector, working to modernise the old Soviet legacy, which has suffered greatly over the years but remains a valuable asset. Conversely, China is building up its military capabilities and making significant inroads. In 2017-21, for instance, the country accounted for 4.6 per cent of total global arms exports. Despite a 31 per cent decline between 2012-16 and 2017-21 (Wezeman et al. 2022), Beijing has also expanded its network of clients in Africa, the Middle East, South Asia, and Latin America. Central Asian countries have also shown a growing interest in acquiring Chinese military technology, particularly unmanned aerial vehicles (UAVs), due to their lower cost and higher reliability than the Russian equivalent. Donations are another tool Beijing often uses to penetrate Central Asian arms markets and weaken Russia's position. Kyrgyzstan has been a particular beneficiary of Chinese military assistance, both before and after the 'Tulip Revolution' that ousted President Askar Akayev in 2005 (Kassenova 2022).

The result is a gradual shift in Sino-Russian relations. At the global level, the two countries continue to share their opposition to the current US-centric 'liberal' international order. In their Joint Statement on International Relations Entering a New Era (4 February 2022), Moscow and Beijing expressed their concern about '[c]ertain States' attempts to impose their own "democratic standards" on other countries, to monopolise the right to assess the level of compliance with democratic criteria, to draw dividing lines based on the grounds of ideology, including by establishing exclusive blocs and alliances of convenience'[8]: a transparent reference to the emphasis the current US administration places on human rights, Western-style democracy, and Western values as the foundations of a peaceful and integrated international system. At the regional level, however, the convergence appears to be weaker. The BRI enhances China's attractiveness and gives Beijing a springboard for its ambitions.

---

8 Joint Statement of the Russian Federation and the People's Republic of China on the International Relations Entering a New Era and the Global Sustainable Development, 4 February 2022, *Official Internet Resources of the President of Russia* <http://en.kremlin.ru/supplement/5770> accessed 20 April 2023.

For the PRC, however, regional stability is a sine qua non for realising the full potential of the BRI. From this perspective, Central Asia is just one ring in a longer chain to extend Beijing's influence westward and south-westward to the Gulf, the Middle East, the Mediterranean and Europe. Russia's vision is more sectoral, focused on securitising its hinterland, reintegrating its 'old' imperial space, and restoring the asymmetric system of core-periphery relations within the former Soviet borders. By courting the 'multi-vector' policies of the Central Asian states, China's more assertive regional presence directly threatens these projects and their implementation. At the same time, the growth of the PRC's global and local rise threatens Russian hegemonic ambitions and endangers the 'axis of convenience' that now links the two countries (Lo 2008).

So far, the Central Asian states have tried to have the best of both worlds. Far from being passive pawns in the tug-of-war between their powerful neighbours, they have shown 'remarkable resilience to external pressure' (Laruelle and Royce 2020), using the Sino-Russian power competition to strengthen their position. It is open to speculation whether this strategy will remain viable in the face of more open rivalry between Moscow and Beijing or their strategic rapprochement. Deeper regional integration, possibly along the lines of ASEAN, has been suggested as a possible solution to this dilemma (Hayat 2021). Since 2018, some initiatives in this area have flourished (Stronski 2018; Zott 2019). However, Central Asian integration – often presented as a possible solution to many regional problems – has always proved elusive, especially without a robust external push. Since 2016, at the initiative of Uzbekistan, attempts to improve regional cooperation have been revived through annual consultative meetings of Central Asian leaders. The 2022 meeting, held in Kyrgyzstan in July, adopted two documents: a Treaty on Friendship, Good Neighbourliness and Cooperation to Promote the Development of Central Asia in the 21st Century and a Roadmap for Regional Cooperation until 2024. Central Asian leaders also agreed to develop a similar roadmap for regional security, create a regional centre for environmental protection, establish a regional television station and develop a common media market. However, just a few weeks later, fresh clashes erupted along the disputed Kyrgyz-Tajik border, confirming the volatility of the current regional security scenario.

Bridging the Persian/Arab gulf

In parallel with a growing presence in Central Asia, the BRI has advanced Beijing's role in the Middle East and the Gulf, with the not-so-veiled ambition of making the PRC a key player in a traditionally US-dominated region. In the 2000s, China established warm relations with several Gulf states to meet its growing energy needs. In 2019, according to the US Energy Information Agency (EIA), oil from Saudi Arabia and Oman accounted for about 16 and 7 per cent of the PRC's oil imports, respectively, and gas from Qatar for 9 per cent of total gas imports. Smaller – but equally significant – amounts of oil also came from Kuwait and the United Arab Emirates (UAE) (4 and 3 per cent of imports, respectively), Iraq, and Iran (10 and 3 per cent of imports, respectively)[9]. But the energy deals were only the Trojan horse for a broader Chinese engagement. Between 2000 and 2017, China's trade with the GCC countries grew from less than $10 billion to nearly $150 billion per year. Since 2004, the parties have also been negotiating (with ups and downs) a free trade agreement that should further boost economic integration. In the financial sector, between 2005 and 2017, Chinese foreign direct investment (FDI) in the GCC countries exceeded $60 billion, while in 2005-21, total Chinese investment in the MENA (Middle East and North Africa) region accounted for $213.9 billion. Chinese companies are active in technology, renewable and nuclear energy, finance, logistics, defence, communications, and infrastructure. According to the American Enterprise Institute's China Global Investment Tracker, between 2005 and 2021, the cumulative value of Chinese investment and construction projects in the Gulf countries reached $43.47 billion in Saudi Arabia, $36.16 billion in the UAE, $30.05 billion in Iraq, $26.56 billion in Iran, $11.75 billion in Kuwait, $7.8 billion in Qatar, $6.62 billion in Oman and $1.42 billion in Bahrain[10].

The Gulf monarchies' need for economic diversification supported China's strategy. In recent years, all GCC countries have adopted long-term development programmes such as Saudi Vision 2030, Abu Dhabi 2030, New Kuwait 2035, Qatar National Vision 2030, Oman Vision 2040, and Bahrain's Economic Vision 2030. These documents open up new possible areas of cooperation (such as green energy and fintech, where the PRC is increasingly active), put China-Gulf relations on a firmer footing, and make them more resilient to the evolving needs of the parties. From a geopolitical perspective, the repositioning of the US and its declining interest in the region is another element that adds value to the China-Gulf partnership. Despite the Trump administration's efforts to refocus US

---

9   U.S. Energy Information Administration (2022). 'Executive Summary', 8 August <https://www.eia.gov/international/analysis/country/chn> accessed 20 April 2023.
10   The American Enterprise Institute, 'China Global Investment Tracker' <https://www. aei.org/china-global-investment-tracker> accessed 20 April 2023. All figures do not include BRI-related projects.

policy on the Gulf, reversing Barack Obama's opening to Iran and strengthening the ambivalent US-Saudi relationship, the trend is towards greater estrangement. The shift in US priorities to the Indo-Pacific has made the traditional Middle East theatre less relevant to Washington's long-term interests. At the same time, the higher level of ambition of the Gulf monarchies has made them less inclined to shape their role according to the US perspective, as they did in the past. The rise of a new generation of Gulf leaders (a trend that began in the mid-2010s) reinforced this process of autonomy, promoting new visions of regional and international politics. Saudi Crown Prince Mohammed bin Salman is only the most prominent among these figures, also including, among else, Qatar's Emir Tamim bin Hamad al-Thani, UAE President and ruler of Abu Dhabi Sheikh Mohamed bin Zayed al-Nahyan, and Abu Dhabi's Crown Prince Sheikh Khaled bin Mohamed al-Nahyan. Within this framework, the PRC's pragmatic approach and (apparent) lack of interest in its partners' internal affairs fits the new scenario better than the 'oil for security' model envisaged in the Ibn Sud-Franklin Delano Roosevelt's Great Bitter Lake Agreement in 1945.

A more robust Chinese presence could also affect the Gulf monarchies' relations with Iran. Iran is a potentially important element in the BRI strategy, linking Central Asia, the Middle East, and the Gulf. As a party to the Joint Comprehensive Plan of Action (JCPOA), the PRC openly criticised the US for withdrawing from the plan in 2018. Beijing and Tehran signed a Comprehensive Strategic Partnership (CSP) in 2016 and a twenty-five-year Strategic Cooperation Agreement (SCA) in 2021, which entered its implementation phase in early 2022. But while Chinese Foreign Minister Wang Yi and his Iranian counterpart Mohammad Javad Zarif have repeatedly stressed the strategic importance of the China-Iran relationship, its actual impact is still to be assessed. The oft-cited figure of $400 billion (about one-third of the estimated investment for the entire BRI project) seems somewhat unrealistic, and the same Chinese sources are vague about the quantitative aspects of the SCA. Reportedly, China would expand its presence in a wide range of sectors, including energy, banking, telecommunications, and infrastructure. Beijing also offered 360-degree military cooperation, including joint training, research, and defence industry cooperation. In return, China would receive a steep discount on its supply of Iranian oil for the next twenty-five years, in defiance of US sanctions on Iran's energy exports. However, it is unclear whether the CSP and the SCA will enhance China's role in the region or strengthen Iran's position vis-à-vis its Arab neighbours. Indeed, beyond the official statements and the resounding rhetoric, the partnership with Tehran does not appear to differ from other Chinese initiatives. Even financially, today's Chinese investment in Iran is less than half of what Beijing invests in Pakistan in the China-Pakistan Economic Corridor.

The PRC's credibility with its Gulf partners depends strictly on its ability not to take sides in their disputes: an approach embodied in its non-interference policy. From this perspective, maintaining an impartial image vis-à-vis the many regional conflicts is crucial, and symbols are essential. The SCA's signing took place during a tour that also took Wang Yi to Saudi Arabia, Turkey, Bahrain, the United Arab Emirates and Oman. The aim was '[to] boost high-quality BRI cooperation […] discuss win-win cooperation […] exchange views on regional affairs, especially hotspot issues with his counterparts […] and contribute China's wisdom to maintain peace in the Middle East'[11]. In a further attempt to promote Beijing's role as an 'honest broker', the trip had more explicit political ambitions than in the past. Although not entirely new, the proposal of a Five-Point Initiative on Achieving Security and Stability in the Middle East[12] marked a further step in the PRC's strategy of presenting itself as a responsible great power willing to play its part in promoting international stability and 'genuine multilateralism'[13]. Beijing has also shown increasing interest in the Israeli-Palestine issue. In 2013, the Chinese authorities unveiled Beijing's first four-point peace plan, which was modified and reiterated several times in the following years. Since then, China has repeatedly spoken out on the issue, stressing the need for a comprehensive solution to the problem and emphasising its importance for the future stability of the Middle East. Despite a positive relationship with both parties, the PRC seems unable to exert any real influence on the issue (Burton 2019). However, Beijing's activism touches the hearts and minds of Arab public opinion (which remains deeply sensitive to the problem) and – at the global level – reinforces the idea of the PRC as a country positively committed to a peaceful and cooperative international order.

---

11 Chinese Ministry of Foreign Affairs (CMFA) (2021). 'Foreign Ministry Spokesperson Hua Chunying's Regular Press Conference', 23 March <https://www.fmprc.gov.cn/mfa_eng/xwfw_665399/s2510_665401/2511_665403/202103/t20210324_9170711.html>, accessed 20 April 2023.

12 Chinese Ministry of Foreign Affairs (CMFA) (2021). 'Wang Yi Proposes a Five-point Initiative on Achieving Security and Stability in the Middle East', 26 March <https://www.fmprc.gov.cn/mfa_eng/wjb_663304/wjbz_663308/activities_663312/202103/t20210327_9168120.html> accessed 20 April 2023.

13 Xinhua (2021). 'Genuine multilateralism, int'l cooperation championed worldwide', 8 May <http://www.xinhuanet.com/english/2021-05/08/c_139933033.htm> accessed 20 April 2023.

The agreement to normalise Saudi-Iranian diplomatic relations, signed in mid-March 2023, was a significant achievement in this area. Although still in its early stages, it 'has the potential to transform the Middle East by realigning its major powers, replacing the current Arab Iranian divide with a complex web of relationships, and weaving the region into China's global ambitions' (Fantappie and Nasr 2023). On the first level, it tackles one of the most urgent and potentially dangerous sources of tension in the region, with possible positive effects on several other crises, starting with Yemen, where Saudi Arabia and its allies are actively engaged. On the other, it strengthens Beijing's political role, especially in front of the US disengagement from the region. The implications are manifold. By brokering the agreement, the Chinese government implicitly advertised Beijing's ability to guarantee its implementation. At the same time, in front of the US failure to revive the JCPOA, China's success highlights Beijing's ability to influence Middle Eastern dynamics and promote and consolidate its regional interests. The possibility that the deal will not hold (Marks 2023) does not affect these considerations. Moreover, even if Beijing's diplomatic feat does not challenge Washington's regional supremacy, it confirms the existence of new space for potential competitors. It also demonstrates the quantum leap in Chinese ambitions to use the influence of the BRI as a tool to promote regional integration. From this perspective, trade, investment, and interdependence are increasingly becoming the linchpin of Beijing's strategy to spread its economic and political influence and promote stability by fostering a shared sense of security among its partners.

Even more than in Central Asia, China's role in the Gulf and the Middle East seems closely linked to the US stance, with Beijing somewhat 'hedging under the US umbrella' (Fulton 2020). On this assumption, Washington's attitude and its evolution since the late 2000s go a long way to explaining how the PRC has been able to expand its regional influence. The US has critical regional allies and partners, but its interests in the MENA region have long been waning. After the Iraq experience, which profoundly shaped George W. Bush's Middle East policy in 2001-2009, both Republicans and Democrats have called for a less prominent role, giving political voice to the attitudes of much of public opinion. With the emergence of the Indo-Pacific theatre as the US strategic priority in the early 2010s, a deep footprint in the Middle East has become less relevant than in the previous two decades. The US strategic rebalance, in turn, offered new opportunities to China and confronted local actors with the need to redefine their roles and reshape their foreign relations. However, these developments have not altered the region's security architecture. Although China's military profile is rising and the US has long sought to develop a more flexible presence,

Washington's assets remain the main guarantors of strategic stability in the Gulf, at least at the military level. Worth noting, despite the opening and gradual expansion of the People's Liberation Army (PLA) naval base in Djibouti, China's overseas military presence is still limited compared to the 40,000-60,000 US troops stationed in the Central Command (CENTCOM) area of responsibility (AOR). Similarly, Chinese arms sales in the Persian Gulf pale compared to those of the US, although Beijing has recently made significant inroads in this area (Ningthoujam 2021; Iddon 2022).

Testifying before the Senate Armed Services Committee in March 2022, then-CENTCOM Commander General Kenneth F. McKenzie noted that competing with Russia and China in its AOR was the third priority for US Central Command after dealing with Iran as a potential adversary in an interstate conflict in the Middle East and violent extremist organisations as the most immediate threat to the American homeland[14]. A posture that recalls the 'three main sets of challengers' identified in the 2017 US National Security Strategy ('the revisionist powers of China and Russia, the rogue states of Iran and North Korea, and transnational threat organisations, particularly jihadist terrorist groups') as 'actively competing against the United States and our allies and partners'[15]. Since then, the strategic relevance of the Chinese challenge has been reaffirmed repeatedly, with increasing emphasis on its military dimension, such as in the 2018 National Defence Strategy[16], the 2020 Expert Group Report to the NATO Secretary General[17], the 2022 NATO Strategic Concept[18], and the

---

14 U.S. Central Command (2022). 'Posture Statement of General Kenneth F. McKenzie, Jr., Commander, United States Central Command, before the Senate Armed Services Committee', 15 March <https://www.centcom.mil/ABOUT-US/POSTURE-STATEM ENT> accessed 20 April 2023.

15 The White House (2017). 'National Security Strategy of the United States of America', 18 December <https://history.defense.gov/Portals/70/Documents/nss/NSS2017. pdf?ver=CnFwURrw09pJ0q5EogFpwg%3d%3d> accessed 20 April 2023.

16 Department of Defense (2018). 'Summary of the 2018 National Defense Strategy of the United States of America. Sharpening the American Military's Competitive Edge', 19 January https://dod.defense.gov/Portals/1/Documents/pubs/2018-National-Defe nse-Strategy-Summary.pdf accessed 20 April 2023.

17 Reflection Group Appointed by the NATO Secretary General (2020). 'NATO 2030: United For a New Era', 25 November, <https://www.nato.int/nato_static_fl2014/ assets/pdf/2020/12/pdf/201201-Reflection-Group-Final-Report-Uni.pdf> accessed 20 April 2023.

18 NATO (2022). 'Strategic Concept', 29 June <https://www.nato.int/nato_static_fl2014/ assets/pdf/2022/6/pdf/290622-strategic-concept.pdf> accessed 20 April 2023.

2022 US National Security Strategy[19]. The possibility of Beijing expanding its naval presence in the Gulf to support its economic and diplomatic engagement is another concern (Herzinger and Lefkowitz 2023), as is Beijing's apparent willingness to establish new overseas military facilities in the region. But, even if China is quickly climbing the list of US priorities, the question is whether Washington will be able to devise a credible containment strategy in the Gulf and whether this strategy could actually engage its (former?) regional allies in the current context of emerging multipolarity.

The US and the Middle Asia challenge

From the US perspective, dealing with China's rising influence in Middle Asia poses multiple problems. While Washington's role in the 'hard' – i.e., military – realm remains undisputed, its political image has suffered more than one setback in recent years. More importantly, 'successive post-Cold War US administrations have struggled to manage a coherent policy towards a reconnected Eurasia that goes beyond the typical regionalisation of policy towards Europe, the Middle East, Russia, South and Central Asia, East Asia and Southeast Asia' (Kuchins 2018: 132). Given the region's geopolitical dynamics (of which the BRI is only one manifestation), the limitations of this approach have become increasingly apparent. At the same time, despite the efforts of the Biden administration, the Build Back Better World (B3W) initiative launched in 2021[20] still lacks not only the appeal of the BRI but also its lower costs, looser standards, and faster timelines. Finally, the attitude of regional players has profoundly changed. In the Gulf, in particular, the US 'pivot to Asia' was widely perceived not only as a sign of its constantly declining interest in Middle Eastern affairs but also as implicit proof of the difficulties Washington faces in maintaining its hegemonic role. Neither the efforts of the Trump administration to revive the 'old' relationship with Israel and Saudi Arabia nor those of President Biden to convey the message that 'America is back' have reversed the trend. On the contrary, Arab Barometer polls show steady – albeit declining – support for China in the MENA region,

19 The White House (2022). 'National Security Strategy', 12 October, <https://www.whi tehouse.gov/wp-content/uploads/2022/10/Biden-Harris-Administrations-National-Security-Strategy-10.2022.pdf> accessed 20 April 2023.

20 The White House (2021). 'Fact Sheet: President Biden and G7 Leaders Launch Build Back Better World (B3W) Partnership', 12 June <https://www.whitehouse.gov/briefing-room/statements-releases/2021/06/12/fact-sheet-president-biden-and-g7-leaders-lau nch-build-back-better-world-b3w-partnership> accessed 20 April 2023.

where Beijing's expansion is still seen as a less critical threat than the US (Robbins 2022).

Unsurprisingly, calls for overhauling the US China strategy are becoming increasingly popular. In an explicit reference to George Frost Kennan's 1946 Long Telegram, for instance, the Atlantic Council presented its 'Longer Telegram' in 2021, calling for a new long-term China strategy based on 'the same disciplined approach [the US] applied to the defeat of the Soviet Union'[21]. While avoiding the Cold War overtones of the 'Longer Telegram', in April 2021, the Middle East Institute spoke of the 'time for a recalibration' of US-Gulf relations to counter the growing influence of China (and to a lesser extent Russia) in the region (Feierstein, Saab and Young 2022). Conversely, in November, the Brookings Institution stressed the need for 'a course correction in America's China policy' and to 'frame the U.S.-China relationship [...] more broadly than the rigid version of competition that exists today' to 'coexist with China on terms favourable to American interests and values' (Hass, Kim and Bader 2022: 7-8, 4). These multiple competing visions highlight the issue's relevance and, at the same time, the lack of consensus on a possible course of action. At a deeper level, they reflect the fragility of current US foreign policy, which suffers from the polarisation of the domestic landscape and the oscillation between different - sometimes incompatible - approaches to Washington's international role. As the 2022 Chicago Council Survey of American Public Opinion and US Foreign Policy pointed out, beyond 'a large degree of consensus that can help form the basis of bipartisan policy on core security issues [...] stark partisan differences remain, both in how partisans see the world and in how they would deal with it most effectively' (Smeltz et al. 2022: 21).

The most obvious consequence of this state of affairs is the decline of the US's global image. Under the Trump administration, the US has suffered a significant loss of prestige and credibility, especially among its key allies in Europe, Canada and, to a lesser extent, Southeast Asia, and the Indo-Pacific. According to the Pew Research Center's June 2022 survey on the global image of the United States, among a panel of seventeen countries in North America, Europe, the Middle East, and the Asia-Pacific, Washington's popularity abroad was at its lowest point

---

21 Atlantic Council (2021). 'Establishing a Long-Term US National China Strategy', in *The Longer Telegram. Toward a new American China strategy*, Washington, DC: Atlantic Council, pp.56-67 <https://www.atlanticcouncil.org/wp-content/uploads/2021/01/ The-Longer-Telegram-Toward-A-New-American-China-Strategy.pdf>   accessed 20 April 2023.

in 2017-21, with the sole exception of Israel, whose popularity declined during the Biden presidency. Despite a rebound after Joe Biden's election and subsequent White House efforts to rebuild allies' confidence, the previous trust was never fully restored (Wilke et al. 2022). With their somewhat protectionist undertones, measures to revive the US economy and contain rising inflation did not help the process and created new tensions with Washington's trading partners. On another front, the renewed US emphasis on human rights and Western-style democratic values as cornerstones of a liberal international order has been somewhat resented by Gulf elites and several Central and Southeast Asian countries and paved the way to criticism of the administration's alleged 'double standard' policy. However, the main concern is about a possible comeback of the US to Trump-like, explicitly unilateral policies and an eventual retreat from its political, economic, and military commitments around the world: a concern that the current deeply polarised US political environment is helping to fuel.

Recent years have been marked by increasing US activism in Central Asian theatre. In the former Soviet republics, Washington has been engaged since the mid-2010s in what has been dubbed the 'Central Asia 3.0' approach (Rumer et al. 2016). In this context, the US developed the C5+1 platform in 2015 as a multilateral framework for its regional engagement, and in early 2020 the Trump administration renewed the US's medium-term Central Asia strategy 'to build [the region's countries] resilience to short and long-term threats to their stability; to strengthen their independence from malign actors; and to develop political, economic, and security partnerships with the United States'[22]. In late 2022/early 2023, State Department officials made several visits to the region, culminating in Secretary of State Anthony Blinken's participation in the first ministerial-level C5+1 meeting in March 2023. President Biden visited Israel and Saudi Arabia in July 2022 with somewhat mixed results. As in Central Asia, the focus was on pragmatic cooperation based on the assumption that regional powers have little or no interest in interfering in the US-China-Russia competition. In the following months, the faltering dialogue with Iran encouraged this kind of pragmatic rapprochement, albeit one that has had its ups and downs. Riyadh's unwillingness to work to lower oil prices is a constant source of frustration for the US administration, while human rights remain a sensitive issue in the bilateral

---

22 U.S. Department of State (2020). 'United States Strategy for Central Asia. 2019-2025. Advancing Sovereignty and Economic Prosperity (Overview)', 5 February <https://www.state.gov/wp-content/uploads/2020/02/FINAL-CEN-Strategy-Glossy-2-10-2020-508.pdf>, accessed 20 April 2023.

relationship, despite President Biden's much-criticised decision to underplay this aspect during his meeting with Crown Prince Mohammed bin Salman.

Washington has also increased its economic and financial presence in the Middle East. For instance, at the Jeddah Security and Development Summit with the leaders of the GCC+3 group in July 2022, President Biden announced a new American Commitment to the Middle East region based on the five pillars of partnership, deterrence, diplomacy, integration, and values, with provisions in areas ranging from global food security to climate change, energy security, information and communication technologies (ICTs), digital connectivity, gender equality, and health care. Promoting cooperation and regional development are among the goals of the Commitment, as well as 'accelerat[ing] ongoing work with its allies and partners in the Middle East to integrate and enhance security cooperation […], advance[ing] a more integrated and regionally-networked air and missile defense architecture and countering the proliferation of unmanned aerial systems and missiles to non-state actors that threaten the peace and security of the region'[23]. A similar approach (with greater attention to infrastructure and a more nuanced position on military and security aspects) underpins the renewed US engagement in Central Asia, where '[t]hrough Working Groups on Economy, Energy and Environment, and Security, the C5+1 will continue to support ongoing regional activities and explore new opportunities for greater collaboration'[24]. The presentation of the Economic Resilience Initiative in Central Asia (ERICEN) in September 2022 fits into the same framework, funding efforts to diversify trade routes, expand investment, and increase employment opportunities.

However, observers have repeatedly pointed out the limits of these efforts. The financial resources supporting Central Asian initiatives are, even in the best-case scenario, only a fraction of the money that Beijing poured – and is pouring, albeit at a lower speed since 2020 – into the region. For instance, ERICEN

---

23 The White House (2022). 'Fact Sheet: The United States Strengthens Cooperation with Middle East Partners to Address 21st Century Challenges', 16 July <https://www.whitehouse.gov/briefing-room/statements-releases/2022/07/16/fact-sheet-the-united-states-strengthens-cooperation-with-middle-east-partners-to-address-21st-century-challenges> accessed 20 April 2023. GCC+3 includes the five GCC member counties (Bahrain, Kuwait, Oman, Qatar, Saudi Arabia, and the UAE), plus Egypt, Iraq, and Jordan.

24 U.S. Department of State (2023). 'Joint Statement on the C5+1 Ministerial in Astana', 9 March <https://www.state.gov/joint-statement-on-the-c51-ministerial-in-astana> accessed 20 April 2023.

received a mere $25 million in FY2022, with another $20 million in the FY2023 budget and $5 million in 'extra cash' to support regional connectivity. Minimal trade incentives are foreseen, and economic cooperation programmes are less ambitious than those offered by other subjects such as the European Union (EU) or Turkey, whose regional footprint increased significantly in the 2020s (Avdaliani 2021; Donnellon-May 2022; Matveeva 2023). The scant attention paid to Afghanistan after 2021 is seen as a further weakness, especially given the ambition to break the region's isolation and the projects already unveiled by Russia and China (Starr 2022). In the Gulf, the problem is more 'political', with the main criticism focusing on the perceived ambiguities of the US-Iran relationship and its negative impact on Washington's reliability in the eyes of its Arab partners. Such ambiguities added to existing divergences, such as those over Riyadh's role in the Yemen war, the US unwillingness to support the development of a Saudi civilian nuclear program or the security guarantee that Riyadh is demanding as a precondition for the normalisation of diplomatic relations with Israel. The consequence would be the de facto end of the 'old' strategic relationship between the US and its Arab allies and its replacement with a new, more fragile and transactional one.

One way out could be deeper cooperation between the US and its partners, such as the EU. The European Union is actively engaged in both Central Asia and the Gulf and has raised its profile in recent years, including announcing a possible strategic partnership agreement with the GCC[25]. Although criticised (Behr and van Genugten 2022; van Veen 2022), the new proposed partnership represents a significant step forward and an attempt to strengthen the Union's presence in the region, including at the political level. Given the growing convergence between the US and the EU on China, the partnership could be a starting point for developing a common approach to the region. The same is true for Central Asia. Here, too, the EU has raised its profile by adopting a new Central Asia strategy in 2019[26]. Moreover, the Central Asian republics have been actively

---

25 European Commission (2022). 'Joint Communication to the European Parliament and the Council. A Strategic Partnership with the Gulf', 18 May <https://www.eeas.europa.eu/sites/default/files/documents/Joint%20Communication%20to%20the%20European%20Parliament%20and%20the%20Council%20-%20A%20Strategic%20Partnership%20with%20the%20Gulf.pdf> accessed 20 April 2023.

26 European Commission (2019). 'Joint Communication to the European Parliament and the Council. The EU and Central Asia: New Opportunities for a Stronger Partnership', 15 May <https://www.eeas.europa.eu/sites/default/files/joint_communication_-_the_eu_and_central_asia_-_new_opportunities_for_a_stronger_partnership.pdf>, accessed 20 April 2023.

involved in the initiatives of the EU Global Gateway 2021-27, which aims to mobilise some €300 million in the digital sector and the fields of climate, energy, transport, health, education, and research. While the EU's initiatives do not aim to compete with the BRI or the Russia-led Eurasian Economic Union (EAEU), they share relevant similarities with the US regarding objectives and approaches. The willingness to include all five Central Asian countries in the programmes, the unstructured and gradual engagement, and the lack of a strong institutional foundation could be a starting point for mutually supportive actions. As in the case of possible cooperation in the Gulf, the main question is the political will of the parties to cooperate at a time when structural divergences between the US and European countries in the economic and commercial spheres are becoming more pronounced.

Concluding remarks

Since the outbreak of the COVID-19 pandemic, the Chinese model seems to have lost part of its appeal. Indeed, 'the net deterioration in the People's Republic of China [...] global image can be considered one of the worst consequences of the outbreak of the coronavirus' (Onnis 2021: 2). China's new negative image also affected the BRI, adding to and fuelling existing doubts. Over time, regional countries became increasingly aware of the hidden political and economic costs of participating in the project, especially after the Kyrgyz and Tajik authorities made public the size of their debts to China and their difficulties in servicing them. On the other hand, the PRC has increasingly revised its initial commitment, partly because of its slowing economy, partly because of growing opposition from abroad, and partly to cope with the riskier international environment. Overall, between the late 2010s and the early 2020s, the BRI has become more risk-averse, reducing investment in problematic countries, and diverting resources to the highest-return sectors. For instance, according to the last BRI Investment Report, in the second half of 2022, fourteen countries saw their commitment to the project fall by cent per cent compared to 2021 (including Russia, once one of the BRI's mainstays), with Beijing's commitment to Pakistan for the flagship China-Pakistan Economic Corridor (CPEC) falling by around 34 per cent. Similarly, while infrastructure – particularly in the energy and transport sectors – remained the BRI's top investment area, finance and technology surged, with investments increasing by 3,450 and 7,536 per cent, respectively, compared to 2021 (Nedopil 2023).

Although Beijing's course remains largely unchanged, the BRI appears less attractive than in the past. This loss of lustre may be one of the reasons for Beijing's recent flurry of 'global' initiatives, beginning with the Global Development Initiative (GDI) in 2021[27] and continuing with the Global Security Initiative (GSI) in 2022[28] and the GSI Concept Paper in 2023[29]. As noted, the GDI is not intended to replace or diminish the importance of the BRI.

> While the BRI is economic growth oriented, the GDI is development oriented. The BRI delivers hardware and economic corridors, while the GDI focuses on software, livelihoods, knowledge transfer and capacity building. The BRI is market oriented [...], the GDI is public oriented, delivering grants and development assistance. While the BRI's pathways are mostly bilateral and regional [...], the GDI promotes diverse partnerships with multilaterals, NGOs and the private sector (Mulakala 2022).

However, the two initiatives are complementary. Moreover, by taking the UN 2030 Agenda for Sustainable Development as a constant reference point, the GDI frames Beijing's regional integration strategy in a broader and more political perspective, rooting the foundation of the international order in China's priorities and worldview. Such a political perspective is also implicit in the GDI, which explicitly aims 'to maintain peace and stability in the world' by rejecting a 'Cold War mentality [that] would only wreck the global peace framework, hegemonism and power politics [that] would only endanger world peace, and bloc confrontation [that] would only exacerbate security challenges in the 21st century'[30].

In this sense, China's 'global' initiatives reinvigorate the geopolitical project behind the BRI while raising its level of ambition and promoting Beijing's role as

---

27 Chinese Ministry of Foreign Affairs (CMFA) (2021). 'Bolstering Confidence and Jointly Overcoming Difficulties to Build a Better World. Statement by H.E. Xi Jinping, President of the People's Republic of China, at the General Debate of the 76th Session of the United Nations General Assembly', 21 September <https://www.fmprc.gov.cn/mfa_eng/wjdt_665385/zyjh_665391/202109/t20210922_9580293.html> accessed 20 April 2023.

28 Chinese Ministry of Foreign Affairs (CMFA) (2022). 'Xi Jinping Delivers a Keynote Speech at the Opening Ceremony of the Boao Forum for Asia Annual Conference 2022', 21 April <https://www.fmprc.gov.cn/mfa_eng/zxxx_662805/202204/t202204 21_10671083.html> accessed 20 April 2023.

29 Chinese Ministry of Foreign Affairs (CMFA) (2023). 'The Global Security Initiative Concept Paper', 21 February <https://www.fmprc.gov.cn/mfa_eng/wjbxw/202302/t20 230221_11028348.html> accessed 20 April 2023.

30 Chinese Ministry of Foreign Affairs (CMFA) (2022). 'Xi Jinping Delivers a Keynote Speech at the Opening Ceremony of the Boao Forum for Asia Annual Conference 2022', 21 April, <https://www.fmprc.gov.cn/mfa_eng/zxxx_662805/202204/t202204 21_10671083.html> accessed 20 April 2023.

a global leader in areas such as climate change, green development, health, and governance that have been almost monopolized by Western policy discourse. Even more than the BRI, the GDI and GSI also aim to build consensus around China's development policy. Within the United Nations General Assembly (UNGA), Beijing has already promoted the creation of a Group of Friends of the GDI, with some fifty-five members, and announced a first set of practical measures to implement the initiative at its ministerial meeting in 2022[31]. Whether the GDI will prioritise development or the projection of Beijing's soft power is open to speculation. But it has raised concerns among those who see it as another effort to spread China's influence abroad and consolidate the PRC's role, especially in the developing world. The foreseeable consequence is increased competition, both within and outside Middle Asia. In the wake of the BRI, development and aid programmes have been widely used as tools to promote a country's image and interests. Initiatives such as the G7's Partnership for Global Infrastructure and Investment, the US-Pacific Partnership, the Indo-Pacific Economic Framework, and the Quad's Sustainability Agenda fit into this picture. In the same vein, the Biden administration has sought to enhance Washington's role in Southeast Asia by reviving dialogue and multilateral cooperation with the Association of Southeast Asian Nations (ASEAN), among others, by signing an ambitious US-ASEAN Comprehensive Strategic Partnership in November 2022[32].

The countries of Middle Asia are only one part of this scenario, but their location and specific traits make them particularly relevant. Situated at the crossroads of Europe and Asia, they link China, Russia, and the Middle East, and integrate the Gulf region – where a complex geopolitical realignment is underway – into this macro-area. These countries have used their status to exploit the great powers' rivalry and balance their competing pressures to maximise their political and economic benefits. This strategy has not always been successful, as the financial problems faced by Kyrgyzstan and Tajikistan since the late 2010s testify. However, the involvement of new players has gradually expanded their room for manoeuvre. Although the BRI has allowed China to make massive

---

31 Chinese Ministry of Foreign Affairs (CMFA) (2022). 'Press Statement of the Ministerial Meeting of the Group of Friends of the Global Development Initiative', 21 September <https://www.fmprc.gov.cn/mfa_eng/wjdt_665385/2649_665393/202209/t20220921_10769142.html>, accessed 20 April 2023 (the list of measures is in annex).

32 U.S. Mission to ASEAN (2022). 'Fact Sheet: President Biden and ASEAN Leaders Launch the U.S.-ASEAN Comprehensive Strategic Partnership', 12 November <https://asean.usmission.gov/fact-sheet-president-biden-and-asean-leaders-launch-the-u-s-asean-comprehensive-strategic-partnership> accessed 20 April 2023.

inroads, Beijing's position has partially been revised since the early 2020s, as the launch of the GDI and the GSI highlights. These developments have had little impact on China's long-term ambitions; on the contrary, they have underlined the People's Republic's apparent willingness to raise its 'political' profile at the local and global levels. From another perspective, they have also shown that the positive influence of the BRI on the attitudes of regional actors cannot be taken for granted. Whether other players (such as the US or the EU) could take advantage of the situation depends on several elements, the most important of which is – probably – their ability to define and support a credible regional strategy. In any case, a simple return to a 'business as usual' scenario is extremely unlikely. As far as Middle Asia is concerned, the BRI has changed the rules of the game, making multipolarity a viable political alternative and opening up the region to the effects of a new power struggle.

Bibliography

Atlantic Council (2021). 'Establishing a Long-Term US National China Strategy', in *The Longer Telegram. Toward a new American China strategy*, Washington, DC: Atlantic Council, pp.56-67 <https://www.atlanticcouncil.org/wp-content/uploads/2021/01/The-Longer-Telegram-Toward-A-New-American-China-Strategy.pdf> accessed 20 April 2023.

Avdaliani, E. (2021). *Turkey's Return to Central Asia*, London: RUSI - The Royal United Services Institute for Defence and Security Studies, 1 April <https://rusi.org/explore-our-research/publications/commentary/turkeys-return-central-asia> accessed 20 April 2023.

Behr, T., and van Genugten, S.M. (2022). *Can a new EU strategy bring EU and Gulf actors closer together?*, Washington, DC: Middle East Institute, 1 June <https://www.mei.edu/publications/can-new-eu-strategy-bring-eu-and-gulf-actors-closer-together> accessed 20 April 2023.

Burton, G. (2019). 'China and the Palestinian-Israeli Conflict', *Confluences Méditerranée*, 109 (2), 147-60.

Davidson, H. and Yu, V. (2023). ' "It was all for nothing": Chinese count cost of Xi's snap decision to let Covid rip', *The Guardian*, 29 January <https://www.theguardian.com/world/2023/jan/29/chinese-cost-covid-xi-lockdowns-china> accessed 20 April 2023.

Donnellon-May, G. (2022). 'Turkey's Growing Influence in Central Asia', *The Diplomat*, 13 October <https://thediplomat.com/2022/10/turkeys-growing-influence-in-central-asia> accessed 20 April 2023.

Dunne, C.W. (2021). 'China's *Belt and Road Initiative and US Middle East Policy*', Washington, DC: Arab Center, 13 January <https://arabcenterdc.org/resou rce/chinas-belt-and-road-initiative-and-us-middle-east-polic> accessed 20 April 2023.

Fantappie, M. and Nasr, V. (2023). 'A New Order in the Middle East?', *Foreign Affairs*, 22 March <https://www.foreignaffairs.com/china/iran-saudi-arabia-middle-east-relations> accessed 20 April 2023.

Feierstein, G.M., Saab, B.Y. and Young, K.E. (2022). 'US-Gulf Relations at the Crossroads: Time for a Recalibration', Washington, DC: Middle East Institut, 5 April <https://www.mei.edu/publications/us-gulf-relations-crossroads-time-recalibration>, accessed 20 April 2023.

Fulton, J. (2020). 'Hedging under the US umbrella', in M. Kamrava (ed.), *Routledge Handbook of Persian Gulf Politics*, pp.492-505. Abingdon and New York: Routledge.

Hass, R., Kim, P.M. and Bader, J.A. (2022). *A Course Correction in America's China Policy*, Washington, DC: Brookings Institution Press.

Hawkins, A. (2023). 'China claims 'decisive victory' over Covid amid doubt over figures', *The Guardian*, 17 February <https://www.theguardian.com/world/2023/feb/17/china-victory-covid-deaths-virus> accessed 20 April 2023.

Hayat, M. (2021). 'Towards an ASEAN Model for Cooperation in Central Asia', *The SAIS Review of International Affairs*, 28 October https://saisreview.sais.jhu.edu/asean-model-for-central-asia accessed 20 April 2023.

Herzinger, B. and Lefkowitz, B. (2023). 'China's Growing Naval Influence in the Middle East', Washington, DC: The Washington Institute for Near East Policy, 17 February <https://www.washingtoninstitute.org/policy-analysis/chinas-growing-naval-influence-middle-east> accessed 20 April 2023.

European Commission (2019). 'Joint Communication to the European Parliament and the Council. The EU and Central Asia: New Opportunities for a Stronger Partnership', 15 May <https://www.eeas.europa.eu/sites/default/files/joint_communication_-_the_eu_and_central_asia_-_new_opportunities_for_a_s tronger_partnership.pdf>, accessed 20 April 2023.

European Commission (2022). 'Joint Communication to the European Parliament and the Council. A Strategic Partnership with the Gulf', 18 May <https://www.eeas.europa.eu/sites/default/files/documents/Joint%20Co mmunication%20to%20the%20European%20Parliament%20and%20the%20 Council%20-%20A%20Strategic%20Partnership%20with%20the%20Gulf. pdf> accessed 20 April 2023.

Iddon, P. (2022). 'China emerges as an arms supplier of choice for many Middle East countries, say analysts', *Middle East Eye*, 22 July https://www.middleeasteye.net/news/china-emerges-major-exporter-weapons-middle-east-north-africa accessed 20 April 2023.

Jardine, B. and Lemon, E. (2020). 'In Russia's Shadow: China's Rising Security Presence in Central Asia', Washington, DC: Wilson Center <https://www.wilsoncenter.org/publication/kennan-cable-no-52-russias-shadow-chinas-rising-security-presence-central-asia> accessed 20 April 2023.

Kassenova, N. (2022). 'How China's Foreign Aid Fosters Social Bonds with Central Asian Ruling Elites', Washington, DC: Carnegie Endowment for International Peace, 7 December https://carnegieendowment.org/2022/12/07/how-china-s-foreign-aid-fosters-social-bonds-with-central-asian-ruling-elites-pub-88579 accessed 20 April 2023.

Kuchins, A.C. (2018). 'What is Eurasia to US (the U.S.)?', *Journal of Eurasian Studies*, 9 (2), 125-33.

Kumakura, J. (2021). 'China's Influence in Central Asia: Sinophobia and the Wave of Anti-China Protests', in B.C.H. Fong, Wu Jieh-min and A.J. Nathan (Eds.), *China's Influence and the Center-periphery Tug of War in Hong Kong, Taiwan and Indo-Pacific*, pp.296-309. Abingdon-New York: Routledge.

Laruelle, M. and Royce, D. (2020). 'No Great Game: Central Asia's Public Opinions on Russia, China, and the U.S.', Washington DC: Wilson Center <https://www.wilsoncenter.org/publication/kennan-cable-no-56-no-great-game-central-asias-public-opinions-russia-china-and-us> accessed 20 April 2023.

Lo, B. (2008). *Axis of Convenience. Moscow, Beijing, and the New Geopolitics.* Baltimore, MD: Brookings Institute Press.

Marks, J. (2023). 'China's Iran-Saudi Deal May Not Stick', *Foreign Policy*, 15 March <https://foreignpolicy.com/2023/03/15/china-iran-saudi-arabia-deal-gcc-diplomacy> accessed 20 April 2023.

Matveeva, A. (2023). 'A New Opening for EU–Central Asia Relations?', Brussels: Carnegie Europe, 13 April <https://carnegieeurope.eu/2023/04/13/new-opening-for-eu-central-asia-relations-pub-89454> accessed 20 April 2023.

Mulakala, A. (2022). 'China's Global Development Initiative: soft power play or serious commitment?', Canberra: Development Policy Centre, Australia National University, 18 October <https://devpolicy.org/chinas-gdi-soft-power-play-or-serious-commitment-20221018> accessed 20 April 2023.

NATO (2022). 'Strategic Concept', 29 June <https://www.nato.int/nato_static_fl2014/assets/pdf/2022/6/pdf/290622-strategic-concept.pdf> accessed 20 April 2023.

Nedopil, C. (2023). 'China Belt and Road Initiative (BRI) Investment Report 2022', Shangai: Green Finance & Development Center, FISF Fudan University.

Ningthoujam, A. (2021). 'The Middle East: An Emerging Market for Chinese Arms Exports', *The Diplomat*, 25 June <https://thediplomat.com/2021/06/the-middle-east-an-emerging-market-for-chinese-arms-exports> accessed 20 April 2023.

Onnis, B. (2021). 'COVID-19 and China's global image', *Policy Briefs*, 57.

Owen C. (2017). '"The Sleeping Dragon Is Gathering Strength": Causes of Sinophobia in Central Asia', *China Quarterly of International Strategic Studies*, 3 (1), 101-19.

Oyen M. (2023). 'The Great Escape: How China's Zero-Covid Boosted Emigration', *ISPI Commentary*, 3 March <https://www.ispionline.it/en/publication/the-great-escape-how-chinas-zero-covid-boosted-emigration-119317> accessed 20 April 2023.

Peyrouse, S. (2016). 'Discussing China: Sinophilia and sinophobia in Central Asia', *Journal of Eurasian Studies*, 7 (1), 14-23.

Robbins M. (2022). *Public Views of the U.S.-China Competition in MENA*, Princeton, NJ: Arab Barometer, <https://www.arabbarometer.org/wp-content/uploads/ABVII_US-China_Report-EN.pdf> accessed 20 April 2023.

Rumer, E., Sokolsky, R. and Stronski, P. (2016). 'U.S. Policy Toward Central Asia 3.0', Washington, DC: Carnegie Endowment for International Peace, 25 January <https://carnegieendowment.org/files/CP_259_Central_Asia_Final.pdf> accessed 20 April 2023.

Smeltz, D. et al. (2022). *Pivot to Europe: US Public Opinion in a Time of War. Results of the 2022 Chicago Council Survey of American Public Opinion and US Foreign Policy*, Chicago: Chicago Council on Global Affairs.

Starr, F.S. (2022). *Rethinking Greater Central Asia: New American and Western Approaches to Continental Trade and Afghanistan*, Washington, DC-Stockholm: Central Asia-Caucasus Institute and Silk Road Studies Program.

Stronski, P. (2018). 'Integration without liberation in Central Asia', *East Asia Forum*, 29 December <https://www.eastasiaforum.org/2018/12/29/integration-without-liberation-in-central-asia> accessed 20 April 2023.

U.S. Department of State (2020). 'United States Strategy for Central Asia. 2019-2025. Advancing Sovereignty and Economic Prosperity (Overview)', 5 February <https://www.state.gov/wp-content/uploads/2020/02/FINAL-CEN-Strategy-Glossy-2-10-2020-508.pdf>, accessed 20 April 2023.

U.S. Energy Information Administration (2022). 'Executive Summary', 8 August <https://www.eia.gov/international/analysis/country/chn> accessed 20 April 2023.

Umarov, T. (2020). 'China Looms Large in Central Asia', Washington, DC: Carnegie Endowment for International Peace, 30 March <https://carnegiemoscow.org/commentary/81402> accessed 20 April 2023.

van Veen, E. (2022). 'What bridges the Gulf and the European Union?', The Hague: Clingendael - The Netherlands Institute of International Relations, 4 July <https://www.clingendael.org/publication/what-bridges-gulf-and-europ ean-union#> accessed 20 April 2023.

Wezeman, P.D., Kuimova, A. and Wezeman, S.T. (2022). 'Trends in International Arms Transfers, 2021', Stockholm: SIPRI - Stockholm International Peace Research Institute <https://www.sipri.org/sites/default/files/2022-03/fs_2 203_at_2021.pdf> accessed 20 April 2023.

White House, The (2017). 'National Security Strategy of the United States of America', 18 December <https://history.defense.gov/Portals/70/Documents/nss/NSS2017.pdf?ver=CnFwURrw09pJ0q5EogFpwg%3d%3d> accessed 20 April 2023.

White House, The (2022). 'National Security Strategy', 12 October, <https://www.whitehouse.gov/wp-content/uploads/2022/10/Biden-Harris-Administ rations-National-Security-Strategy-10.2022.pdf> accessed 20 April 2023.

Wilke, R. et al. (2022). 'International Attitudes Toward the U.S., NATO and Russia in a Time of Crisis', Washington, DC: Pew Research Center, 22 June <https://www.pewresearch.org/global/wp-content/uploads/sites/2/2022/06/PG_2022.07.22_U.S.-Image_FINAL.pdf> accessed 20 April 2023.

Zott, B. (2019). 'Central Asian States: Is Intra-Regional Integration Possible?', ISPI Commentary, 1 October <https://www.ispionline.it/en/publication/central-asian-states-intra-regional-integration-possible-24070> accessed 20 April 2023.

List of Contributors

Mireno Berrettini - Full Professor of History of International Relations at the Catholic University of the Sacred Heart (Milan). His studies currently focus on the genesis of the Cold War in Asian perspective. His volumes include: Verso un nuovo equilibrio globale: le relazioni internazionali in prospettiva storica, (Rome: Carocci, 2017).

Davide Borsani – Researcher in History of International Relations and Lecturer at the Catholic University of the Sacred Heart, Milan. He is also Associate Research Fellow in Transatlantic Relations at the Italian Institute for International Political Studies (ISPI). Since 2015, he has been the Academic Assistant to the President of the International Commission of Military History (ICMH); he is also a member of the ICMH Bibliographic Committee. In addition, he has been a member of the Editorial Board of the International Journal of Military History and Historiography since 2021. He has published books and contributed for Italian and international think tanks, institutes and journals, and co-edited international volumes.

Francesca Frassineti – Postdoctoral Research Fellow at the University of Bologna, and Associate Research Fellow at the Italian Institute for International Political Studies (ISPI) in Milan. She is also Lecturer of History of Contemporary East Asia at Ca' Foscari University in Venice. Her research mostly focuses on the domestic, foreign, and security policies of the Korean Peninsula, EU-Korea relations, and public diplomacy in East Asia. She has been named a member of the Next Generation Korea Peninsula Specialists at the National Committee on American Foreign Policy (NCAFP) and a Next Generation Policy Expert for the Korea Foundation Network with Chatham House.

Lorenzo Medici - Associate Professor of History of International Relations at the University of Perugia. Among his main publications is: Dalla propaganda alla cooperazione. La diplomazia culturale italiana nel secondo dopoguerra (1944-1950) (Padova: Cedam, 2009). His current research focuses on the role of culture in international relations.

Raimondo Neironi – Lecturer in History of Japan at the University of Turin, in History of East Asia at the University of Bologna 'Alma Mater Studiorum' and in Political Institutions of East Asia at the International College of University of

Ca' Foscari of Venice. He is also Research Fellow at T.wai – Torino World Affairs Institute ('Asia Prospects' programme) and Managing Editor of RISE – Relazioni Internazionali e International Political Economy del Sud-Est asiatico (T.wai's journal focusing on South-East Asia and ASEAN studies). His current research interests span Cold War in Southeast Asia, Philippines' foreign policy and US-Japan-Australia diplomatic relations.

Barbara Onnis – Associate Professor of History and Institution of Asia at the Department of Political and Social Sciences (Cagliari University), where she teaches Contemporary China and International Politics of Asia. Her research interests are mainly focused on the international relations and foreign policy of PRC. Her most recent publications include: (with F. Congiu) Fino all'ultimo Stato. La battaglia diplomatica tra Cina e Taiwan (Rome: Carocci, 2022); "COVID-19 and China's global image', in G. Pugliese, A. Fischetti, and M. Torri (eds.), US-China competition, COVID19, and democratic backsliding in Asia, Asia Maior (special issue), 2/2022; La politica estera della RPC. Principi, politiche e obiettivi (Rome: Aracne, 2020).

Gianluca Pastori – Associate Professor of History of Political Relations between North America and Europe at the Catholic University of the Sacred Heart of Milan. He collaborates with several public and private research structures; among them, the Italian Institute for International Political Studies (ISPI), Milan. He is author or editor of several books and essays, both in Italy and abroad, on the history of international relations, security issues, and military history.

Valentina Sommella - Associate Professor of History of International Relations. She teaches East Asian History and Culture and Global Governance and International Organizations. Before joining the Department of Political Science at the University of Perugia, she taught History of International Relations at La Sapienza University of Rome and was Visiting Research Fellow at University College Dublin. Her main research interests lie in the foreign policy of liberal Italy; Italian foreign policy in the interwar years; relations between the Allies during and after WWII; and, more recently, the rise of China as a global power in the international system. She has participated in several research projects and has published three monographs and numerous essays in international journals, among them Un console in trincea. Carlo Galli e la politica estera dell'Italia liberale, 1905–1922 (Soveria Mannelli: Rubbettino, 2016); Dalla non belligeranza alla resa incondizionata. Le relazioni politico-diplomatiche italo-francesi tra

Asse e Alleati (Rome: Aracne, 2008); Un'alleanza difficile. Churchill, de Gaulle e Roosevelt negli anni della guerra (Rome: Aracne, 2005).

Simone Zuccarelli - PhD student and Teaching assistant at the Catholic University of the Sacred Heart (Milan) and Head of the Transatlantic Program at the Italian Atlantic Committee. After graduating with honours in International Relations (2016), he started working as a researcher at the Italian Institute for International Political Studies (ISPI). Meanwhile, he founded and became President of the Italian chapter of the Youth Atlantic Treaty Association, an international association of young professionals interested in Euro-Atlantic and international security policies. In 2017, he started working as a researcher at the Italian Atlantic Committee, where he was appointed Head of the Transatlantic Program in 2020. From 2018 to 2020, he was President of the international chapter of the Youth Atlantic Treaty Association: in this capacity, he had the opportunity to discuss frequently with policymakers, academics, civilian and military officers on the main issues related to transatlantic security.

Printed in Great Britain
by Amazon

43846805R00118